THE EMOTIONAL POLITICS OF SOCIAL WORK AND CHILD PROTECTION

Joanne Warner

First published in Great Britain in 2015 by

Policy Press
University of Bristol
1-9 Old Park Hill
Clifton
Bristol BS2 8BB
UK
t: +44 (0)117 954 5940
pp-info@bristol.ac.uk
www.policypress.co.uk

North America office:
Policy Press
c/o The University of Chicago Press
1427 East 60th Street
Chicago, IL 60637, USA
t: +1 773 702 7700
f: +1 773-702-9756
sales@press.uchicago.edu
www.press.uchicago.edu

To my mother, Norma, and my late father, Derek, with love and thanks for everything; and to David, Daniel, Henry and Catherine, with much love

Acknowledgements

There are many people to thank for their help with this book and for their support along the way.

My sister, Jane Nellist, kept me in touch with unfolding events in Coventry and my brother-in-law, Richard Draeger, carried out some newspaper research for me in Norfolk. Liz Beddoe was a great help in the research on New Zealand. Katrina and Duncan, and Maria and Ria, have all been a much-needed source of practical help and support.

Thank you to my colleagues in the School of Social Policy, Sociology and Social Research at the University of Kent, particularly to the social work team – especially Anne Kelly and Alisoun Milne – for enabling the study leave that made this book possible. Julia Twigg was a source of encouragement concerning the basic idea for the book, and has been an invaluable informal mentor to me at Kent. Thanks also to Nigel Parton.

Thanks to the team at Policy Press, who have been brilliant, especially Isobel Bainton. The comments by the anonymous reviewer of the first draft were helpful and constructive.

Finally, thank you to my partner, Eleanor Draeger, who has been so tolerant in living with the rollercoaster I have been on in the course of writing this book and who proofread everything. Our two young children, Henry and Catherine, were a major source of inspiration for this book but the price of it has been that we have missed far too much playtime. The final big thank you goes to them.

Some of the material in this book first appeared in two previously published journal articles: Warner, J. (2013) 'Social work, class politics and risk in the moral panic over Baby P', *Health, Risk and Society*, 15(3), 217-33 (www.tandfonline.com/doi/full/10.1080/13698575. 2013.776018); and Warner, J. (2013) '"Heads must roll"? Emotional politics, the press, and the death of Baby P', *British Journal of Social Work*, first published online 4 March 2013 (www.bjsw.oxfordjournals. org/content/44/6/1637).

ONE

Introducing emotional politics

Introduction

For some 40 years, social work and child protection in Britain and elsewhere have been subject to an accelerating cycle of crisis and reform. Each crisis phase involves intense media and political scrutiny and public outcry following the serious harm or death of a child through extreme abuse or neglect. Media reports are often characterised by detailed accounts of the child's suffering, together with hostile coverage of the social workers and agencies that failed to protect them from harm. Further intensive media coverage follows the publication of any inquiry or serious case review into the role and conduct of agencies and professionals in the case, and the circumstances surrounding what happened. The reform phase of the cycle is usually marked by a fresh political commitment to make changes to ensure that such events do not happen in the future. Paradoxically, despite its apparent abject failures and the intense anger and hostility directed towards it, social work's role in child protection appears to remain secure.

My aim in this book is to add to our understanding of what drives the seemingly relentless cycle of crisis and reform in social work and child protection and to consider new ways in which it can be challenged. By introducing the concept of 'emotional politics', I explore the way in which emotions such as anger, disgust and shame over the abuse of children are not only personally and subjectively felt, but are also generated and experienced collectively. Emotions are thereby relational, cultural and deeply political. They are embedded in the entire child protection system and in the wider context for its development, including:

- policy making;
- government and political institutions;
- media stories;
- official documents such as inquiry reports and serious case reviews;
- child protection agencies;
- social work education;
- families and communities.

I argue that emotions in this sense are not free-floating and haphazard but structured and stratified, such that they constitute an emotional regime.

The book is concerned with the way politics and emotions operate together, both to generate crises and to compel political leaders to promise a future in which 'this child's death will be the last'. Rather than seeing emotions as the mere by-products of events, my focus is on how emotions are generated, mobilised and reflected in the public sphere; principally through political leaders, the media and official documents. Emotions can thus be seen as *the* driving force behind policy and practice as currently constituted. But just as emotions drive the current system, they can also drive change, and in this book I consider how a different emotional politics might operate.

While those involved in the social work profession might be the most obvious audience for this book (whether it be as practitioners, academics, researchers or students), this is not just a book for them. It is also a book for other professional groups involved in child welfare and child protection, and for people from a range of disciplines and fields for whom the relationship between politics and emotion in shaping policy and practice is of interest. Furthermore, as I suggest in Chapter Seven, the concept of emotional politics is also one that is of relevance beyond the British context.

Most of the ideas in the book are based on original research involving the qualitative analysis of documents; mainly newspaper articles, official documents, political speeches and debates. Further information about my approach to the research can be found in the Appendix.

In the next section I provide a brief account of the background and context for the book. Then, in the rest of the chapter I set out in considerable detail how the concept of emotional politics can be understood in theoretical terms and how it relates to other key conceptual and theoretical areas, including risk, social class and gender. As in the book as a whole, I have drawn on literature from a wide range of sources and disciplines, including social work, sociology, cultural studies, politics, social policy and criminology. The final section of this chapter outlines the structure of the book as a whole.

Background and context

Hostile media coverage of social work in relation to child abuse in Britain can be traced back to the death of Maria Colwell in 1973,[1] when as a relatively new profession, social work was first linked to a child's death that was perceived to have been preventable (Butler and

Drakeford, 2011, p 193). Throughout the last four decades there has been a series of cases involving high-profile inquiries and aggressive media coverage of social work (Ayre, 2001). The multiple layers of reform that have followed have each held out the 'false hope of eliminating risk', rooted in unrealistic expectations on the part of the media and public (Munro, 2011, p 134).

In 2008 there was a step-change in the intensity of the cycle of crisis and reform after the death of Peter Connelly[2] ('Baby P') at the age of 17 months, who was found to have suffered extensive injuries over several months. The horrific story, which emerged in late 2008, reached 'entirely new levels of irrationality' in terms of the scale of hostility directed at social workers (Butler and Drakeford, 2011, p 199). The story was characterised by a 'striking and complex narrative' (Elsley, 2010, p 1) and involved a powerful convergence between the interests of politicians, the media and others (Warner, 2013; Jones, 2014). Media attention was sustained over a longer period than in previous cases, as was its apparent effects on services. The crisis period following the media and political reaction saw increases in demand across all levels of the child protection system in England, including a significant rise in initial referrals and demand for care proceedings (Parton and Berridge, 2011). It was asserted in Parliament and elsewhere that thresholds for care proceedings were too high (Parton and Berridge, 2011). The period was also marked by difficulties in retaining and recruiting social workers at a time when morale was at its lowest level (Parton and Berridge, 2011, p 80).

Reaction to the death of Peter Connelly led to change and reform in England on an unprecedented scale. In the swathe of reforms and reviews of social work that followed, significant attention was paid to the role of the media. The Munro review of child protection (Munro, 2011) – initiated by the new coalition government of 2010 – reflected on the issue at some length (see Munro, 2011, pp 121-7). The newly established College of Social Work established a media centre, published a media guide for social workers (College of Social Work, 2011), and also commissioned and published research into media ethics (College of Social Work, 2012). There has been an ongoing effort to explain why and in what way the media attack social work and how this might be changed in favour of producing more 'good' stories about social work. For example, Lucie Heyes (2014) from The College of Social Work asks in *The Guardian*: 'Social work needs positive news stories – why are they so hard to tell?' Through such means, there have been considerable efforts to encourage the media to project more positive images of social work and to engage with the everyday realities of child protection and its complexity. In her review of child protection, Munro (2011, p 124) explicitly highlights the need for politicians and other public figures to avoid 'knee-jerk reactions or conclusions' and for 'actions to be thoughtfully reviewed'; a thinly veiled allusion to the occasions when this has not been so. However, there has been little detailed analysis of the role played by politicians in relation to media stories about social work.

The politics of social work and child protection

In order to understand how the media operate in relation to social work, I argue that we need to understand the nature of the politics that is at work and the place of emotion in relation to this politics. The nature of news values and the power of politicians to shape the way news stories are told and to thereby generate and reflect particular public responses are central. Media stories about child abuse and social work, particularly those concerning the deaths of children, are first and foremost news stories. As such, they are intimately connected to the political environment and, specifically, to the 'politics–media–politics' cycle through which news stories circulate and are shaped (Wolfsfeld, 2011). They are stories that are concerned with deeply vexing questions regarding the nature of the family and childhood, the state and even more fundamentally 'the good society'. As Dingwall et al (1983) have long observed, it is in the context of a particular set of answers to these questions that child protection agencies develop.

The politics that underpins the cycle of crisis and reform in social work and child protection reflect the powerful nature of social work's position, as described by Parton:

> The key defining feature of social work is that it operates in the intermediary zone between the private sphere of the family and the public sphere of the state and the wider society in order that the child can be protected but also that the privacy of the family is not undermined. In doing so it plays a key role in 'governing the family' in advanced Western societies. (Parton, 2012, p 98)

In mediating between the privacy of the family and protecting children on behalf of the state, the child protection system carries an inherent degree of 'agency failure', meaning that it is 'fully effective neither in preventing mistreatment nor in respecting family privacy' and 'lurches between these two poles' (Dingwall et al, 1983, p 220). Operating between the public state and intimate family life therefore makes child protection 'perhaps the most demanding, conflict-ridden, worrying and controversial of modern public services' (Cooper et al, 2003, p 16). The family and the state – particularly the *welfare* state – represent 'two streams of chronic social anxiety and moral ambiguity' (Martin, 1987, p 129). However, social work does not only arouse anxieties through the powerful 'liminal' position it occupies between the state and the family. Social work is also charged with mediating 'between those who are accorded political and discursive rights and those who are excluded through fear, censure, mistrust or superstition' (Philp, 1979, p 97). As such, it is also poised dangerously between 'us' and 'them'. The focus of this book is the emotional politics that shapes the relationship between the state, social work and the family as embodied by the child protection system. To understand 'emotional politics', I mean to show how emotions are political and how politics is emotional and, as such, how the two go together.

How emotions are political

There has been considerable debate in sociology about what emotions are and how they can be studied. A central issue has been the relationship between biological and social conceptions of emotion (Williams and Bendelow, 1998). Attention has focused on the way in which emotions can be understood *both* as embodied, physiological experiences *and* as social and relational in character. Williams and Bendelow (1998) argue that the sociology of emotions does not leave behind the physiological basis for emotions but goes beyond the realm of the body to explore emotions in the cultural, social, institutional and ideological realms. Emotions can thus be understood as important for both micro and macro – private and public – modes of analysis:

> In short, the emphasis here is on the active, emotionally expressive body, as the basis of self, sociality, meaning and order, located within the broader sociocultural realms of everyday life and the ritualized forms of interaction and exchange they involve. Seen in these terms, emotions provide the 'missing link' between 'personal troubles' and broader 'public issues' of social structure. (Williams and Bendelow, 1998, p xvii)

Emotions that are experienced personally are 'part of a transaction between myself and another. The emotion is *in* the social relationship'

(Barbalet, 2002, p 4). It is in this way that 'emotion is a necessary link between social structure and social actor' (Barbalet, 2002, p 4). Emotions can be understood as political, not least because they have the potential to generate political action. While emotions are generally thought of as being experienced by individuals and often as being brief and episodic, the emotions that are politically important are experienced collectively and embedded in political institutions (Berezin, 2002); they are also enduring rather than short-lived (Barbalet, 2006). Anger, for example, is a major force in the mobilisation of collective action in response to social injustice (Holmes, 2004; Thompson, 2006). In terms of understanding social conformity, Scheff (1994) stressed the significance of two emotions – pride and shame – which he saw as supporting a 'code of deference' in everyday social interaction. In this sense, '[e]motions are as constitutive of macro-level social processes as they are of individual psychology' (Berezin, 2002, p 33). The relationship between emotion at the micro level of individual experience and the collective, macro level of politics is key to the arguments developed in this book.

Collective responses to children's suffering

The idea of a collective, emotional response to the death of a child from severe abuse and neglect is suggested by Munro (2011, p 21) in her review of child protection, when she observes, simply: 'We should expect the public to be upset by children's suffering.' But what constitutes 'the public' in this collective response, how does it relate to the mediation of that child's suffering and what does it *do* in political terms?

The concept of the 'audience' in the literature on media has swung between accounts that emphasise the dominance of the media in shaping the audience to the influence of the audience in shaping the media (Schneider, 2014). In her study of media influence on public understanding of violence towards children, Kitzinger (2004) analysed the way audiences engage with media. Like previous research on the issue, her study refuted the idea that audiences uncritically absorbed what they were told by the media. However, she argued that as well as understanding audience responses, the textual analysis of media accounts continues to be important because such texts are of central importance in defining public issues and shaping ideas.

Increasingly, the way audiences are conceptualised has become more complex. This is particularly the case as media have become all-encompassing, such as through rolling news coverage and social media such as Twitter. This produces an effect whereby 'the media are inextricably interwoven into everyday life and everyone is an audience member all the time' (Schneider, 2014, p 3). Crucially, as Schneider (2014) indicates, discourses from the media can enter social interaction even in the absence of direct exposure to them via text. This includes 'emotion discourse' whereby feelings about issues of common concern circulate and are made available through discourse.

Accounts of human suffering in the media do not necessarily elicit strong emotional responses from their audience and it has become popular to argue that audiences suffer from 'compassion fatigue' (Wilkinson, 2005). However, stories of children's suffering continue to have the capacity to invoke powerful responses. In the competition for attention among news agencies, 'children are perceived to be one of the sure fire ways to attract eye-balls' (Moeller, 2002, p 37), especially when stories are illustrated by graphic images. In the 'hierarchy of innocence', children are *the* moral referent and the face of the child has the ultimate power to transcend boundaries between 'us' and 'them'. Ahmed makes this point eloquently in relation to British press coverage of the Iraq war, and the focus on one particular child, Ali, in media accounts of the conflict:

> The child represents the face of innocence; through the child, the threat of difference is transformed into the promise or hope of likeness. That child *could* be mine; his pain is universalised through the imagined loss of *any* child as a loss that could be my loss. (Ahmed, 2004, p 196)

Ahmed develops the point further with reference to the child's family in Iraq, and the Iraqi people as a whole, to show how such reports can generate an emotional response that reaches beyond the child to his family and wider community to produce a *universal parent*: 'The child's pain is what brings us closer to the others, because I can identify with the pain another must feel when faced by the child's pain' (2004, pp 192-3). The face of a child can be identified with *any* child, including my own. Furthermore, the expression of a shared emotional response can produce a positive national identity, which defines 'us' as compassionate in relation to suffering. Alongside images of suffering, the news therefore also provides us with an image of *ourselves*. It does this 'by providing an account or model of ourselves which identifies our responses to world events....' (Richards, 2007, p 60).

News stories of children who have died from the suffering deliberately inflicted on them by their parents or carers clearly threaten the possibility for collective positive identification, since the parent we might identify with is the direct source of the suffering. I argue that the photographic images of children that are used in the news stories about their deaths are of particular significance in this respect. As Kleinman and Kleinman (1997) argue, an image of suffering causes the reader to want to know more and to want answers to questions, and can mobilise social action. However, the photographs of children who have died from abuse are not images of the suffering child but of the ordinary child in poses that we can readily identify as normal and everyday. The photograph of Daniel Pelka,[3] who died in 2012, is of him smiling, dressed in his clean, red, primary school uniform. Peter Connelly's image in the photograph most often used in reports about his death is of a blond, tousled-haired toddler reaching out towards someone beyond the camera's lens. The photograph of Victoria Climbié,[4] who died in 2000, shows her with a wide smile that conveys a sense of excitement. All of these are everyday images of children that might occupy the mantelpiece and wall of any home, epitomising what Marina Warner (1994, p 35) has called the 'utopian childhood state'.

Yet these images are juxtaposed with accounts of the most appalling suffering and abuse that led to the child's death. In terms of the meaning the photographs have in relation to the news story (Altheide, 1996), it is this juxtaposition that gives the news story its power. The photograph produces an instantly imagined future and tells its own story about the life that child *might* have had in contrast with the chronicle of horrific events. It is in this sense of an imagined future that I argue media and political discourses about the deaths of children generate a universal, symbolic child that occupies an imaginary realm as understood by Hoggett (2006). Of particular importance here is the distinction Hoggett draws between pity and compassion and how this relates implicitly to different forms of social and political action:

> Pity requires an object whereas compassion requires a subject. The object of pity is innocent, a 'pure' victim, without subjectivity. Compassion, in contrast, does not require innocence. The object of pity exists primarily within the realm of the imaginary; it is an impossible condition – a pure, helpless, innocent being. (Hoggett, 2006, p 154)

Children and nation

For politicians and the media, stories about children can be used to convey profound messages about political and social wellbeing. Children represent a country's future (Moeller, 2002) and are ultimately 'the keepers and the guarantors of humanity's reputation' (Warner, 1994, p 35). The death of a child through severe neglect and abuse is not only horrific in its own right; it also 'represents the collision between the fantasy of the nation as a universal safe childhood, and the rejected, abject elements that render this fantasy impossible' (Provan, 2012, p 186). Fantasies about who 'we' are collectively are of central importance in political vocabulary (Rose, 1998). Rose (1998, p 6) argues that fantasy can be understood as constitutive in binding groups together by reaching out 'to the unspoken components of social belonging', including nation states. When a collective, national identity as 'caring parents' is disrupted, searching questions must then be asked about:

- who or *what*, in moral terms, the dead child's parents are;
- how they could do – or be allowed to do – such a thing;
- how the child could have been invisible or their suffering 'hidden in plain sight' and the implications of this for the whole community;
- how the child was both 'seen and not seen' by social workers (Cooper, 2005) and, crucially, who the next ones *among us* might be.

In the concluding comments of the report of the Committee of Inquiry into the death of Maria Colwell, the links between collective emotional reactions to child abuse and collective *responsibility* are succinctly expressed:

> The overall impression created by Maria's sad history is that while individuals made mistakes it was 'the system', using the word in the widest sense, which failed her. Because that system is the product of society it is upon society as a whole that the ultimate blame must rest; indeed the highly emotional and angry reaction of the public in this case may indicate society's troubled conscience. (Field-Fisher, 1974, p 86)

It is in terms of this collective response to it that child abuse might be understood as a 'nationed crime', with its origins in, and reflecting 'some deep disturbance within the nation' (Provan, 2012, p 189). Expressions of revulsion at the nature of the abuse inflicted, compassion and shared guilt for the child's suffering, intense anger at those responsible for it and demands for political action, are responses that define 'who we are' to ourselves – as a community, a society, a nation and as parents collectively in the face of this deep disturbance. Operating within this deep disturbance is the knowledge that the particular story can be taken to represent other, similar stories. As Cooper in his analysis of the Victoria Climbié Inquiry report observes:

> At the level of both the particular case and the general responsibility, we know that terrible things are happening, but the pain of knowing is too great for us to be able to sustain our attention … we know that cases not so dissimilar to Victoria's are being reported to the authorities on a regular basis, and yet do not become the object of public attention or political hand-wringing. (Cooper, 2005, p 9)

The idea of 'political hand-wringing' hints at the central importance of political leaders as well as the media in generating, appropriating or redefining collective emotional responses to child abuse deaths. Along with inputs from the media, it is statements from public figures – especially political leaders – that are a major source of public feeling about any news event (Richards, 2007).

How politics is emotional

Writing in 1999, Mayo observed that '[f]rom the vantage point of its closing years, the politics of emotions emerge as one of the key themes of twentieth century history' (p 144). Appeals to emotion have been critiqued by both left and right of the political sphere as displays of sentimentality, or of 'false empathy' (Mayo, 1999). The media have a key role to play in the perceived authenticity or otherwise of politicians in this regard, particularly since the communication of empathy is vital to political survival. In this context, empathy can be understood as 'the visceral connection between politician and voter, the strand of communication that makes the latter believe – or half-believe – that the former grasps what life is really like for him [sic]' (d'Ancona, 2011, p 2). This is a now a constant theme in public narratives about the capacity of different political leaders – both left and right – for 'political empathy'.

While 'politics and emotion have always gone together' (Barbalet, 2006, p 31), understanding the nature of the relationship in analytic terms is a challenge. It represents a relatively new area for social scientists because political theorists and sociologists have regarded emotions as being largely irrelevant to the study of politics. The issues with which they are concerned, ranging from the nation state to individual voting behaviour, 'are predicated on a conception of rationality' (Berezin, 2002, p 34). Political judgement based on reason and self-control has traditionally been evaluated more positively than that influenced by emotions, which have been regarded as having a distorting effect (Marcus, 2000, p 237). However, this conventional view has ignored the fact that appropriate emotions are a prerequisite, not only for successful action but also for reason itself (Barbalet, 2002, p 2). In essence, to make judgements requires a sense of what is right and wrong and such moral evaluations are shaped by how we *feel* about the issue. Anger in particular can be considered the 'essential political emotion' (Lyman, 1981, p 61). The role of politicians and the media in generating anger through moralising talk was particularly evident in the political call to action over the death of Peter Connelly, and I explore this in depth in Chapter Two. Alongside anger, compassion is perhaps the key moral sentiment in politics, where it is a 'slippery emotion' that has been deployed in a variety of political discourses, ranging from 'compassionate Conservatism' to New Labour's 'tough love' (Hoggett, 2006, p 145).

Political empathy and the 'emotionalisation' of politics

Richards (2007) argues that the place of emotion in civic life has become more central and that '[w]e have been moving away from the emotional inattentiveness which has previously characterised public discourse' (2007, p 30). Richards describes this as a process of 'emotionalisation' and it includes the emergence of a new form of political leadership in which there is a 'growing concern for the emotional dimensions of the public and its opinions' (2007, p 5). Tony Blair's speech as Prime Minister following the death of Princess Diana in 1997 exemplified this shift, in which he had the 'political acumen to recognise the depth of personal connection felt by "the people" for "their" princess' (Hey, 1999, p 72). Fairclough (2000) locates the growing 'mediatisation' of politics and government in the rhetoric of New Labour and, specifically, Tony Blair's rhetorical style. Blair's carefully constructed leadership style and personality succeeded in anchoring 'the public politician in the "normal" person' (Fairclough, 2000, p 7). In his campaign for the leadership of the Conservative Party, David Cameron explicitly used 'his ability to create a sense of empathic contact with his audience' in seeking to promise a new, caring brand of Conservatism (Richards, 2007, p 96). In the run-up to the election of 2015, at the time of writing, there is considerable debate about Ed Miliband, as leader of the Labour Party. Minogue (2014) noted Miliband's perceived 'incredible inability to connect with people' but also argued that the focus falls on personality in the absence of engagement with *ideas*, or more specifically, ideology. In short, the focus on emotional engagement by politicians can be understood as indicative of a deeper malaise in politics and the democratic process. Thompson (2000) argues that there has been a shift in politics towards 'mediated visibility' involving a greater premium being placed on the personal integrity of politicians. Matters of principle have diminished in their importance in terms of the struggle for parties to differentiate themselves and gain political advantage. Questions of character have become more politicised in the quest for differentiation, where parties 'seek more and more to make political capital out of the character failings of others' (Thompson, 2000, p 113). In moments of national crisis, the role and character of political leaders becomes particularly central.

Political leadership and national crisis

In a paper given shortly after the attack on the World Trade Center in New York in September 2001, Hochschild (2002) reflected on the importance of political leaders in such periods of turmoil. After 9/11, Americans and others looked to national figures of authority – particularly senior politicians – 'for guidance about what we ought to feel' (2002, p 119). Hochschild argued that periods of crisis are moments when people turn to leaders as feeling legislators in order to re-establish trust in the world around them and 'for a sense that we live in an environment where things make sense' (2002, p 121). Furthermore, the catastrophic nature of 9/11 exposed an emotional regime, which is a structure that always exists but is seldom seen. I draw on this and related concepts at intervals throughout the book and so it is important to be clear what it means:

> This emotional regime includes a set of taken-for-granted feeling rules (rules about how we imagine we should feel) and framing rules (rules about the way we should see and think). Together these rules shape how we see and feel about everyday reality. (Hochschild, 2002, p 118)

After 9/11, Hochschild argued, new feeling rules concerning blame, fear and suspicion quickly emerged, with a new emotional stratification system in which different groups from before became targets of suspicion and fear. Her analysis highlights the power that political leaders have to become feeling legislators, particularly over events that evoke deep social anxieties. Drawing directly on psychoanalytic theory and also on Hochschild's work, Richards (2007) argues that politicians (and the media) should engage more proactively in containing public anxiety about threats such as terrorism through 'emotional governance'. He highlights the importance of the 'emotional labour' that is undertaken by both politicians and journalists.

In responding to the stories of the deaths of children from extreme abuse and neglect, there is a moral mandate for politicians to respond in emotional terms. As one judge observed with reference to the death of Peter Connelly: 'Any decent person who heard the catalogue of medical conditions and non-accidental injuries ... cannot fail to have been appalled' (*R v B, C & Jason Owen*, 2009). There is also a political mandate if, as I have argued, fatal child abuse is understood as a 'nationed crime' (Provan, 2012). Beyond being appalled, the question of how politicians respond and in what way is of central importance. In Chapter Four, I develop the concept of 'emotional interest representation' in politics. I argue that, as well as generating emotional responses, politicians such as Members of Parliament (MPs) act as envoys or tribunes for feelings that are more widely shared among their constituents, as suggested by Drewry:

> Child abuse is a subject liable to arouse strong emotions and its political salience is very volatile. In this and other areas, the House of Commons can be seen as a sensitive, if somewhat temperamental, instrument for measuring the temperature of transient and diffuse public emotion. (Drewry, 1987, p 105)

How *shame* over child abuse is felt or not felt and by whom, and how it is attributed to others as being shameful or shameless, is central to the emotional politics of child protection. At particular moments, the state or community bears witness to the child's suffering and how 'we should all feel ashamed'. More often, blame is quickly apportioned to social workers and the agencies they work in. While politicians are heavily implicated in this blaming system, the media, and especially newspapers, are normally regarded as its chief architects.

The emotional politics of the news

More than 25 years ago, it was observed that since the death of Maria Colwell in 1973, hostility towards social work from the press had already become 'an occupational hazard' (Greenland, 1986). As already emphasised, this concern has intensified still further since late 2008 and the apparently new standards of hostility set by media coverage after the death of Peter Connelly. It has been argued by many commentators that social work needs to be much more proactive to improve its image in the media and in particular for there to be a greater focus on positive stories about what social workers do. While this is important and has merit, it betrays a particular view about news values that I argue underestimates their nature and also the particular appeal that news stories about social work carry. First, it fails to reflect the fact that stories about the deaths of children from abuse are *news stories* and therefore conform to the specific narrative forms that apply to all news stories. Fundamentally, all news is bad news in the sense that the criteria for the selection, treatment and presentation of news items are weighted towards the troubling, dramatic, violent and frightening. In essence, 'the media are better at scaring than reassuring' (Waisbord, 2002, p 209). It is social work's misfortune to be attached to and implicated in the kinds of stories that routinely appeal to the media. As Franklin and Parton (1991, p 39) put it: 'For a journalist or broadcaster seeking a sensational story, [social work] offers a rich lode to mine.'

Given their potentially sensational quality, the value that stories about child abuse and social work can offer the media has increased in recent years. This is partly because of radical changes to the mainstream media, resulting largely from growing internet use and reduced numbers of readers, viewers and advertisers. The mainstream media have consequently gone from being 'a big, bad, uncontrolled beast' to a 'fatally wounded stag' (Dean, 2013, p 50), albeit with continued power in the political sphere. British newspapers in particular have been subject to increasing tabloidisation and what Greer and McLaughlin (2012, p 274) have termed a 'press politics of outrage'. The pressure to deliver dramatic headlines for commercial reasons has signalled a new culture of journalism where the appeal of scandal is proactively embraced, even by newspapers that would not have used such tactics in the past. For Greer and McLaughlin, these changes also signal a shifting relationship between the press and institutional power. The relationship between the press and politicians, specifically in terms of stories about social work and child protection, is explored in greater detail in Chapter Two. While there are undoubtedly changes affecting the newsworthiness of stories about children, such stories have features that are repetitive and which resonate with meaning well beyond their immediate concerns. It is in this sense that I argue they resemble myths. Crucially, this does not mean that the stories are not real, but that they come to have a particular *meaning* culturally.

According to Bird and Dardenne (1997), it is as myths that news stories create order out of disorder and provide credible answers to difficult questions. They 'do not tell it like it is but rather "tell it like it means"' (Bird and Dardenne, 1997, p 337). The news genre entails stories of good and evil and can be understood as an enduring symbolic system (Bird and Dardenne, 1997). News values are 'culturally specific story-telling codes', which produce narrative structures that are recognisable as stories and have a logical structure of cause and effect (Bird and Dardenne, 1997, p 342). Myths in the form of news stories are not repeated but rather retold and it is in this sense that they retain their power. I argue that this is how news stories about the deaths of children can be understood as mythological. They have the qualities of myths because 'while news is not fiction, it is a story about reality not reality itself' (Bird and Dardenne, 1997, p 246). In more specific terms, as argued by Martin (1987, p 129) in her analysis of media reaction to the death of Jasmine Beckford,[5] the media create order out of the intense confusion and contradictions that arise from 'the confluence of two streams of chronic social anxiety and moral ambiguity – the family and the welfare state'. The role of social work in this confluence is to act as 'symbolic lightening conductor on behalf of all of us' (Martin, 1987, p 130).

Gender, class and 'race'

The emotional regime that underpins the cycle of crisis and reform in child protection is bound up with stories of good and evil that have been told and retold through media accounts. While a story about the death of a child immediately appeals to the media and their audiences as a story of innocence and evil, such stories also carry a complex array of meanings at structural, political and cultural levels. News stories about the death of a child are, for one thing, deeply gendered. Even where there are also men implicated in the death of a child – as is often the case – it is normally the child's mother who is the central focus for vilification; if not for her role in actively harming the child then for failing to protect them. Gender norms associated with femininity are chiefly concerned with caring and particularly childcare, where mothering is seen as the 'archetypal caring relationship'

(Turney, 2004, p 256). As Gillies (2007, p 9) argues, the increasing use of the gender-neutral term 'parenting' masks the fact that looking after children remains principally the concern of women and is thus a 'highly gendered activity'. When a woman kills a child it represents a crime in the cultural as well as legal sense. It is a symbolically important act as well one that is literally grave, as Motz articulates with respect to infanticide:

> Violating those taboos held most sacred, infanticide is an offence which bewilders and appals both the general public and professionals. In this crime the attributes conventionally assigned to motherhood are grotesquely distorted. The twin taboos of child killing and female violence are dramatically and irrevocably interwoven in this offence. (Motz, 2001, p 113)

While the mother who kills her own child is the worst example of the 'bad mother', this extreme case speaks to a much wider, political agenda about bad mothers (Warner, 1994). This agenda is in turn linked to the classed sexuality of working-class or so-called 'underclass' women.

In this book, the idea of 'the emotional politics of class' is utilised in which class operates in a dynamic and relational way so that it is concerned with 'measurements made against others' (Skeggs, 1997, p 74). Such measurements involve moral judgements that are experienced in emotional terms:

> People experience class in relation to others partly via moral and immoral sentiments or emotions such as benevolence, respect, compassion, pride and envy, contempt and shame. Such emotions should not be seen as counterposed to reason: as many philosophers have argued, they are about something; they are embodied evaluative judgements of matters influencing people's well-being and that of others. (Sayer, 2005, p 3)

Class and gender are central themes in this book because of the powerful emotions that attach to them: feelings such as shame, fear, pride and disgust (Skeggs, 1997, 2004; Lawler, 2005; Sayer, 2005; Gillies, 2007). This book shows how powerful emotions that relate to the dynamics of social class, gender and 'race' can all be identified in news stories and political discourse about social work and the death of a child from extreme abuse or neglect. The emotional politics of social class and gender are explored in depth in Chapters Three and Five, where the twin themes of disgust and respectability are the focus. How these intersect with racism and with legacies of colonialism is the focus of sections in Chapter Seven. The focus in the book on 'middle-class respectability' is important. I argue that the audience invoked by political and media discourse about social work and child protection can be defined by the notion of respectability. In sociocultural terms, politicians and the media are talking to 'us', the respectable, about 'them', the disreputable.

Risk and emotion in practice and politics

Not only has politics been under-theorised with regard to emotion, so too has risk. Despite the rich literatures in sociology on both risk and emotion, there has been little engagement between the two (Lupton, 2013). Yet the embodied experiences that are called emotions are an integral part of how we perceive the world around us and therefore how we experience possible threats. Both 'risks' and 'emotions' rely on us naming them as such, depending on how they are interpreted, and they are both the product of social relations, as Lupton emphasises:

> The concepts of risk and emotion express moral judgements within a specific historical, cultural, social and political context. Both emotion and risk are intersubjective, produced through social relations. They are ways of making sense of situations, naming responses, part of the diverse cultural meaning systems that we use to try and understand the world. (Lupton, 2013, p 638)

As Lupton (2013, p 641) observes, risks and emotions constitute each other: 'Emotions create risks and risks create emotions.' In terms of the arguments of this book, this mutual constitution of risk and emotion is important on two levels – both micro and macro: first, as it relates to social work practice vis-à-vis risk; and second, as it relates to the wider political sphere in which social work and child protection operate. I shall visit both briefly here.

With regard to the dominant paradigm of risk in social work practice, there are important connections between risk and emotion. Broadhurst et al (2010), for example, provide a detailed critique of the dominance of instrumental approaches to risk management in child safeguarding. They argue that the formal technologies of risk reduction systems and audit are at odds with the complex, negotiated and contingent nature of social work activity, which remains fundamentally relationship-based. *Informal* processes are fundamental to judgement and decision making in this context, and emotions form an integral part of the '*multiplicity* of risk rationalities' that are in operation (Broadhurst et al, 2010, p 1060, emphasis added). Informal, *emotional* rationalities relate directly to the operation of social work's delicate political task in mediating between the state and family, as follows:

> [W]ithout relationships between worker and service user that can 'withstand' the intrusion of the home visit, procedures would be impossible to implement. In conducting the home visit, a multiplicity of risk rationalities operate that are to do with following procedure, but also a respectful awareness of the worker's position within the family home. (Broadhurst et al, 2010, p 1060)

Politics and risk

The dominance of an instrumental and bureaucratic risk paradigm in social work and child protection cannot be understood in isolation from the wider processes at work. The ambiguity of social work as an occupation, its messiness and the fact that it carries with it an inherent degree of 'agency failure' (Dingwall et al, 1983, p 220) means that it is a 'high-risk' activity. Importantly, it seems that social work attracts critical attention even when it functions 'as well as might be expected' (Franklin and Parton, 1991, p 39). This means that child protection presents particular dilemmas for political leaders. In his attempt to argue for a 'new politics of uncertainty', Power (2004) has provided a useful and detailed account of the 'explosion' of risk management in organisational and institutional life in general, and specifically the way this hinges on 'reputation risk'.

> The UK government, like many others, is concerned to manage public expectations with improved service delivery and project management. The gap between these expectations and actual performance constitutes a reputational, and ultimately political risk for government and its agencies, such as regulatory bodies. (Power, 2004, p 20)

The relationship between politics and risk is underpinned by a fundamental contradiction between, on the one hand, the need to 'maintain myths of control and manageability' and, on the other, the seemingly endless supply of disasters, 'suggesting a world which is out of control and where failure may be endemic' (Power, 2004, p 10). This does not mean that *all* industries or sectors are subject to a political zero tolerance of risk. Sometimes politicians are willing to give voice to the view that there are 'high-risk' domains and that some bad outcomes – including significant loss of life – are compatible with systems that remain effective and fundamentally 'safe'. This stance in relation to risk is illustrated by the following exchange in the House of Commons in 2011 following a major event at the Pembrokeshire Oil Refinery:

> Simon Hart (Carmarthen West and South Pembrokeshire) (Con): The Prime Minister will be aware of the terrible explosion at the Chevron refinery in Pembroke last week, as a result of which four people died and one was seriously injured. Will he join me in extending condolences to the families and colleagues of those concerned, and also in commending the safety record of Chevron and its new owner, Valero, in what is a pretty difficult industry?
>
> The Prime Minister [David Cameron]: I will certainly do that. This was a tragic incident, and, on behalf of the whole House, may I join my hon. Friend in paying tribute to his constituents and expressing our deepest sympathies to the families of those who have been affected? I am sure there will be lessons to learn, but as my hon. Friend said, the company has had a good safety record, and in an industry in which there are inherent risks. I will be happy to discuss the issue with him. (House of Commons Debates, 2011, col 158)

The nature of risk in child protection means that the concept of a 'good safety record' seems impossible for anyone, inside or outside the field, to gauge. In many ways, the most fundamental moral and philosophical question concerning risk as it relates to the political context for risk and child protection can be put in the starkest terms as follows: 'How many children should be allowed to perish in order to defend the autonomy of families and the basis of the liberal state?' (Dingwall et al, 1983, p 244). This question throws into sharp relief the tensions and contradictions that are inherent in the *political* system as well as in child protection practice and which, in either sphere, can only ever be held in an unsatisfactory balance rather than resolved. The question goes far beyond the sphere of social work practice and reaches into the very nature of an effective democratic state. It is in this sense I argue there has been an abdication of political and social responsibility. This abdication is most evident in the operation of the rule of optimism. For the rule of optimism is not a psychological property of individuals such as social workers, as currently represented in political and media discourse; it is 'a practical reflection of a *political* philosophy' (Dingwall, 1986, p 505, emphasis added). The implications of this argument are a focus in the final chapter of the book.

The chapters

In Chapter Two the focus is on the politics of anger and how media and political reaction to the death of Peter Connelly generated as well as reflected intense collective emotions. The nation – Britain – was constructed as a feeling subject that was angry and social workers were portrayed as unfeeling and inured to suffering. In Chapter Three I turn attention to the emotions of disgust and contempt. I argue that media coverage of social work and the deaths of children from abuse reflects anxieties about certain groups and social work's capacity to morally regulate them. Chapter Four considers the cultural and symbolic importance of commemorating children who have died and how this is linked to the political impulse to rescue children. The concept of 'emotional interest representation' is introduced to show how politicians act as envoys of feelings as well as generate them. Chapter Five explores the 'other side' of class disgust and considers the fears that social work holds for the middle-class respectable parent. I argue that anxieties over the potential for social work to enter *any* home loom large, particularly under conditions of socioeconomic uncertainty and a middle-class 'fear of falling'. Chapter Six is concerned with the emotionality and political action of texts, specifically serious case reviews. I argue that these documents can be understood as activating powerful emotions such as regret relating to hindsight. They also activate 'new' forms of authoritative social work practice. In Chapter Seven I analyse emotional politics in comparative perspective using four short case studies. In the concluding chapter, Chapter Eight, I present a number of ideas for how the current form taken by emotional politics might be challenged. This includes a 'new' emotional politics of social work based on a solidaristic notion of compassion and reclaiming its public institutional role. I also argue for strategies that would close the widening gap between the political sphere, social work and the wider communities in which the families that social workers work with live.

Notes

[1] Maria Colwell died in 1973, aged seven years, of severe internal injuries and brain damage. Prior to her death she also suffered severe neglect. Maria had been returned to her biological mother by social workers, having been fostered from an early age. Her stepfather, William Kepple, was convicted of her manslaughter. Maria's death led to a major public inquiry chaired by T.G. Field-Fisher (1974).

[2] Peter Connelly (also known as 'Baby P') died in August 2007, aged 17 months, in the London Borough of Haringey. He had suffered extensive injuries over a number of months, which included a broken back, eight broken ribs and damage to his fingertips. Peter had been the subject of a child protection plan under the categories of physical abuse and neglect since December 2006. On 11 November 2008, his mother, Tracey Connelly, her boyfriend, Steven Barker, and his brother, Jason Owen, were all convicted of causing or allowing his death.

[3] Daniel Pelka died from a blow to the head in March 2012, aged four years. In the six months prior to his death, he had been starved, neglected and abused. His mother, Magdalena Łuczak, and his stepfather, Mariusz Krężołek, were both convicted of his murder.

[4] Victoria Climbié died in February 2000, aged eight years, in the London Borough of Haringey. Multiple agencies had contact with Victoria over repeated concerns about her welfare in the months preceding her death. On admission to hospital Victoria's body was found to be bruised, deformed and severely malnourished with extensive scarring from injuries sustained over a long period. Her great-aunt, Marie-Thérèse Kouao, and Carl John Manning were convicted of her murder. Victoria's death was the subject of a major public inquiry (Laming, 2003) and reforms to policy and legislation.

[5] Jasmine Beckford died in 1984, aged four years. The cause of her death was brain damage but the post-mortem revealed malnourishment and extensive injuries, including burns and several broken bones, some of which had been sustained over a period of months. Her stepfather, Morris Beckford, was convicted of manslaughter and her mother, Beverley Lorrington, received a sentence of 18 months for wilful neglect and cruelty. Jasmine's death was the subject of a major public inquiry (Blom-Cooper, 1985), which concluded that her death had been predictable and preventable and that her social workers had failed to act with sufficient authority.

TWO

'Heads must roll'? The politics of national anger and the press

Introduction

In this chapter I analyse the immediate political and media reaction following the death of Peter Connelly (also known as 'Baby P'). Peter Connelly was killed in August 2007 in the London Borough of Haringey after suffering more than 50 injuries over an eight-month period. During this time he was seen repeatedly by children's services, police and health professionals, and he was the subject of a child protection plan with Haringey Children's Services. It has been argued that reaction to Peter Connelly's death marked a watershed in the politics of child protection in England (Parton, 2014). In this chapter I argue that this watershed was characterised by a significant crystallisation of the emotional structure that underpins social work and child protection. In terms of this process of crystallisation, my main focus is on anger as a political emotion, which facilitates the creation of binary moral categories such as 'good' and 'evil'. Through political rhetoric, public anger is reflected and mobilised by constructing the nation – Britain – as a feeling subject that is sickened and angry.

As the 'politics–media–politics' cycle unfolded from the start of the news story in November 2008, certain framing and feeling rules about how to think and feel about Peter Connelly's death were quickly established. The rules about who should be the proper target for anger and blame over the death of children hardened, with social work the chief focus. I argue that the story of Peter Connelly also crystallised the idea of the empathic, heroic politician who is personally identified with child protection as an instinctive form of child rescue. When child protection is viewed in these terms, it constructs risk in a form in which all deaths are preventable. Prevention hinges on professionals deploying the personal and humanitarian instincts that 'any parent' would recognise. As I show in Chapter Four, this aspect of emotional politics has continued to shape reform in the sector long after the crisis period following the death of Peter Connelly.

Bird and Dardenne (1997) argue that news is best understood as narrative in which a symbolic system operates. The detailed accounts of Peter Connelly's suffering touched profound social, cultural and political anxieties that reached far beyond the terrible facts of his individual story. In this sense, while his story was all too real, it also produced a *metaphorical* child that has deep symbolic and cultural meaning, and images that have continued to resonate. As Vallely (2013, p 39) observed, more than five years after the events, 'This is a saga of competing icons.' In the context of this book and its concern with emotional politics, it is the '*political corpse* of Baby P' (Hoggart, 2008, emphasis added) that is the central focus of this chapter. Understanding the political context for the events under scrutiny is important. By late 2008, the left-of-centre government under Prime Minister Gordon Brown was unpopular in the polls and, with a General Election due in 2010 at the latest, all political parties were keen to foster the support of the press, in particular *The Sun* newspaper.

The arguments in this chapter and the next are based largely on original research involving a qualitative document analysis of articles published in UK national newspapers during the period immediately after the news story began on 11 November 2008.[1] To set these arguments in theoretical context, the chapter draws on a range of literature including politics, sociology and criminology. This literature points to the changing nature of the relationship between politics and the media – specifically the press – and the general trend towards the 'emotionalisation' of politics. I explore the particular importance of anger as *the* political emotion in this respect.

'A ghastly affected intimacy': the power of the press in the politics–media–politics cycle

As Wolfsfeld (2011, p 1) observes, 'politics is above all a contest' in which political actors compete for attention and influence over the news media and where political power can generally be translated into power over the media. However, while political power lends significant influence or control over media sources, such influence is dependent on control over the political environment, and when this is lost the news media can 'go from being lap dogs to attack dogs' (Wolfsfeld, 2011, p 23). Political control – or lack of it – can be understood in relation to three elements:

- control over events;
- control over the flow of information;

- the ability to mobilise a consensus within the political elite.

The relationship between elite politicians and journalists can be characterised as one of 'competitive symbiosis'. This means that political leaders and the news media exist in a permanently moving 'politics–media–politics' cycle whereby one shapes and is in turn shaped by the other (Wolfsfeld, 2011, p 10). Even where a news event does not originate in politics, it is important to analyse activity in the political sphere because the media seldom create events themselves; they transform events that are initiated elsewhere and look to political leaders to articulate their meaning. In this way, '[j]ournalists construct news stories about an issue by turning to their usual elite sources and trying to gauge the public mood about the topic' (Wolfsfeld, 2011, p 24). According to Richards (2007), the main sources of public feeling are:

- events;
- statements – especially those from public figures such as politicians;
- mediations (or inputs from the media).

Mediations have two overlapping types of input: first, the way statements by key actors are framed, contextualised and so forth; and second, the contribution that journalists themselves make to the debate.

Turning to the power of the press specifically, the Leveson Inquiry into the culture, practices and ethics of the British press (Leveson, 2012) emphasised three factors. First is the capacity of the press for mass communication; or what the inquiry refers to as its 'megaphone effect' (2012, p 76). Within this is the power to block dissenting voices. Second, the dominance of viewpoints expressed in the press is attributed to the fact that 'the press is considered a voice of authority in society' (2012, p 77). The press thereby has the capacity to set agendas and 'shape culture' (2012, p 78). Third, perhaps most significantly for the arguments being developed in this chapter, is the cumulative effect of the press, as expressed by the following witness statement quoted by Leveson (2012, p 78): 'This megaphone effect is a kind of culture-shaping effect ... it exerts much greater influence and power on people, how they're perceived by others, creating stereotypes or creating certain assumptions in society.'

There are profound changes taking place that affect the relationship between politicians and the press. Not least of these is the reported decline in public engagement with mainstream politics, notably among young people, and declining newspaper sales. Also significant is the proliferation of new media, including 24/7 television news channels, online reporting such as blogs, and simultaneous reporting of news events via social media such as Facebook and Twitter. However, there is good reason to reject the idea that these changes have necessarily diminished the power of the press, particular with regard to what Greer and McLaughlin (2012) term 'the press politics of outrage'.

Greer and McLaughlin (2012) argue that print journalism has retained control of the 'tagging' of news developments over television journalism. Furthermore, the response to crisis in the industry has brought tabloid and broadsheet newspapers closer together, taking greater risks in which they have 'proactively embraced the combined cultural and commercial appeal of scandal' (Greer and McLaughlin, 2012, p 277). Milne (2005) has argued that the interrelated trends of rapid falls in newspaper circulation and declining public engagement with the conventional political arena have also led the press to engage with protest movements in 'manufacturing dissent'. This involves 'dramatic surges of single-issue sentiment that occur outside party politics' (2005, p 10).

The proliferation of new media offers ways for politicians to communicate directly with their electorate and 'constitute new, lively fora of political debate in their own right' (Leveson, 2012, p 1443). These changes also mean that control over information has ebbed away from both the press and politicians, thereby affecting the nature of their relationship, although in unpredictable ways:

> The print press is no longer the unique medium through which public reputation and political partisanship is contested and is no longer the all-surrounding sea in which political fish must sink or swim. But paradoxically, this may enhance the relative power of what remains unique about the press: a powerful mediated partisanship which may indeed contain unspoken expectations of a tangible return. (Leveson, 2012, p 1444)

With regard to the expectation of a tangible return, the Leveson Inquiry concluded that political parties of government and opposition in the UK 'have had or developed too close a relationship with the press' (2012, p 1439). This relationship has been succinctly characterised by Boris Johnson, prominent Conservative politician and Mayor of London at the time, as a 'ghastly affected intimacy' (quoted in Hope, 2012). It is important to emphasise that the intimacy between politics and the press is not specific to one political party but was symptomatic of a cultural shift in the relationship that evolved over several years.

The various shades of over-involvement with powerful elements of the media by Tony Blair, Gordon Brown and other senior political figures is also well documented in the Leveson Inquiry report (2012).

The Sun *and Andy Coulson*

The historical context for this chapter is 2008 and the political contest for the support of the press, in particular *The Sun*, in the run-up to the 2010 General Election. In terms of the news story about the death of Peter Connelly, it is the role of politicians in the Conservative Party in opposition and *The Sun* that is my specific interest. *The Sun* continued in its support for the Labour Party that had begun under Blair's premiership until formally transferring its backing to the Conservatives in late 2009. However, it has since become evident that David Cameron had been confident for some months prior to this that the editor of the newspaper was 'on side' (Leveson, 2012, p 1192).

The developing nature of the relationship during 2008 between Rebekah Brooks (née Wade), then editor of *The Sun*, and David Cameron, Leader of the Conservative Party in opposition, is documented in detail in the Leveson Report:

> In 2008, Mr Cameron and Ms Wade lunched on 23 April 2008.... Relations between Mr Cameron and Ms Wade were already warm by this stage. She accepted that by then she was 'quite friendly' with Mr Cameron. Ms Wade and colleagues from The Sun dined with Mr Cameron on 29 September 2008. (Leveson, 2012, p 1191)

Andy Coulson, a former close colleague of Rebekah Brooks at the *News of the World*, had been appointed as the Conservative Party's Director of Communications and Planning in 2007. He was appointed primarily due to his background as editor of a large tabloid newspaper. His role for the Conservative Party was to oversee all party communications across the press, broadcast and online media, including articles, press conferences, interviews and speeches written or given by David Cameron (Leveson, 2012, p 1177). Apart from his strengths in terms of knowledge and experience of the newspaper industry, Coulson also brought to the role a keen awareness of cultural shifts that he perceived to have taken place in politics, as observed by Leveson:

> I was also struck by what Mr Coulson said in his evidence about the inexorable growth of the importance of individual

personality at the highest level (indeed at all levels) in politics. Mr Coulson spoke of the significant investment needed to ensure that the public has an 'authentic view' of senior politicians. That can involve a work of portraiture in which colour and background are provided by well-chosen and sympathetic insights into aspects of character, and private family life. (Leveson, 2012, p 1444)

Thompson (2000) has argued that the politics of ideology has been replaced by a 'politics of trust', which is performative and which places greater emphasis on the personal credibility of individual public figures. Stress has been put on the capacity for politicians to empathise and 'tap into' the public mood on issues. The importance of individual personality also points to the generalised process of 'emotionalisation' in politics. In the emotional politics of social work and child protection, I argue that there a particularly important role is played by anger, as 'the essential political emotion' (Lyman, 1981, p 61).

Anger and the emotionalisation of politics

In terms of manifest displays of emotion by individual politicians, there are clearly dangers. Just as an emotional display can enhance an image, it can also damage it (Shields and MacDowell, 1987) and it can result in politicians being seen as a liability (Clarke et al, 2006). But while a display might signal irrationality, there are moments when 'the presence of emotion seems to signal an *increased* legitimacy of one's words or deeds' (Shields and MacDowell, 1987). Logically, there are also occasions when *not* displaying an emotional response is politically disadvantageous. In this sense, emotionality can be understood as a moral resource that can be an asset or a liability, depending on the context (Lowe, 2002, p 116). The main element in measuring the effect of emotional displays by politicians on those observing them appears to be appropriateness (Shields and MacDowell, 1987, p 78). Ideas about what might be deemed appropriate are fluid rather than static.

Anger in politics has traditionally been associated with social movements and their campaigns on specific issues. However, anger underpins *all* politics, including the dynamics of power between mainstream political elites. Political parties that already hold power need to maintain it and parties in opposition seek to gain it, with anger being key to this process. As Ost (2004, p 230) argues: 'Politics does not become angry only when non-elites shout. Anger is built into politics through the everyday activities of political parties, which continually both stoke and mobilize anger in order to gain and maintain support.'

The process of organising anger involves the articulation by political parties of an identity in which they are distinguishable from other parties. This means that: 'The chief axis of distinction is not what you're for but what you're against' (Ost, 2004, p 238). The distinctiveness of a political position on any topic is therefore essentially a moral one, presenting a binary distinction between 'good' and 'bad'; 'with us' or 'against us'. Moeller (2002) has observed that children play an increasingly central role in political power struggles between elites because calls to action on behalf of children are particularly effective in engaging the public imagination and eliciting emotional responses. In the process, political leaders can appropriate a 'community of feeling', which arises spontaneously in response to particular events, producing solidarity and a sense of security (Berezin, 2002). Crucially, this security is achieved partly through the exclusion of those perceived as posing a threat to it (Holmes, 2004).

Political communication that is explicitly employed to harness or mobilise emotional responses such as anger inevitably involves 'moralising talk', which is defined as 'social behaviour which lifts decisions out of the context of tolerated differences of opinion, into choices between polarized positions in a moral conflict' (Lee and Ungar, 1989, p 712). Political leaders help citizens in making choices between these polarised positions, 'by giving them an Other: someone to blame, something or someone to be angry at' (Ost, 2004, p 241). Setting these choices out is undertaken largely through the media and specifically through the news media, since news is the 'heart of the mediated public sphere' (Richards, 2007, p 59).

The main news events concerning the death of Peter Connelly were the conclusion of the criminal trial on 11 November 2008, followed later the same day by the press conference at which Sharon Shoesmith, who was Director of Children's Services in Haringey at the time, spoke. In the rest of this chapter I analyse political and newspaper accounts published during the immediate period following these events. During the three-week period from 11 November to 2 December 2008, there were 2,054 articles about Peter Connelly (then known only as 'Baby P') in local and national newspapers. Of these, 1,002 were in the national press, 630 of them in tabloids. Of these 630, a third (216) were published in *The Sun* – the UK newspaper with the highest national circulation figures (3 million in November 2008; *The Guardian*, 2008b). *The Sun* was to be particularly important in the way the story unfolded over the critical period. Its coverage included the launch of a petition to campaign for the dismissal both of Sharon Shoesmith and of the social workers in the case, and articles written by David Cameron and Ed Balls, Secretary of State for Children, Schools and Families at the time.

The alchemy of emotional politics: how sadness becomes anger

The focus in this section is an article by David Cameron (then Leader of the Conservative Party in opposition), which was published in the first edition of the *London Evening Standard* on 12 November 2008 (Cameron, 2008a). It is important because it is a longer version of an article that appeared in *The Sun* the following day, in support of *The Sun's* campaign launch. The article was also directly quoted in other national press reports on 13 November (although not accredited to the *London Evening Standard*). The moral structure of this lengthy (794-word) article and the feeling rules it seeks to establish make it important as a reference point. The themes in it mirror, or are reflected in, the subsequent political debates; and in statements made by other national politicians, including Lynne Featherstone (Liberal Democrat MP for Hornsey and Wood Green in Haringey, where Peter Connelly and Victoria Climbié had lived) and later Ed Balls. The same themes are also to be found in political responses to child deaths that have occurred since Peter Connelly, for example in an article by Diane Abbott MP in *The Guardian* following the death of Daniel Pelka in 2012 (Abbott, 2013).

The focus of David Cameron's article is his reaction to television news coverage of the death of Peter Connelly and the Haringey press conference on 11 November. The article as a whole is notable for the force of feeling – particularly anger – that characterises the language used and his appeal to affinity with the whole country. The article begins with a visceral emotional and deeply personal identification as a parent with Peter Connelly's suffering: 'Watching the news last night took my breath away. My wife Sam couldn't watch and left the room.... As a father of three young children who I would do anything to protect, I am sickened to the core by these crimes' (Cameron, 2008a).

The language used is not the formal, public language of political leadership. It is personal, using the first-person singular, and it is vernacular, using everyday language ('took my breath away'; 'sickened to the core'). In his analysis of Tony Blair's speeches, Fairclough (2000, p 7) describes such language as the 'vernacular language of affect'. Cameron's article places him in an everyday setting – in his living room, watching television with his wife, reacting to the news along with every other viewer. By explicitly positioning his reaction as one that comes, not from the politician, but from the father of children 'who I would do anything to protect', Cameron is able to represent himself as speaking on behalf of *all* parents in the country who love their children. This shift from Cameron's personal emotional reaction to Peter Connelly's horrific death to the stance he adopts of speaking for all parents *universally* is of central importance in the feeling rule that is then set out in his piece.

Cameron's articulation of his immediate reaction to the details of Peter Connelly's death is followed by intense anger at the agencies involved and, crucially, an invocation of past child abuse tragedies. As I argue in Chapter Four, the 'roll-call' of names of children who have died in the past plays a centrally important role in political rhetoric on child protection. In this appeal to the national collective memory, his moral rhetoric of feeling urges action, not only over Peter Connelly's suffering, but also the deaths of *all* children under apparently similar circumstances: 'After the shock and sadness comes anger. It is an outrage that less than 10 years after the murder of Victoria Climbié – and more than three decades since the case of Maria Colwell – another child was left to slip through the safety net to their death' (Cameron, 2008a). This sense of accumulated anger illustrates how '[t]he ghost of each successive scandal haunts the next' in child abuse cases dating back to Maria Colwell (Butler and Drakeford, 2011, p 194). Cameron's emotional responses of sadness then anger at the repeated failure of Haringey's 'safety net', mirror almost exactly Featherstone's (2008a) comments in her blog published on the previous evening, where she states: 'My initial reaction as more and more details come to light is that my horror and sadness turning to anger [sic]. How after the Victoria Climbié tragedy can a poor child fall through safety net after safety net?'

In the next passage of Cameron's article, the language shifts to address the collective 'we' with an explicit appeal to affinity. Use of the pronoun 'we' to signal connection to others and attachment to community is a particularly powerful tool, which simultaneously builds trust and constructs outsiders (Sreberny, 2002). The sentiments in this section of the article introduce the logic of a feeling rule that equates compassion for suffering with anger and blame. Cameron is now speaking on behalf of the country and moral action is logically equated with the argument that 'the buck has got to stop somewhere':

> We've had a raft of excuses and not one apology. Everyone says they followed protocol to the letter and that the fault

lies with some systemic failure. But we cannot allow the words 'systemic failure' to absolve anyone of responsibility. Systems are made up of people and the buck has got to stop somewhere. (Cameron, 2008a)

An important feature of the logical moral rhetoric at work here is the reverse logic that it implies: to not be *angry* is to not be appalled by Peter Connelly's death and therefore to feel no *compassion* for his suffering. The feeling rule that underpins the moral equation is that pity or compassion for Peter Connelly's suffering *necessitates* anger that should be directed largely at those charged by the state with responsibility for protecting him.

Cameron's sentiment on responsibility again mirrors Featherstone's (2008a): 'Haringey Council should have prevented this death. I refuse to stand by and watch them squirm out of responsibility again.' The phrase 'heads must roll', which quickly became a leitmotif in press reports, was accredited to Featherstone, speaking on *Sky News* on 11 November, and appears in an article she wrote for the *Eastern Daily Press* 10 days later (Featherstone, 2008b). In this article, Featherstone describes the Haringey press conference as 'grotesque' under the headline: 'Why heads must roll over Baby P failures'. The phrase was also invoked three years later by the High Court in its judgment on the dismissal of Sharon Shoesmith: '"Accountability" is not synonymous with "Heads must roll"' (*Shoesmith v Ofsted & Ors* [2011], para 66).

In the final section of his article, Cameron (2008a) positions the social workers in the case as blameworthy *specifically* for following bureaucratic procedures and failing to act on 'common sense'. Managerialism – and the protocol-driven and standardised forms of assessment associated with it – has of course been widely criticised from within social work (see for example White et al, 2009). In Cameron's article it is presented as the barrier against an empathic, compassionate engagement with Peter Connelly's suffering that virtually *anyone* else in the country *other than a social worker* would have overcome. In this binary 'us/them' discourse, social workers have failed, not as the social workers of old, with their 'soft, "namby-pamby" attitudes' (Parton, 1985, p 84). They have failed as the modern, 'cold hearted bureaucrat' folk devil social workers (Cohen, 2002, p xv) who have become disconnected from humane responses to suffering. Invoking common sense reinforces an 'us/them' divide because the message is clear: any of 'us' would have acted, but 'they' did not:

But let's be frank this child was seen not once, not twice, but 60 times. The whistle should have been blown, the child should have been taken into care, the repeated cruelty should have been stopped. It's about responsibility, not just in procedure and protocol.

No amount of child protection legislation is a substitute for properly trained and supported professionals at the sharp end, social workers who can spend time with vulnerable children and not in front of computer screens collecting data and ticking boxes.

But more than that, there's no substitute for common sense and responsibility. The common sense that says this child is being abused, and the responsibility to do something about it.

...

It's these instincts we need to lead child protection for the sake of all children who are at risk, and in memory of Baby P. (Cameron, 2008a)

In press coverage in the days that followed, the vilification of social workers and particularly Sharon Shoesmith (who was not a social worker) reflected the same themes of bureaucracy supplanting common sense and empathy: 'If Miss Shoesmith had used common sense, a baby might be alive. She has to go' (Mackenzie, 2008).

In the final sentence of his article, Cameron makes a call to action to make Peter Connelly's death the last of the long line of child abuse tragedies. The collective 'we' generates the idea of the whole nation as having instincts that, if only mirrored by professionals, would protect children. The promise is, as ever, that such incidents would end if social workers could only 'get it right'. I argue that the idea of common sense based on an instinctive impulse to rescue children underpins what Munro (2011: 134) describes as the 'false hope of eliminating risk' in child protection. In the next section I explore how the emotional reaction of politicians became an integral part of the story of Peter Connelly.

When wounded feelings become public consciousness

National press coverage of what had happened to Peter Connelly rose sharply from the 35 articles that were published on 12 November in immediate response to the story, to 61 on 13 November. While the reports on 12 November made barely any reference to politicians, there was widespread reference to senior politicians in the press coverage a day later. This coverage chiefly comprised reaction to the angry debate about Peter Connelly's death that took place in the House of Commons at Prime Minister's Questions on 12 November. The media story about Peter Connelly's death thereby also became a news story about politics; specifically the emotional reaction to his death by politicians and questions concerning the appropriateness and authenticity of this reaction. Regardless of whether newspapers judged his intervention to be appropriate or not, 'Cameron was able to press his wounded feelings into the public consciousness' (Carr, 2008, p 12).

In Prime Minister's Questions that day, David Cameron began his questions to Gordon Brown by linking Peter Connelly's death to that of Victoria Climbié, questioning the absence of resignations and apologies, and also questioning the appropriateness of Sharon Shoesmith conducting the local review (House of Commons Debates, 2008a, col 761). Brown responded with his own call to affinity about the emotional impact of the case for the whole country, identifying the recurrent theme of sadness turning to anger. However, he did so without the visceral personal engagement that Cameron had deployed and he rebuffed the call for immediate action, stating that 'we will make a decision about what procedures and processes we will adopt in relation to Haringey'. The argument escalated dramatically when Brown accused Cameron of 'making a party political issue of this matter' and reached its climax when Brown rejected Cameron's repeated and increasingly desperate requests for him to withdraw the allegation: 'I ask the Prime Minister one more time: please just withdraw the accusation that I was playing party politics, because he knows I was not' (House of Commons Debates, 2008b, col 763).

The potential impact of the exchange was immediately clear to observers. David Lammy (Labour MP for Tottenham in Haringey) telephoned Sharon Shoesmith immediately after the session 'to warn her that "something dreadful" had happened in the House of Commons' (Butler, 2009). The government's Department for Children, Schools and Families (DCSF; subsequently reorganised and renamed) sent an email to Haringey's press office, which read: 'There was a fierce exchange at PMQs [Prime Minister's Questions] re Baby P. *Story is being ramped up* and we're being asked to "take over" Haringey. Early heads up' (*Shoesmith v Ofsted & Ors* [2010], para 129, emphasis added). This email clearly suggests that, from the perspective of the DCSF at least, a deliberate attempt had been made to intensify coverage of the story.

On the following day, 13 November, press coverage of Prime Minister's Questions was woven into the continued coverage of

Peter Connelly's story. Newspapers analysed the rights and wrongs of the political row, particularly its emotional nature. There were several moral narratives in the press accounts of the row but three emerged most clearly. The first was that the row had brought shame on the House of Commons and politicians in general. The second was that Cameron's performance was heroic and a success in political terms. The third was that Brown's display had further exposed supposed flaws in his emotional character. Gordon Brown's personality had already been an ongoing subject of critical scrutiny in the press (see for example Blair, 2008).

In terms of the row being shameful, Simon Hoggart of *The Guardian* was unambiguous in his moral condemnation of all involved:

> It was the House of Commons at its very worst. Ghastly, embarrassing, shameful. As they discussed the case of the tortured and mutilated Baby P, you could almost see the baby's body hurled from one side to another. We're always hearing about political footballs. This was a political corpse. (Hoggart, 2008, p 2)

The Times journalist Ann Treneman (2008, p 10) used similarly powerful metaphors to draw the same conclusion, describing it as an 'Hogarthian scene' and MPs as 'punchdrunk on politics'; 'baying at each other like bloodhounds over the battered body of Baby P'. Ironically, as a tabloid, *The Mirror* reached the same verdict but in more prosaic terms: 'Politics sank to a new low yesterday when both the Tories and Labour tried to score points over the death of baby P' (Roberts, 2008).

The pattern of reporting generally reflected the findings of research on judgements of emotionality in politicians, which is that the display of emotion will be judged according to whether the speaker already has the observer's support (Shields and MacDowell, 1987, p 88). For the politically right-of-centre press such as the *Daily Mail*, the *Express* and *The Sun*, Cameron's emotional display was seen as capturing the national mood about the story. The theme of his stance as heroic was exemplified by the *Daily Mail's* headline: 'Mr Cameron's vehemence was spontaneous ... and magnificent' (Letts, 2008, p 10).

In contrast with Cameron, Brown was perceived as being more concerned with procedures than with the suffering of Peter Connelly. Hoggart (2008) in *The Guardian* described him as 'Gordo the unflinching bureaucrat'. More forgivingly, in its Leader column, *The Guardian* (2008a) explained that Brown 'is not the most comfortable of performers on such emotive terrain'. For *The Telegraph*, it was the contrast with Tony Blair's assured performances on 'emotive terrain' that was notable. Unlike Blair, Brown was unable to make his words 'sound as if they came from the heart' (Gimson, 2008, p 8). In the next section, I argue that the status of fatherhood and public declarations by individual politicians of what this meant in emotional terms was to be of continued rhetorical importance in the way the story developed.

'The power of your feeling is clear': the nation as the subject of feeling

The campaign launched by *The Sun* on 13 November took the form of a petition demanding the dismissal of Sharon Shoesmith and the social workers involved with Peter Connelly's care. It was consistent in many respects with its traditional strategy of addressing its readers collectively and inviting them to participate in often jingoistic or xenophobic activity (Aldridge, 1994). It 'whipped up and unleashed harassment and hatred' for those targeted in its campaign (Jones, 2014, p 90). In key respects, this campaign also offered a potent illustration of what Milne (2005, p 9) describes as 'the conjunction of media power and popular protest that is reshaping the terms of political engagement'. The power of this type of conjunction is in evidence in David Cameron's (2008b) article for the newspaper, in which he explicitly forms an alliance with *The Sun* in its campaign. In Milne's (2005) terms, this is a mainstream opposition party adopting the position of popular protest. It has been argued that this alliance was a deliberate political strategy coordinated by the Conservative Party's then Director of Communications, Andy Coulson, which had the broader objective of winning the newspaper's support for the forthcoming General Election (Jones, 2011).

Cameron's (2008b) article in *The Sun* was a shorter (129-word), crystallised version of his *London Evening Standard* piece (Cameron, 2008a) analysed earlier in this chapter. It began: 'Britain's sickened and we're angry too − outraged at the failures that left a child to die' (Cameron, 2008b). Cameron explicitly generates the idea of the nation as a feeling subject that is sickened and angry in the sense articulated here by Ahmed in relation to mourning:

> What does it do to say the nation 'mourns'? This is a claim both that the nation has a feeling (the nation is the subject of feeling), but also that generates the nation as the object of 'our feeling' (we might mourn on behalf of the nation). (Ahmed, 2004, p 13)

It is not only Cameron personally who is 'sickened to the core by these crimes', as in his longer piece (Cameron, 2008a); it is now *Britain* as a *nation* that is sickened and angry. The death of Peter Connelly is generated as a 'nationed crime' as understood by Provan (2012) and responses to his death define who 'we' are to ourselves as a nation.

The call for action by the 'we' in Cameron's article is to avenge Peter Connelly's death by ensuring that professionals 'pay the price with their jobs' (Cameron, 2008b). While not explicitly referring to the Prime Minister's Questions debate, he obliquely returns to the accusation that he may be using Peter Connelly's death to political advantage in his reassertion in this article that 'this is not about politics' (2008b). The moral rhetoric of feelings specifically urges action *out of anger.* 'All of us should be angry when 17 months on this earth are lived in misery and end in horrific pain. Baby P was cruelly let down in life, but we won't let him down in death' (2008b).

In parallel, elsewhere in the same edition of *The Sun*, there is an explicit call in personal terms for Brown to take moral action *as a father*, which echoes the stance asserted by Cameron in his *London Evening Standard* article the day before:

> Yesterday was a low moment for Gordon Brown. He is a loving father himself, yet he seemed to be the only parent in Britain *whose blood was not boiling* at those who should have saved Baby P from the merciless savages who killed him.... Heads must roll. (*The Sun*, 2008, emphasis added)

This call to emotional affinity was echoed by Ed Balls the next day. In his MP's column in the local *Wakefield Express*, Balls mirrored *The Sun*'s language exactly: 'The details of how that little boy had been treated by his mum and step-father *made my blood boil* and my heart bleed' (Balls, 2008a, emphasis added). While the target of his moral outrage is still the killers rather than agencies, Balls' mirroring of emotional language lends some credibility to the argument by the *Daily Express* in its Leader article that 'ministers were running to catch up with public opinion' (*Daily Express*, 2008, p 12).

As Wolfsfeld (2011, p 32) has observed, identifying when politicians are behaving defensively is 'one way to understand which direction the political wind is blowing in'. The successive press announcements and ministerial statements from Ed Balls and the DCSF reflected their growing concern with the media and political reaction. On the morning of 12 November, in Ed Balls' written ministerial statement in the House of Commons, there was acknowledgement of the emotional reaction to the case nationally. But the moral 'us' is deployed to lay blame on those who had been responsible for Peter Connelly's death and their readiness to deceive professionals: 'The death of Baby P in Haringey is a very tragic case that will have shocked and appalled the country. It makes all of us question how someone could do such a terrible thing to a child and set out to deceive the very people trying to help' (House of Commons Written Ministerial Statements, 2008, col 58WS).

After this, the statement adopts a factual tone to emphasise that the serious case review will be considered and reiterates that the progress of the Laming reforms will be reviewed. It is notable that the option to institute a public inquiry into Peter Connelly's death, by which it may have been possible to recover political control or at least a pause in the pace of events, was in effect unavailable to the government at this point. This was because the Laming Inquiry into the death of Victoria Climbié in 2001 in the same London borough, and all the reforms under the New Labour government that had followed the inquiry, had been expressly presented as reforms that would prevent a similar event ever happening again. As Parton (2014, p 79) suggests: 'The death of Baby P seemed to demonstrate the absolute failure of these reforms.'

The absence of anger in Ed Balls' statement is noticeable; this is the rational, managerial language of government. However, the growing tension between the need to 'keep up with' the emotional politics while sustaining a rational-bureaucratic response becomes ever more evident. The continuing press interest, political pressure and enormous 'success' of *The Sun*'s petition eventually sees the publication by Balls of his own piece in *The Sun* two weeks later under the headline: 'Power of your feeling is clear' (Balls, 2008b), together with coverage of the petition being delivered to No 10 Downing Street. His article states: 'The whole nation has been shocked and moved by the tragic and horrific death of Baby P.... And the huge strength of feeling across Britain is clear to see from the million plus readers – including many teachers and social workers – who have already signed *The Sun*'s petition' (Balls, 2008b).

In many senses, Balls' moral voice is heard more forcefully elsewhere in the same edition of *The Sun*, in a report of an exclusive interview with him. The tension between his emotional response as a father and the responsibility to sustain a rational-managerial political stance, or at least the impression of one, is clearly articulated. By using direct quotations, this representation of Balls identifies him as a public figure who can *both* reflect the authentic emotional response of a father, shared with the nation's parents, *and* operate as a rational politician carrying the responsibilities of government:

Mr Balls made it clear he will wait until he receives the report into the failings on Monday before acting. He refused to single out individuals. And he insisted he would not act out of anger – but after a full study of the report…. 'I have to separate the emotion I feel as a father from my job as Secretary of State…. I feel revulsion that adults could do this to a child…. But I should not make decisions on the basis of my own emotional reaction or the anger we all feel.' (Pascoe-Watson, 2008)

On national television four days later, Ed Balls announced that Sharon Shoesmith was to be removed from her post and some days later *The Sun* (2008) was able to declare: 'Baby P victory at last'. Long after the immediate media outrage had ended, the Appeal Court gave its own moral verdict on the manner of this outcome: 'It seems that the making of a public sacrifice to deflect press and public obloquy … remains an accepted expedient of public administration in this country' (*Shoesmith v Ofsted & Ors* [2011]: para 134).

After a series of court cases over a number of years, Sharon Shoesmith was eventually awarded compensation for unfair dismissal; a decision that was met with derision by the media.

Three fathers and a shameless woman

A recurrent theme in the political and media accounts was Sharon Shoesmith's reported refusal to apologise at the press conference held on the day the trial ended. Her stance appeared to provoke particular outrage in the press and later from individual politicians, notably David Cameron as outlined above. Vilification of her in the press focused in part on her insistence on stating that it was Peter Connelly's own family members who were responsible for his death. It is evident in the following extract from the *Daily Mail* that her refusal to carry shame herself for what had happened was wholly unpalatable: 'The horror of Baby Ps death … should have made her hang her head in shame. Instead she twice refused to apologise and certainly had no intention of … resigning … saying brazenly "The child was killed by members of his own family"' (Reid, 2008).

Haringey also attempted to demonstrate in the press conference that its children's services department was achieving positive outcomes. The data shown to reporters were the source for hostile reports of Sharon Shoesmith personally as: 'The woman who puts performance graphs before a baby's life' (Reid, 2008). An interesting observation on the issue of apology is made by Gaber (2008), who was involved in handling public relations in Haringey at the time of the death of Victoria Climbié. He argues that the apology issued over Victoria Climbié, together with acceptance by the authority that no 'good' coverage from the case was possible, resulted in far less damaging media coverage.

An apology can be understood as conveying three main messages:

- admission of a wrongful act;
- an expression of remorse for the wrongdoing;
- an implicit commitment to avoid such acts in future (Davis, 2002).

Sharon Shoesmith's reported failure to apologise prompted a particularly angry response on all three counts:

- First, it was interpreted as a refusal to acknowledge wrongdoing in Haringey in relation to the case and so – de facto – no one in Haringey but the killers themselves could be held responsible.
- Second, it signified an absence of remorse and shame – and thereby an absence of any significant emotional response to what had happened. This was in stark contrast to what was to be a visceral emotional engagement with the details of Peter Connelly's suffering by others, particularly politicians.
- Third, and perhaps most significantly, it offered no assurances that what had happened (both to Peter Connelly and to Victoria Climbié before that) would not happen to other children. Unlike the political promise to make this death the last, Shoesmith's prediction of the future is bleakly realist: 'You can't stop people who are determined to kill their children.... None of the agencies involved with the family are responsible for the death' (Edemariam, 2009).

There is an important distinction between the *act* of apologising and the feelings that may or may not be reflected in the act. It is not enough merely to apologise; there must be evidence of appropriate authentic feelings to go with the act of the apology. As Davis (2002, p 170) observes: 'The consummate apologiser is affected by feelings of self-reproach. If the transgression is sufficiently serious, then this reproach might glissade into disgust or even revulsion towards one's self'. Parton (2014, p 86) points to the way that the 'public apology has become required practice', which is a further reflection of the 'performative politics of trust' linked to the 'mediated visibility' of the public sphere as argued by Thompson (2000).

In contrast to the moral and emotional status of Sharon Shoesmith as unrepentant and shameless, the moral and emotional position of all three senior politicians – David Cameron, Ed Balls and Gordon Brown – is articulated in very different ways. All three men had a young family in 2008 and so could claim a natural affinity with the nation's parents in the complex identification with Peter Connelly's suffering. Underpinning this universal identification as parents is a basic assumption about parental love for a child. It is, paradoxically, the same assumption that constitutes the operational framing of social work in child protection, which is that 'all parents love their children as a fact of nature' (Dingwall et al, 1983, p 99). In 2008, both David Cameron and Gordon Brown had a son aged two, so just a little older than 17-month-old Peter Connelly, and Ed Balls' youngest child was aged four. The increasing presence of young families in the lives of senior male politicians had drawn frequent comment from the media and it is almost certainly a factor in the perceived emotionalisation of politics. For example, David Cameron's decision to take paternity leave at the birth of his child born while he was in office attracted a good deal of public comment. While David Cameron publicly expressed his anger as a father at the details of Peter Connelly's death, the absence of an equivalent expression by Gordon Brown was presented in some press reports as signifying a deeper lack on his part: 'he seemed to be the only parent in Britain *whose blood was not boiling* at those who should have saved Baby P' (*The Sun*, 2008, emphasis added). But more comprehensively, Brown stood accused of 'being unable to speak from the heart' on the issue. His performance, in emotional terms, was contrasted poorly with what some members of the press, such as *The Telegraph*, imagined Tony Blair's would have been: 'Tony Blair would likewise have conveyed, by his face and the catch in his voice, his understanding that the story of that baby's suffering must move anyone to grief and rage' (Gimson, 2008).

However, while Brown is described as being 'unable to speak from the heart' in the political exchanges about Peter Connelly's death, in quite another context his emotional authenticity is regarded without question. Some four months after the political row over Peter Connelly's death in the House of Commons, Cameron's own young son, Ivan, died. On the following morning, Brown made a statement in the House of Commons and Cameron's response to this statement on his return to politics two weeks later was poignant: 'I particularly want to thank the Prime Minister for what he said. It came straight from the heart and it meant a great deal to Samantha and to me' (House of Commons Debates, 2009, *Hansard*, 11 March, col 287).

Cameron's tone here was deeply personal, reflecting the mutual empathy these two men – momentarily at least – felt towards one another, having each experienced the serious illness and death of a young child. Gordon Brown's daughter, Jennifer, had died aged 10 days in 2002 and his son Fraser had a potentially life-limiting condition. Cameron had no interest in denigrating Brown's emotional response to his son's death. The children who had died or were suffering were all too real – not metaphors in a political drama. The 'emotion work' on display here is specifically detached from the wider public sphere, with the language confined to the intimacy of the House of Commons and its members rather than the nation. Press coverage on the day after Cameron's return to the House of Commons was based on the assumption that this expression of 'authentic' emotion – for good or ill – is at odds with normal political behaviour: 'It was weird and at the same time wonderful to hear at the Commons dispatch box something utterly personal, clearly wrenched from inside himself, words that were being spoken because they were true, not because they might win a couple of votes or a quick debating point' (Hoggart, 2009).

The same Quentin Letts who had praised Cameron's high emotion over Peter Connelly's death in the *Daily Mail* concludes simply: 'That's enough grief. Let the mêlée resume' (Letts, 2009).

Conclusion

In this chapter I have argued that reaction to Peter Connelly's death served a powerful function in allowing politicians to articulate a particular moral and emotional stance. Their appeals to moral feeling simultaneously constructed politicians and social workers in starkly polarised terms. Just as politicians reflected and also mobilised strong empathic identification with extreme human suffering, social workers were constructed – paradoxically – as cold, detached and inhumane. An important feature of the emotional politics that the chapter has highlighted is the feeling rule that can be seen to underpin it. The compassion or pity felt for Peter Connelly's suffering was quickly equated with intense anger at those charged *by the state* with responsibility for protecting him from his own family members. The political appeals to moral feeling invoked a national feeling of solidarity as parents based on rage towards, not only Peter Connelly's social workers, but also social work as a whole, as it embodies the state in relation to family life.

These arguments are not inconsistent with the long-stated argument that 'bad' stories about social work in the UK serve the press because of their newsworthiness and also serve political parties and newspapers on the political right of centre because they facilitate wider ideological attacks on state welfare and the 'loony left' (Galilee, 2005, p 5). In this sense, social workers continue to be presented in the media 'as a metaphor or symbol for the entire public sector, personifying the "evil" which the political new right presumes to be inherent therein' (Franklin and Parton, 1991, p 9). However, by focusing on the way collective emotions are reflected, generated and structured through political and media discourse, I argue that it is important to attend to deeper processes that are at work. While the emotional politics at work after the death of Peter Connelly served the interests of politicians and the press, it can also be understood at a deeper cultural level as an attempt to define a nation's idealised sense of who 'we' are collectively in the face of a child's suffering.

The focus of this chapter has been largely on the reflection and generation of public anger by politicians and the press. In the next chapter my attention turns to the way media accounts of the deaths of children from abuse and neglect reflect deep disturbance about the social groups to which these children are seen to have belonged. The emotional response to these groups is also reflected in cultural anxieties about social work's capacity to fulfil its function of moral regulation on behalf of the state.

Note

[1] UK national newspapers incorporate the so-called 'quality press' of broadsheet newspapers such as *The Guardian* and *The Times* and the 'popular press' of tabloids such as *The Sun* and *Daily Mail*. The latter generally have significantly higher circulation figures compared with broadsheets. In November 2008, circulation figures for *The Sun* and *Daily Mail* were 3 million and 2.2 million respectively, while the highest circulation for a daily broadsheet was *The Daily Telegraph* at 835,479. Each newspaper has a 'sister' Sunday edition, with *The Sunday Times'* circulation being notably high for a broadsheet at 1.2 million (*The Guardian*, 2008b).

In terms of the political affiliation of individual newspapers, the picture is complex. For an accessible guide to the politics of British newspapers during the 2008-09 period, see: http://news.bbc.co.uk/1/hi/uk_politics/8282189.stm

THREE

Hidden in plain sight: poverty and the politics of disgust

Introduction

In this chapter I extend the analysis of the concept of emotional politics. I show how social work's role in relation to the public state on the one hand, and the privacy of family life on the other, is bound up with other powerful collective emotions. I argue that understanding the cycle of crisis and reform in child protection hinges on understanding the powerful role played by contempt and disgust directed towards particular groups, and the notion of respectability that these feelings mobilise. These feelings in turn relate to collective anxieties about social work's capacity – both imagined and real – to recognise and regulate particular groups.

The chapter draws on critical moral panic theory and cultural class analysis to argue that reactions to fatal child abuse are much more than a visceral response to an individual child's suffering. They also represent deep social and cultural anxieties about imagined dangerous and perplexing social groups to which these children are seen to have belonged. These groups include people living in poverty, particularly the so-called 'underclass', and those who are categorised as 'Other'. Social work's role – both in real terms and symbolically – is to maintain its proximity to these groups and, in the process, police the divide between 'us' and 'them' by regulating and managing the risks that such groups are deemed to represent.

The chapter is based on analysis of newspaper articles following the criminal trials of the mothers and carers of Peter Connelly in 2008 and Hamzah Khan[1] in 2013. The chapter shows how the vilification of Peter Connelly's mother emphasised disgust for the living conditions in the family home. This coverage made associations between the underclass – particularly mothers – and evil. The chapter explores how social workers were constructed in the story of Peter Connelly as tick-box, cold-hearted bureaucrats, which made his suffering invisible to them even as they saw him. The chapter then turns to the portrayal in the media of Hamzah Khan's mother as an object of disgust who transgressed all maternal instincts. The social workers in this case were portrayed as ineffectual because they did not find out what was going on behind the closed doors of the family home and did not possess an instinctive impulse to rescue the child. The chapter begins by exploring the nature of social work's relationship to people living in poverty and the underclass, and its assumed role in terms of moral regulation and risk surveillance.

Social work, the underclass and moral regulation of the dangerous Other

Since its earliest incarnations, social work has been inextricably bound up with poverty and with the complex and contradictory attitudes towards people living in poverty that have characterised social policy since the late 19th century. From its beginnings to the present day, the wide range of explanations for the causes of poverty can be mapped onto the range of activities that have been termed 'social work'. As Walkowitz (1999, p 19) puts it: 'Social workers often find themselves acting as lightning rods for the political storms that swirl around the welfare state.' From explanations that locate causes in the structural inequalities that bear down upon individuals, to those explanations that locate the causes of poverty within the flawed character of individual behaviour – these are all reflected in the broad field of activities that can be called social work. Such explanations can, in turn, be mapped onto the political sphere as 'the old and problematic binaries of structure (old Labour) versus character (Right)' (Morris and Featherstone, 2010, p 563).

Of particular relevance for this chapter is the long history of political concerns with a perceived underclass and the moral threat that this 'undeserving poor' have been judged to pose to wider society. In his analysis of Keith Joseph's 'cycle of deprivation' theories, Macnicol highlights the continuities between this and much earlier articulations of the same concerns:

> The concept of an intergenerational underclass displaying a high concentration of social problems – remaining outwith the boundaries of citizenship, alienated from cultural norms and stubbornly impervious to the normal incentives of the market, social work intervention or state welfare – has been reconstructed periodically over at least the past one hundred years. (Macnicol, 1987, p 296)

The history of concern about this underclass has a lineage that can be traced from the focus on the social residuum of the late 19th century; through the problem family of the 1950s and the cycle of deprivation theories of the 1970s; to the underclass of the 1980s (Macnicol, 1987; Welshman, 2013). While there have undoubtedly been changes in the specific focus of concern along the way, the argument that there has been more continuity than change is strong enough to assert that '[u]nderclass stereotypes have always been a part of the discourse on poverty in advanced industrial societies' (Macnicol, 1987, p 296). Even more bluntly it can be argued that '[t]he social residuum of the 1880s is the troubled family of the present day' (Welshman, 2013, p 14).

In terms of attitudes to people living in poverty, the ongoing role of the media, particularly the press, has been to operate a 'continuous performance morality play' (Golding and Middleton, 1982, p 237). They have served to connect cultural legacies from the past with contemporary anxieties through the use of culturally resonant stereotypes that are again framed as binary opposites: 'the sturdy beggar, the rogue, the stranger (the alien presence) on one side; on the other, the shopkeeper-hero distilling a mixture of thrift, enterprise and decency' (1982, pp 238-9). The media act as 'switchmen' that selectively reinforce or orchestrate from a mix of contradictory attitudes: 'As social change accelerates or throws up disorders or dislocations the media divert attention to a limited range of the available metaphors and explanations' (1982, p 237). Golding and Middleton (1982) identify two periods of social dislocation during which the press has evolved particular presentational devices: one period in the early 19th century and the second between the First and Second World Wars. The first device is the rendering of structural poverty as invisible, with the result that individual factors are thrown into the foreground. Second is the reinforcement of the concepts of 'efficiency' (of the labour market), 'morality' (of the work ethic) and 'pathology' (of individual inadequacy) as the 'lens' through which poverty is perceived. Third is the presentation of the welfare state as 'a thing apart' (1982, p 241) and thus subversive, rather than an integral part of the socioeconomic system. Under the continued ascendancy of neoliberalism, these devices have become a more rather than less prominent feature.

In its apparent imperviousness to social work interventions (Macnicol, 1987, p 296), the concept of the underclass has posed a particular problem for social work and the way it, in turn, is perceived. This is particularly so when anxieties about the believed expansion of the underclass and its potential threat to a respectable 'us' are high. The link between media and political discourse in this respect is important.

In her article on parenting and the media, for example, Millar (2007, p 46) identifies the distinction made in many media accounts between crude parenting types and the significance of this differentiation in political discourse: 'On one side the feckless, welfare-scrounging begetters of feral yobs, teenage mums and vandals; on the other the hard-working, middle Englanders that so many politicians cite these days as their target audience and whose lives are presumed to be ruined by their less responsible peers.'

In September 2008, two months before the story of 'Baby P' emerged, The Centre for Social Justice think tank published *Early intervention: Good parents, great kids, better citizens* (Allen and Smith, 2008). The report was co-authored by Iain Duncan-Smith, later the Secretary of State for Work and Pensions in the coalition government that came to power in 2010. The focus of the 2008 report was the 'dysfunctional base' of society 'where life is characterised by dependency, addiction, debt and family breakdown' (2008, p 9). The report emerged during the latter stages of the New Labour government and largely signalled continuity with this period. Along with the destigmatising approaches of the Sure Start reforms introduced by New Labour, there had been a focus on targeting the 'dysfunctional home', with clear echoes of the cycle of deprivation policies of much earlier (Morris and Featherstone, 2010; Parton, 2014). There was also a shift under New Labour towards a more assertive interventionist stance, particularly towards those seen as being 'members of a hard-core underclass' (Frost and Parton, 2009, p 165). The focus of New Labour had been on relieving poverty rather than addressing inequality (Parton, 2014). One focus of the 2008 report was a deep anxiety about the dangers of contamination and pollution posed by 'the creeping expansion of this underclass: the way decent people … are sucked into and governed by the "code of the street"' (Allen and Smith, 2008, p 9).

The authors also specifically referred to the effects of this expansion on social work practice, where they argued that levels of 'acceptable risk' had shifted and thresholds for intervention had become higher (Allen and Smith, 2008, p 26). The overwhelming picture painted in the report was of a crisis of *parenting* that threatens the *moral* order of society itself, and against which social work is unable to provide a bulwark. The report positioned a decent, respectable 'us', which was clearly delineated from a threatening, dangerous 'them'. Critical moral panic theory offers useful insights into the processes at work in this report and others like it.

Moral panic, social class and the Other

In his later theoretical work, one of the earliest moral panic theorists, Jock Young, emphasised that moral panics were borne out of 'significant structural and value changes within society', which provoked moral disturbance (Young, 2009, p 4). In this broader terrain of moral disturbance, moral indignation can be seen as the underlying long-term state while a moral panic is a more visible short-term outburst. Moral panics have been conceptualised in the political sociology of emotions as fleeting reactions that belong to simulated feelings of 'the post-emotional' society (Clarke et al, 2006). In contrast, Young sees them as an extreme expression of an ongoing emotional state of *indignation*. More specifically, Young sees moral panics as 'a dramatic form of othering' that otherwise exists in the form of (chronic) moral indignation in society (Young, 2011, p 250).

The concept of 'otherness' is central to explaining the way risk is associated with certain groups rather than others and can be defined as 'that which is conceptualised as different from the self' (Lupton, 1999, p 124). The concept has been used to explain the way different social groups are targeted through discourses of risk so that they come to be seen as 'the marginalised and stigmatised risky other' (Lupton, 1999, p 124). Processes of othering involve identification of strangeness and danger in 'them' in binary opposition to the safety and familiarity associated with 'us'. The Other is 'a symbol of fear, depravity and disgust that all respectable citizens must avoid be(com)ing at all costs' (Ferguson, 2004, p 98). The designation of the objectified Other is always produced by reference to the self (Skeggs, 1997) and so there exists an '[i]ntimate relationship between the Other and the Otherer' (Young, 2011, p 251). As well as fear, processes of Othering also generate shame. As Ahmed (2004, p 107) observes, 'some identities become stigmatised or shaming within the social order, so that the subject in assuming such identities becomes committed to a life that is read by others as shameful'. Crucially, in terms of the arguments developed in this chapter, such groups are also constructed as having the potential to pollute or extend their reach at the same time as they are marginalised, expunged and excluded from the mainstream. The fear that 'decent people' may be 'sucked into the code of the street' (Allen and Smith, 2008, p 9) is evident across both political and media discourses. The position of social work 'in between' the mainstream and those who are excluded from it is central to the way social work is perceived and the anxieties it provokes.

Moral panics in the early sociological work of the 1960s were largely concerned with post-war intergenerational conflict – as exemplified by Cohen's (1972) seminal study of youth subculture and moral panic. However, Young (2011) observed that moral panics have in recent years reflected the fears and anxieties associated with post-9/11 ontological insecurity and economic collapse. As such, he sees moral panics more latterly as being concerned with diversity and social class. The pernicious effects of growing social inequality are of particular importance here (Wilkinson and Pickett, 2009). Young has specifically located a 'prime site for moral panics' as being middle-class insecurity and detachment from the rest of society and their dearth of direct social knowledge and experience of people who are living in poverty and people who are dispossessed: 'The poor have been reconstructed into a service class … they support and subsidize the dual-career, middle-class family. Yet they are somehow invisible' (Young, 2011, p 250).

This estrangement is part of, or perhaps accounts for, 'the erosion of affective solidarities between social groups and classes' (Hoggett, 2006, p 153). For Young, this middle-class detachment, combined with a tendency towards moral indignation, means that the 'discipline necessary to maintain their class position has with it a consequent *fear of falling*' (2011, p 250, emphasis added). The anxiety and anger of the middle class, while repressed, reflect the fact that its 'members' status and class power are forever at risk because it is suspended between rich and poor in a "middle class" based upon educational attainment' (Lyman, 2004, p 139). A series of diffuse feelings of insecurity afflict large sections of the middle class, including fear of the future, anguish at the uncertain prospects facing the next generation and dread of social degradation (Wacquant, 2009). Under such conditions of insecurity, emotions relating to respectable middle-class identities in class politics become central.

Contempt has special significance in distinguishing the respectable from the disreputable. It 'ranges from visceral revulsion, disgust and sneering, through the tendency not to see or hear others as people, to the subtlest form of aversion…. It responds to accent, language, appearance, comportment, demeanour, values, actions, possessions, and lifestyle' (Sayer, 2005, p 163).

Disgust – 'a sickening feeling of revulsion, loathing or nausea' (Tyler, 2008, p 19) – is a key mechanism that underpins processes of Othering and it is also a feature of the historical development of poverty and child protection discourses in social work (Ferguson, 2004). Just as 'disgust hinges on proximity' (Lawler, 2005, p 440), so social work action hinges on proximity too. In the next subsection, the focus is the nature of moral disturbance as it relates to class politics and parenting and, specifically, the role of social work in the moral regulation of the dangerous Other.

Moral regulation of the problem mother and her home

Just as Young conceptualised moral panic as a dramatic form of Othering and an acute form of moral disturbance, Critcher sees moral panic as representing 'an extreme form of a much wider, more diffuse and less volatile process of *moral regulation*' (2009, p 31, emphasis added). This is helpful because moral panic as a process is then more readily linked to *both* ethical regulation of the *self and* moral regulation of the *Other*. In terms of parenting, the focus for regulation in either case is mothers, 'since it is mothers who are the guarantors of the social order, charged with the task of bringing up a generation of new citizens' (Lawler, 2002, p 109). As argued by Lawler (2002), the 'good middle-class mother' founds her identity on *not* being working-class. Working-class mothers are subject to being constituted as Other to the good middle-class mother and as 'bad, neglectful mothers, oversexualized and with the "wrong" kind of relation to men' (Lawler, 2002, p 109). As such, they are subject to moral regulation by social work. This dialectical construction of class identities of 'them' and 'us', 'bad parents' and 'good parents', underpins processes of moral regulation and therefore also the operation of social work.

Since it is largely concerned with working-class mothers, the moral regulation of parenting by social work is therefore both gendered and classed (Scourfield and Welsh, 2003). The site for its operation is the home, which can also be regarded as a classed space (Gillies, 2007, p 95). However, in terms of its relations with marginalised people, social work has always been associated with both control *and* care, reflecting its mediating role between the excluded and mainstream of society (Parton, 2008). It is through the creation of a subject out of the objectified individual and in the role of advocate for the marginalised that the control functions of social work are realised (Philp, 1979). To control through the operation of surveillance, the 'gaze' of social work operates through relationships in which it 'rejects anonymity in favour of a highly personalized relation with the observed' (Margolin, 1997, p 24). In the post-war period, social work was constituted by its proponents as 'friendship with a purpose' (Starkey, 2000, p 539). In crude terms, this closeness is the 'social' that produces social work. The embodied proximity of social work to 'risky' families positions it paradoxically. Social work needs to be close in order to achieve its dual aims of offering support and establishing order, but by its proximity it too represents a potential threat. As Ferguson (2004, p 121) has noted: 'Because of its closeness to and structurally ambiguous relationship with those dirty, dangerous Others who abuse children, social work itself represents a threat to ontological security and becomes a focus of the blaming system.'

In his book on the history of child protection, Ferguson documented the privatisation of practice that was a feature of the development of social work from the late 19th century to the present day, emphasising the spatial dimension of these developments and in particular the importance of the home:

> [T]he key encounters in social work and child protection took place in the home, which had gained a kind of sacred status in the symbolic ordering of everyday life. The metaphor of dirt and obsession with smell speaks to the twentieth and twenty-first century about its fears of contamination by the underclass of excluded 'problem families' and the individualized 'Other'. (Ferguson, 2004, p 67)

According to Ferguson, embodied experiences shape what is 'seen' in encounters between social workers and families. Smell in particular evokes danger while also provoking fears of contamination, such as in the case of Victoria Climbié (Ferguson, 2004, p 73). Largey and Watson (1972, p 1028) stress the significance of smell in bearing social meaning. They argue that racial identity and social class 'are often imputed in terms of odors'. Smell reflected the identification of risk to children (and society more widely) with 'marginal, "dirty" families such that in their pursuit of them it was the dirt and smell that first hit practitioners in the face and caught their nostrils' (Ferguson, 2004, p 68). In her account of social work and the stigmatisation of poor mothers as 'feckless', Starkey (2000) similarly emphasises the importance of dirt. She cites a visceral account of the 'typical problem family' by a health visitor in 1939 as follows:

> [T]he following up at home reveals dirt and neglect; if there is any decent bedding it is usually on the parents' bed, the children's accommodation being a filthy, holey flock bed or palliasse, flock or straw protruding on to the floor and soaked with urine ... the pillow ticking is usually grimy after months of use by unclean heads and much stained

from discharging and sore eyes, running ears etc. (Starkey,
2000, p 542)

Such accounts led to a sense of national disgust. This emphasis on
the physical condition of the home reflected the fact that 'problem
family' really meant 'problem mother', and the values to be instilled
in rehabilitation were 'middle-class, suburban values' (Starkey, 2000,
p 550). Starkey goes on to describe how social work during and after the
Second World War was focused on intensive family casework involving
close supervision. This closely resembled the model of intervention
currently adopted under the Troubled Families agenda (DCLG, 2012).

Following Douglas's (1966/69) work on purity and danger, Ferguson
observes that the key to understanding the link between narratives of
dirt and smell and social work action is an appreciation that 'the entire
discourse … is not really about dirt, but *order*' (2004, p 71, emphasis
in original). The operation of social work to penetrate and to cleanse
the 'most private cells' of social problems has positioned the home
as 'the final layer of resistance: it is the target, the object of scrutiny
and judgement, the target for renewal and transformation' (Margolin,
1997, p 85).

As a result, the home visit in social work became a totem that assumed
magical powers (Margolin, 1997, p 175). In relation to contemporary
social work practice, penetration of the home has become more and
not less important, with '"risks" of every description' being the focus,
especially in the homes of people living in poverty (Margolin, 1997,
p 172) with the continued focus on mothers as targets for regulation.
However, the home is also implicitly the site of the compromise that
the liberal state makes with its citizens, underpinned by the 'rule of
optimism': 'The family will be laid open for inspection PROVIDED
the state makes the best of what its agents find' (Dingwall et al, 1983,
p 92; emphasis added).

Moral panics involving social work are therefore inextricably bound
up with the moral disturbance that arises, first from its necessary
proximity to 'the dangerous Other' and, second, the fear of what it
might make of what it finds in even the most respectable homes. The
theme of respectability and the class politics of parenting is the focus
of attention in Chapter Five. In the rest of this chapter I draw on my
analysis of newspaper articles about the deaths of two children, Peter
Connelly and Hamzah Khan. This analysis highlights the significance
of the processes of class disgust and Othering that have so far in this
chapter been discussed in theoretical terms.

'Glimpses of an earthly hell'

Analysis of newspaper articles from 2008 about the death of Peter
Connelly indicated that the circumstances in which he had lived caused
as much moral outrage as the horrific way in which he had died. In
the newspaper articles there was explicit reference to the secret and
hidden nature of the child's life, and the way in which his death had
permitted 'glimpses of a world that most of us in society's comfortable
middle rarely see' (Heawood, in the *The Independent on Sunday*, 16
November 2008, p 42). Articles and editorials invoked the idea of a
pathologised underclass to differentiate this world, not only from that
of 'society's comfortable middle', but also from that of the 'normal'
conditions of deprivation that surrounded it:

> [Y]ou won't find the world of Baby P and others like him
> by merely glancing around. Theirs is a world apart even
> from the residents of this deprived area ... they are part
> of an underclass that is increasingly detached from normal
> society. (Editorial, in *The Times*, 15 November 2008b, p 6)

One of the key elements in the coverage was the visceral disgust
directed at the living conditions in Peter Connelly's family home.
These accounts reflected the longstanding idea that dirt and smell
evoke danger for both children and society at large (Ferguson, 2004).
The profoundly embodied nature of the underclass in terms of the
dirt and smell associated with it was not only presented as an 'earthly
hell' in which to raise a child. It also represented aspects of Peter
Connelly's carers' dysfunctional lifestyle choices shaped by their welfare
dependency; a life lived by 'them' through a plentiful supply of 'other
people's money' (for which can be read 'our money'). Contrasting Peter
Connelly's existence with that of a child of respectable, middle-class
parents, Hitchens writes: 'But things are different in the earthly hell
inhabited by Baby P – life financed by £450 a month of other people's
money, filthy rooms and clothes, infestations of lice, the house stinking
of human waste and overrun by smelly, aggressive dogs' (Hitchens, in
Mail on Sunday, 16 November 2008). Journalists cited the dirt and
smell of these living conditions in their vilification of Peter Connelly's
mother, including a direct association with council house occupancy:

> [H]ow is it that this disgusting piece of humanity, in the
> shape of the mother, was ever allowed to have the child in
> the first place? She came from a family of drunks, never

worked and watched porn all day. Her council house – she had to have one didn't she? – stank. Why wasn't the child taken away from her at birth? (MacKenzie, in *The Sun*, 13 November 2008)

Journalists also used the moral embodiment of the underclass that Peter Connelly's home life represented to evoke the past, specifically through comparisons with 19th-century 'Dickensian' forms of deprivation: 'In his 17 months of life he lived as the children of the Victorian slums did ... neglected and unloved and subject to arbitrary abuse' (Tweedie, in *The Daily Telegraph*, 15 November 2008). The newspapers, particularly right-leaning ones, were able to tap into powerful and well-worn negative discourses on poverty and social class. Such discourses have been explored in depth in other studies such as that by Golding and Middleton (1982), along with the hatred of 'welfarism' linked to the suffering of others (Hoggett, 2006).

Crucially, in the account of Peter Connelly's death, discourses on welfare were combined with a story of underclass parenting as 'evil'. Where evil can be unambiguously identified it permits social control at its most aggressive and punitive, since '[e]vil represents a challenge to the moral order of such magnitude that it must be identified, named, cast out' (Critcher, 2009, p 27). In this case, a story of evil acts became virtually synonymous with the status of 'welfare dependency', reflecting the hatred of dependency that has become a feature of many Western democracies (Hoggett, 2000). In the *News of the World*, under the headline 'Evil and the idle', Nelson (2008) made the link explicitly in stating: 'When a truly abhorrent crime happens, you can be sure of one thing: it'll have taken place in a welfare ghetto.' In an editorial in *The Times*, the point may have been less starkly made, but it was there nonetheless:

> The unspeakable case of Baby P raises profound questions about the state of Britain today. The welfare state has created some communities with no morality ... this is not just a story about Haringey, or the child protection system. It is a story about Britain today.... The story of Baby P provides a glimpse into the colossal failure of community, in which dependency on the State is a way of life. (*The Times*, 2008a, p 2)

As Butler and Drakeford (2011, p 84) have argued, the earliest appearance of sustained press attention on the figure of the 'benefit cheat' was reflected in coverage of the death of Maria Colwell in 1973. Questions were asked about the employment status of her stepfather, even after his conviction for her manslaughter (Butler and Drakeford, 2011). Press accounts of Peter Connelly's death also reflected deep moral disturbance about family, fathers and blood ties, again with echoes from the Maria Colwell case. The accounts identified an inability/unwillingness to sustain a stable family environment; another of the 'pathological dispositions' that characterise the underclass, and from which all other 'behavioural problems', such as delinquency, emanate (Hayward and Yar, 2006). In his article about Peter Connelly's death in *The Guardian*, Iain Duncan Smith (2008), leading Conservative politician, later Secretary of State for Work and Pensions, was clear about the diagnosis. He stated: 'Dysfunctional family life lies at the heart of the problem' (2008, p 32).

Writing in *The Sunday Telegraph* on the emergence of an underclass during the 'affluent decades', Anderson (2008, p 31) argued: 'There is a simple explanation for this: the disintegration of the family and the collapse of fatherhood.' In the newspaper accounts the male presence in the form of the mother's boyfriend epitomised 'evil', not only because of what he ultimately did, but also because of his very nature as a transient, hidden, 'unknowable' figure associated with dependency culture and sexual promiscuity. The boyfriend was one of 'an ever-shifting queue of serial boyfriends lurking just out of view, hoping for a slice of the benefits' (Hitchens, in *Mail on Sunday*, 16 November 2008). The fact that his presence was actively disguised by the mother was an important aspect of the moral condemnation of her in the press. She 'hid not only her own neglect but the presence in her filthy, flea-infested home of a boyfriend' (Riddell, in *The Daily Telegraph*, 13 November 2008a).

Press accounts of Peter Connelly's fate were permeated by moral disturbance about the underclass. This also reflected powerful and deeply contradictory anxieties about social work and its role in moral regulation and social control, which is examined in the next section of the chapter.

'Tick-box' social work, common sense and the invisibility of suffering

A particularly dominant theme in press reports concerned the overlapping domains of 'tick-box/procedural approaches' and 'common sense', which were presented as interlinked fault lines running through social work practice. The relationship between the two domains was presented in contradictory ways: in some accounts, tick-boxes had supplanted common sense, while in others, tick-boxes had only become necessary because professionals had no common sense and were incompetent to begin with. But all accounts shared the strong moral condemnation of social workers as the 'cold hearted bureaucrat' type of folk devil (Cohen, 2002, p xv). For example, Malone in *The News of the World* blamed all the social workers involved. In his article under the headline 'Baby P: They're ALL guilty', he stated: 'They [social workers] just left him there while they went off to fill in their forms, tick their boxes and cover their cowardly backsides' (Malone, 2008). Similarly, in a *Sunday Mirror* piece that ran with the headline, 'They ticked their boxes but let Baby P die in pain', McIntosh (2008, p 27) wrote: 'What is now painfully clear is that the box ticking culture of council bureaucracy is so ferociously out of control it has squashed any form of judgement or plain common sense.'

The *Daily Mail* (2008, p 16)in its Comment on the death of Baby P asserted that '[t]he correct boxes had been ticked, rules followed. To hell with the common sense that could have saved Baby Ps life.' Commentaries that argued that adherence to procedural approaches was evidence of the incompetence of the professionals involved asserted that these professionals – by implication unintelligent and lacking in humanity compared with the 'average person' – had failed to exercise common sense. For example, a leading article in *The Daily Telegraph* (2008, p 27) asserted that '[n]o one is capable of making a decision that is based on common sense rather than what is in the rule book'. Some journalists did acknowledge that the development of tick-box procedural approaches was a by-product of social services and social work responses to the reforms initiated by previous child abuse inquiries. For example, Leapman, in an article in *The Sunday Telegraph* in which he reflected on the ways in which the child protection system should develop, argued that:

> At its best, social work relies on human judgement, which can always be wrong. At its worst it is a tick-box exercise in which little judgement is exercised – and critics say this is increasingly the case, since Lord Laming's 2003 report on the murder of Victoria Climbié recommended additional layers of bureaucracy. (Leapman, 2008, p 9)

Munro, later to chair a review of child protection (2011), wrote an article for *The Independent* headlined 'Lessons learned, boxes ticked, families ignored' (Munro, 2008). However, Heffer (2008, p 28), in an article in *The Daily Telegraph*, claimed that the lack of common sense was a product of government policy: 'It [the government] has bureaucratised common sense out of social work.'

A central issue in these accounts is what constituted common sense and how it was evident that it was lacking in the case of Peter Connelly. Common sense is not a new theme in this context. In their analysis of the inquiry into the death of Maria Colwell, Butler and Drakeford (2011, p 116) highlight how common sense came to be 'a powerful lens through which to view what had happened to Maria Colwell'. Social work practice in the case was measured against 'ordinary standards of social or moral concern' and 'the accepted tenets of common sense' (Butler and Drakeford, 2011, p 116). In an article in *The Sunday Times*, Driscoll et al (2008) noted that the living conditions alone – particularly the dirt and smell – should, from a 'common sense' perspective, be sufficient evidence to warrant immediate intervention by the social worker:

> You have to brace yourself to even imagine the smell that greeted police as they entered the council flat where baby P lived and died. There was dog mess and human faeces on the floor, along with the bodies of dead chicks, mice and dismembered rabbits – food for a hungry Rottweiler and three other dogs. The living room was littered with pornography. In short it was the sort of place that would make you want to scoop up a child and get it out as quickly as possible. But when Maria Ward, Baby P's social worker, saw him for the last time four days before his death, she simply noted that he smiled and 'appeared well'. (Driscoll et al, 2008, p 15)

The message of the article was that virtually anyone in the country *except* Peter Connelly's social worker would have wanted to rescue him from the living conditions to which he was exposed. As Tweedie (2008) argued in a *Daily Telegraph* article, common sense was the common humanitarianism which he claimed social workers were lacking because 'procedure rather than human reality' was what mattered to these social workers. This mirrors the assertion by David Cameron (2008a), discussed in the previous chapter, that 'there's no substitute for common sense and responsibility.... It's these instincts we need to lead child protection for the sake of all children who are at risk.'

In the deep moral disturbance over the life and death of Peter Connelly, the discursive construction of the 'us' that would have rescued him is as powerful as that of the social workers who failed to. Similarly powerful themes are found in the media accounts from 2013 of the death of Hamzah Khan, who had died on 15 December 2009 but whose body had lain undiscovered in the family home for almost two years. These themes are explored in the next section, particularly the moral narratives relating to the perplexing figure of Hamzah Khan's mother, Amanda Hutton.

A mother's instinct, transgression and the impulse to rescue

The second half of 2013 signalled an increasingly intense crisis period for social work and child protection. It culminated in autumn 2013 in a 'perfect storm' of national media and political commentary following a sequence of interrelated events. On 31 July, Daniel Pelka's mother and stepfather were convicted of his murder in Coventry. On 3 October, a serious case review into the death of Keanu Williams[2] in Birmingham was published and the trial of Amanda Hutton ended with her conviction for the manslaughter and neglect of her son, Hamzah Khan, in Bradford. During the same period, there was intensely angry further coverage of the story of Peter Connelly when, in late October, Sharon Shoesmith received a compensation award for her dismissal from Haringey Council in 2008. Just a few days afterwards, Tracey Connelly, Peter Connelly's mother, was released from prison. What had already been a set of complex and multilayered narratives was made still more complex by the interweaving of new accounts of cruelty, suffering and professional failings into those from five years before.

Crucially, however, these events were not only locked together in the symbolic narratives of the political and media sphere. They were also deeply connected to the real world of practice and in the reordering of priorities for action arising directly from reaction to the death of Peter Connelly. This is a point made most poignantly in the introductory section of the serious case review into the death of Hamzah Khan, as follows:

> The review has set out to understand what was happening and why and to explore the various influences and contributory factors. For example, mention is made in later sections of the report about how the aftermath of the 'Baby P' case had very significant consequences in the increased level of contacts and referrals and how some of the measures designed to help ameliorate workload pressures

had consequences in how information was being recorded at the time and the capacity to follow up less urgent or unresolved information such as when Hamzah was first identified as missing from education and health services. (Bradford Safeguarding Children Board, 2013, p 9)

Media and political reaction to the deaths of Hamzah Khan, Daniel Pelka and Keanu Williams reflected different anxieties from those seen in relation to the death of Peter Connelly. However, what they share are the questions each of their deaths raised about their visibility as children in their communities, to wider society and to the agencies that might have intervened to prevent their deaths. Coverage of Peter Connelly's death was characterised by a focus on entire 'hidden communities of immorality' in Britain. Reaction to the death of Hamzah Khan was characterised by revulsion and shock at the degree to which he had been neglected by his mother and how it had remained hidden behind the closed door of the family home, as illustrated in the following *Daily Mail* piece:

> It is barely believable that a family in 21st century Britain could live in such horrific conditions. Almost every room was littered with plastic bags of household rubbish, bottles, filthy nappies, newspapers, vomit and mouldy food.... Hidden in a travel cot, beneath clothes, shoes and bedding, was the body of Hamzah Khan. The little boy had been starved to death by his cruel alcoholic and cannabis-addicted mother. (Brooke, in *Daily Mail*, 4 October 2013)

Unlike Peter Connelly, who had repeatedly been seen – at home and elsewhere – by a range of services but had apparently remained 'unseen', or 'hidden in plain sight', Hamzah Khan had been entirely invisible, not only to health and social care agencies, but also to those within his immediate community and street: 'When news of [Hamzah Khan's] death became public, neighbours said they had never seen him. He may as well have not existed' (Pidd, in *The Guardian*, 4 October 2013).

Press accounts during the days following the conviction of Amanda Hutton for her son's manslaughter reflect the moral voice of the trial judge, Judge Thomas, in his summing up of the case. As illustrated by the following two quotes, the focus is on Amanda Hutton's abject failure as a mother, on her 'deviousness' in her avoidance of various agencies and on her 'selfish addiction' to drink and drugs, which she prioritised above the care of her children. The explanation that is privileged is not the modern, medical conception of severe alcohol addiction, but the centuries-old, archetypal account of the woman who pursues alcohol for her own selfish gratification in deliberate neglect of her children (Waterson, 2000):

> Judge Thomas sentenced her to 12 years in prison for manslaughter and added three years for child cruelty. He told her that her 'wicked conduct' happened 'through your purposeful, persistent and gross conduct in failing in that most basic and fundamental requirement that is upon every parent, to feed her child adequately'. (Higgens, in *The Independent*, 5 October 2013, p 7)

> Judge Roger Thomas, QC, said that he was sentencing Hutton for her 'terrible failures to fulfil the most basic responsibilities that you, as a mother, should have fulfilled'. He added that she 'must be regarded as a real danger to any child with whom you may live, or in any way have care of in the future'. Hutton showed no emotion as she was led from the dock. (Brown, in *The Times*, 5 October 2013, p 31)

The newspaper reports also give moral voice to the downplaying of the possible impact of the domestic violence to which Amanda Hutton was subjected over many years. The domestic violence in the case was constructed as something that should not arouse compassion for Hutton but as something she was using to deflect attention from her accountability, since '[u]nder cross-examination she accepted that other women with violent partners had managed to bring up healthy children who were not neglected' (Pidd, in *The Guardian*, 4 October 2013). The position of the adult male family members in relation to Hamzah Khan's invisibility is presented largely in morally neutral terms. A strong moral voice is afforded in some press reports to Aftab Khan, Hamzah Khan's father and Amanda Hutton's ex-partner, despite his history of violence within the family. In the coverage of the accounts given in court of their violent relationship, any suggestion of Amanda Hutton's suffering is neutralised by the simple statement of facts. The last word in the following *Daily Mail* piece is given through the voice of her ex-partner and his vitriolic moral condemnation of her:

> The court heard she was beaten by Khan throughout the 20-year relationship. Her personal problems worsened dramatically a few months after Hamzah was born when

Hutton's mother Ann died from breast cancer in December 2005, leaving her heartbroken. She was on anti-depressants for post-natal depression and turned increasingly to alcohol. Police were regularly called to the house, but Hutton refused to make a complaint against her violent partner. She changed her mind and they finally split up in December 2008 after Khan attacked Tariq [their eldest son]. Khan was later convicted of beating Hutton. During police interviews, he told officers: 'She's a bitter and twisted woman and there's something seriously wrong with her. She don't brush her teeth, she don't clean herself, she don't look after herself. She's an alcoholic.' (Brooke, in *Daily Mail*, 4 October 2013)

The disgust attached to Amanda Hutton at the end of this piece is significant because it introduces deep moral ambiguity over the violence she was subjected to by her partner. Details of the estrangement of Amanda Hutton from family members such as her father are presented factually and therefore also in morally ambiguous terms. This is again in contrast with the moral voice given to him in the report, in which he condemns his daughter and social services outright:

But Hutton was also so cut off from relatives that her father [Alan] didn't know Hamzah had been born. Alan Hutton, a phone installation engineer living in the Scottish Borders, said he was ashamed of his wayward daughter and they lost touch a decade ago. 'What she has done is evil,' he said. What kind of mother starves her own child to death? Can she even be a part of the human race? He died all on his own, a painful death. Social services should have taken him away. They should have intervened. There was an apathy there. It is better to do too much than too little. They let him down. (Brooke, in *Daily Mail*, 4 October 2013)

The question of what he may have done or not done is clearly a moral question that such articles were not prepared to ask. Compassion is extended to both the father and the grandfather of the child so that questions over what they may have done differently are simply not asked. In the midst of the details provided about Amanda Hutton and failures to intervene by services, the discussion of any possible role that might have been played by family members in preventing or contributing to the eventual tragedy is notable by its absence. The father and grandfather remain very much on the sidelines except in offering further condemnation of Amanda Hutton and services. As the serious case review was to later observe: 'Neither the trial nor the SCR [serious case review] has satisfactorily reconciled how and why Hamzah's disappearance for almost two years was not a matter of curiosity or inquiry for the father or any other adults in Hamzah's family' (Bradford Safeguarding Children Board, 2013, p 7).

A mother's instinct

Just as Amanda Hutton's failings as a mother were the focus of press reports, the transgression of maternal instinct was also implicitly a theme in the accounts of social work failings in the case. This was evident in the presentation of the heroic figure of the woman police community support officer (PCSO) who found Hamzah Khan's body. The PCSO gave an account of having followed her 'mother's instinct' and so personifies the 'common sense' of an emotional, visceral urge to rescue a child at risk of maltreatment. Her assertiveness based on maternal instinct throws the lack of such qualities among professionals into sharp relief, as exemplified in the following extract from *The Daily Telegraph*:

> His death might have remained undetected had it not been for the 'mother's instinct' of a police community support officer who visited the house on her second day in the job and sensed that something was wrong. She opened a 'terrible Pandora's Box', the court was told. Jodie Dunsmore felt Hutton was 'hiding something' when she refused to let her in, but would not take no for an answer, leading to the discovery of Hamzah's corpse in September 2011. Her curiosity, concern and tenacity appeared to have been signally lacking in other professionals who missed at least nine opportunities to intervene while Hamzah was alive. His story was so heartbreaking that Hutton's trial at Bradford Crown Court had to be restarted with a new jury after one of the original panel broke down as the evidence was read, and could not continue. (Rayner, in *The Daily Telegraph*, 4 October 2013, front page)

The PCSO was assertive in gaining access to the home based on an instinctive response that something was wrong. The fact that she had only recently started her job brings her closer to 'us' and distances her from the professionals whose experiences have blunted their instincts. The figure of the PCSO personifies what constitutes an appropriate professional response as reflected in political and media discourses on child protection. It again brings to mind the injunction by David Cameron (2008a) in his newspaper article noted in the last chapter: 'It's these instincts we need to lead child protection for the sake of all children who are at risk.'

More deeply buried in the story of Hamzah Khan's death are the wider possible causes of his mother's decline into severe alcoholism and social isolation that ultimately led to her extreme neglect of him and his invisibility to others. In contrast to the individual failings and character flaws that are the sole focus of many of the press reports, the serious case review asserts that 'Amanda Hutton was not always such an inadequate or a dangerous parent' (Bradford Safeguarding Children Board, 2013, p 6). It includes the domestic violence as a significant cause of her social isolation, but also extends its analysis to consider her position as a perplexing, liminal figure in terms of her racial and cultural identity and, by extension, that of her children too. The report comments on the negative reaction that Amanda Hutton seemed to provoke from other people, as a white woman married to an Asian man. The following account suggests that she was perhaps first marginalised and ostracised by others before shutting herself away:

> The cultural and religious complexity of the family was not enquired into. This is surprising for a service working in a metropolitan district with a rich history and diversity of culture, religion and language. It is of some note that there are occasions when Amanda Hutton appears to be the victim of racial or cultural inspired violence. The BDCT [Bradford and District Care Trust] author comments that Amanda Hutton was isolated from both the white and Asian communities. (Bradford Safeguarding Children Board, 2013, p 52)

Not only was Amanda Hutton apparently a perplexing figure in terms of her cultural and racial identity, her class status and the respectability it might confer on her also served to confuse people with whom she came into contact: 'Hutton, 43, the daughter of a nurse, came from a middle class background and was "well-spoken", something which appeared to have thrown some of those who came into contact with her' (Rayner, in *The Daily Telegraph*, 4 October 2013, front page).

These factors bring to the fore the sense in which Amanda Hutton was a marginalised and vulnerable figure in the community. I argue that the invisibility of her son can *only* be understood in this context.

Conclusion

In this chapter I have argued that political and media reactions to the death of a child are characterised by deep disturbance, not only at the horrific nature of the child's death, but also at the worlds they are perceived to have occupied when alive and which have been exposed to public view by their deaths. It is important to recognise that, while alive, such children occupy a very different imaginary realm from that of the 'pure, helpless, innocent being' (Hoggett, 2006, p 154) that they come to occupy in death. Along with their parents and perhaps their entire community – as in Peter Connelly's case – they are very likely to be designated Other and undeserving, are deeply stigmatised and, most significantly, are deemed to pose a threat.

While almost all political and media discourse about the deaths of children reflects themes of children being invisible or hidden, the reality is that the poor conditions, hardships and challenges in which they and their families *live* represent forms of suffering that 'we' do not wish to see. Research from other fields shows that the social organisation of denial arises because thinking about unpleasant things raises 'fears of ontological security, emotions of helplessness and guilt, and [is] a threat to individual and collective senses of identity' (Norgaard, 2006, p 372). The state functions as part of the social organisation of denial and routinely protects 'us' from the suffering of others. In this sense, the state serves to 'create an impermeable membrane which is resistant to disturbance, to be both "thick-skinned" and unresponsive to the suffering of some of its citizens (particularly those regarded as "undeserving") whilst trying to appear responsive to the demands of the deserving' (Hoggett, 2006, p 151).

Social work forms part of this attempt to be responsive to the suffering of others, but in its dealings with people living in poverty, it too is caught up in the delineation between deserving and undeserving. Furthermore, social workers do not always have the vocabulary for the complex emotional effects of poverty and structural inequality that they encounter, especially shame (Featherstone et al, 2014). Social work operates in the context of a wider feeling of moral condemnation of people living in poverty rather than compassion. This is particularly true of people living in poverty close to home: 'If only our own poor could present themselves as innocents, essentially virtuous but the victims of forces beyond their control, then they could receive our fellow feeling. But, increasingly, they do not' (Hoggett, 2006, p 152). This is equally true of the most vulnerable children. English social policy since the Tudors has constituted abused children as a threat to civil order rather than as victims (Dingwall et al, 1983). As Ferguson (2007, p 137) observed in his study of abuses of children in care: 'while there have been some important changes, the construction of abused and looked after children as a grotesque "Other", as "moral dirt", lingers'. Martin Narey of Barnardo's made the link directly and explicitly in relation to Peter Connelly:

> The tragic probability, is that had Baby P survived, he would probably have been unruly by the time he was 13 or 14, at which he wouldn't have been Baby P any longer, he'd have become 'feral', a 'parasite', a 'yob', helping to infest our streets. All terms used on newspaper websites very recently, about children. And what would our response have been to an unruly Baby P at 13 or 14? We'd have locked him up. (Narey, 2008)

A recurring theme in accounts of the deaths of children is that what was happening should have been obvious to those in proximity to the families concerned, but that the child was invisible, or 'hidden in plain sight'. I have argued that their invisibility can only be understood in a wider cultural context and the way their families and communities are marginalised and hidden from view.

In the next chapter, I focus in greater depth on the process by which media and political discourses about the deaths of children generate a universal, symbolic child. I argue that it is this symbolic child that drives political reform in social work and child protection and which has become the main focus of the political impulse to rescue.

Notes

[1] Hamzah Khan died in Bradford in December 2009, aged four years. His body was discovered at the family home in September 2011, almost two years after his death. He had died from starvation and severe neglect. His mother, Amanda Hutton, was convicted of his manslaughter and of child cruelty.

[2] Keanu Williams died in Birmingham in 2011, aged two years. He was found to have sustained multiple non-accidental injuries due to assaults over a period of weeks prior to his death. He had been the subject of an assessment by child protection agencies and defined as a 'child in need'.

Keanu's mother, Rebecca Shuttleworth, was convicted of his murder and her boyfriend, Luke Southerton, was convicted of child cruelty.

FOUR

From crisis to reform: the emotional politics of child rescue and commemoration

Introduction

In the previous two chapters I have argued that emotional politics in its current form is characterised by the mobilisation of anger, disgust and shame by politicians and by the media towards social work and the so-called 'underclass' – particularly mothers. In this chapter I extend the concept of emotional politics and illustrate other processes that characterise it. In the first section, I highlight the importance of collective remembering, which can be understood as a form of social action through commemoration. I argue that processes of commemoration are of deep significance in driving the impetus for reform. Through commemoration, particular ways of making sense of the past – and therefore, implicitly, the future – are sustained. The rhetorical device of listing the names of children who have died in the past in a 'roll-call' is explored, together with processes of inquiry and case review.

The politics of the impulse to rescue children is illustrated in the second section of the chapter, this time in relation to the relevant ministerial portfolio. Through analysis of a political speech in which reform measures are announced, the chapter shows how binary discourse and the roll-call of children's names are used to code reforms in moral terms that link them to the prevention of any future deaths, thereby casting any opposition to them as morally wrong. The link that is made in the speech between the urge to reform and the personal experience of the politician also suggests that such speech acts can be understood as a form of emotional labour. One specific element of the reform agenda announced in the speech is briefly analysed, which is the creation of an alternative training route for social workers. In this initiative, I argue that the creation of a newly idealised, heroic social worker can be seen as the antidote to the toxic, folk-devil social worker that was constructed through reaction to the death of Peter Connelly.

The chapter then moves on in the third section to explore the idea of emotional interest representation. A brief account is given of the ancient concept of 'interest representation' in parliamentary politics, which enjoyed a revival in the post-war period and has continued to expand since. This is where the primary role of MPs is to seek redress for grievances on behalf of their constituents. I develop this concept in terms of its emotional dimension. I argue that politicians can be understood as envoys of the emotions that are both personally felt by and expressed among their constituents, which they then seek to convert into political action. Feelings of constituents in response to the death of a child are expressed through personal correspondence (including social media and email), face-to-face in MP surgeries, by word of mouth on the street and in the local press and other media. The chapter focuses on two examples where these processes of emotional interest representation can be observed: first in relation to the death of Lauren Wright in 2001[1] and second in relation to the death of Daniel Pelka in 2012. In both cases, the myth of political control and the impulse to rescue are also in evidence, where reforms to legislation and guidance are invested in as measures that will prevent another child's death and where risk is regarded as politically unacceptable.

A 'sad army of little children': collective memory and the politics of false hope

Political and media accounts of the death of a child from abuse frequently invoke events from the past, often collecting together children who have died under apparently similar, appalling circumstances in a 'roll-call' of their names. In terms of media coverage, the death of Maria Colwell in 1973 was of particular significance, as emphasised by Butler and Drakeford:

> It [the Colwell case] provided the first entry in the cuttings file for any journalist faced with an apparently similar case. Thus, whenever a child dies, the name of a previous child to die is invoked: Peter Connelly invokes Victoria Climbié, who invokes Tyra Henry, who invokes Jasmine Beckford, who invokes Maria Colwell. (Butler and Drakeford, 2011, pp 193-4)

The way children's deaths in the past are woven through time into the present (and, implicitly, the future) can be demonstrated in a simple, if crude measure of the co-occurrence of children's names in newspaper articles. In the 12 months between January 2007 and January 2008, articles in newspapers referring to Victoria Climbié numbered 109. During the 12-month period when coverage of the death of Peter Connelly was at its most intense, from November 2008 to November 2009, references to Victoria Climbié rose to 333. More than a tenth of the articles about Peter Connelly also referred to Victoria Climbié. Similarly, following the conviction in July 2013 of those responsible for Daniel Pelka's death, there were 255 newspapers items regarding the story up to January 2014. A fifth of these also referred to Peter Connelly. This effect was even more marked in the case of the reporting of the Hamzah Khan case, where, following the conviction of his mother in early October 2013, almost a third of the 93 newspaper articles about his death published up to January 2014 also referred to Peter Connelly.

Butler and Drakeford rightly argue that the process of invoking the past has served to emphasise similarities and mask important differences: 'Even when no obvious similarities exist, irrelevant, ahistorical but also potentially misleading comparisons may be made and dwelt on, not least in the pages of newspapers, especially if they are in campaigning mode. The ghost of each successive scandal haunts the next' (Butler and Drakeford, 2011, pp 193-4).

The same can be said of political rhetoric, in which the process of bringing names together is evident from the mid- to late-1980s, as illustrated by the following statement by an MP in a debate in the House of Commons in 1985. During this period, the public response to the death of Jasmine Beckford and other children had served to focus political attention, with a notable increase in debates and parliamentary questions in the House of Commons (Drewry, 1987):

> I wish to highlight one or two points that have put this issue so high in the public concern. In this year alone, there has been the case of the 22-month-old girl who was killed by a ball of wool being pushed into her mouth; the case of Jasmine Beckford, aged four, who after 10 months of terror, was finally beaten to death by her stepfather; the 21-month-old baby Tyra Henry, who was battered and covered with 57 bites; the child Christopher Stock who was bitten and beaten by his mother; Heidi Koseda, whom many hon. Members mentioned; and Charlene Salt, who was shut in a drawer and died of brain haemorrhage. Against such a background, the public concern, which we all share, is not only entirely understandable, but well accepted on both sides of the House. (Whitney, 1985, col 1162)

From the mid-1980s onwards, more names were added to the lists that invoked the names of children from the past, forming what one MP described as a 'sad army of little children who have died' (Lestor, 1989, col 1155).

In assessing the recommendations made by the Laming Inquiry into the death of Victoria Climbié, the House of Commons Health Select Committee report that was published shortly afterwards serves to illustrate the obvious point that what these children shared, first and foremost, was the way they suffered:

> Since 1948 there have been around 70 public inquiries into major cases of child abuse. The names of many of the children who have died have become well known, simply because of the terrible nature of their deaths. From Maria Colwell in 1973, to Jasmine Beckford and Tyra Henry (both in 1984), Kimberley Carlile (1986), Leanne White (1992), and Chelsea Brown in 1999, the deaths of these children all share many points of similarity. (House of Commons Health Select Committee, 2003, p 5)

While Butler and Drakeford are right that important differences between cases are masked by easy comparisons, it is equally clear that what these children shared is of overriding significance in *cultural* terms. The fact that their suffering and death were the consequence of parental abuse or neglect is the source of particularly deep disturbance. I argue that the nature of the suffering experienced by each child brought them together in cultural terms as an infinite set, defined as 'a collection where the counting of its elements or members does not, conceptually, come to an end' (Rayner, 1995, p 56). This aggregation of children into an infinite set produces a symbolic, or mythological, child that can stand for all others, where one name can represent many children, moving backwards or forwards through time. In this sense, as I have already argued, the stories of child deaths in the media function as myths that are important for being 'the same story retold'. The listing of names serves as a chronicle of events and, as Bird and Dardenne (1997, p 340) put it: 'Through chronicle, the overall structure of the myth is emphasized, although individual stories are not.'

News stories, however dysfunctional, constitute part of the search for meaning in the midst of the disturbance raised by the death of children. News stories constantly draw on stories from the past in order to build a specific set of cultural meanings and through which the news 'provides credible answers to baffling questions and ready explanations of complex phenomena' (Bird and Dardenne, 1997, p 336). A 'credible answer' in cultural terms to the question of how children could die under such circumstances appears to avoid altogether the unfathomable questions regarding what their parents did to them. It focuses instead on the failure of state agents to adequately intervene to prevent their deaths and the possibilities for reform to prevent it happening again. This is a valuable displacement not only in cultural terms, but also politically.

Alongside the roll-call of children's names is the message that the same professional failings have been repeated over and over again. In 1985, *The Times* epitomised this in its account under the headline 'Catalogue of failure in infant abuse deaths':

> From Maria Colwell, the seven-year-old girl battered to death by her stepfather in 1973, to the inquiries into the deaths of Tyra Henry and Jasmine Beckford, there have now been more than 20 public and formal inquiries into deaths from child abuse since 1973 ... From the list of inquiries the same factors emerge time and again in the failures that led to children's deaths – communication breakdowns between social workers or other departments and agencies, failures to review cases regularly and comprehensively, and misunderstandings of the job of other professionals. (*The Times*, 27 July 1985)

The account of repeated failures given in *The Times* article, and the thousands of similar accounts in the press since, can easily be interpreted as despairing about the future. However, the fact that each child's death is understood as being the consequence of failures means that such articles encapsulate infinite *hope*:

- communication systems can be improved;
- social workers and others can be made to review cases regularly and comprehensively;
- understanding between professionals can be modified.

But rather than a hope based on a rational appraisal of the possibility for improving services, it is a politicised hope that reform is possible 'to make this child's death the last'. This hope is mirrored in the perpetual reforms that 'hold out the false hope of eliminating risk' (Munro, 2011, p 134). I argue that it is in this sense we can understand the naming of children from the past as a form of collective remembering and commemoration, which has important political and institutional consequences.

Collective remembering and commemoration

Activities of remembering and forgetting are inherently social and cultural (Middleton and Edwards, 1990) and they are rooted in a range of collective emotional experiences. The social practice of commemoration embodies the tension between viewing the past as fixed and 'conserved in the present', and the past as susceptible to new and different interpretations (Middleton and Edwards, 1990, p 8). The rhetorical and institutional organisation of remembering and forgetting involves 'telling the right kind of story' about the past, in which accounts about what happened and who might be honoured, blamed, trusted and so forth are evident. For example, when service men and women who have died in world wars and other conflicts are symbolically represented in war memorials and at formal services on Remembrance Sunday, their memory is invoked in a *particular* story about the past. Contrary interpretations of that past are not represented and '[t]he silent remembrance of those who died in battle also silences outrage at the courses of action entailing such loss' (Middleton and Edwards, 1990, p 8).

In the case of children who have died from abuse, institutional forms of collective remembering reflect a paradoxical set of tensions between the universal child that is produced and the desire to remember each child individually. As already argued, the rhetorical organisation of remembering in the form of a roll-call of children's names produces a universal child, where each child can stand for other children (crucially, even those who are never named). The sad army of little children not only reaches into the past; it also implicitly reaches into the future, to children as yet unnamed and unknown, and a meaning that will be given to their deaths that is already prescribed. However, there is also a desire to commemorate each individual child. This desire is most keenly reflected in the pressure for inquiry or review processes to be held into a child's death, as illustrated later in this chapter and in Chapter Six of the book. It is through an inquiry or case review that the details of the child's life and suffering can be *publicly* witnessed, when the biographies of individual children are, possibly for the only time, coherently articulated. This impulse is poignantly expressed in the dedication to Victoria Climbié at the beginning of the Victoria Climbié Inquiry report. It features a colour photograph of Victoria smiling, apparently happy and healthy. Beneath the photograph is the dedication, which incorporates a translated extract from *The Little Prince* by Antoine de Saint-Exupéry:

> 'I have suffered too much grief in setting down these heartrending memories. If I try to describe him, it is to make sure that I shall not forget him.'

This sentiment applies also to Victoria Climbié.

This report is dedicated to her memory. (Laming, 2003, p iii)

Cooper (2005, p 5) argues that, while the report begins with a 'clear sense of political passion for change', reflecting this deep identification with Victoria's suffering, it ends with 'the same kind of terse, lifeless, abstract series of recommendations that has flowed from every other similar exercise'. The catalogue of suffering and institutional failings documented through processes of inquiry and review, while particular at the level of detail, secures that individual child's place in the infinite set of children who have died through abuse and neglect. Both the roll-call of names and processes of inquiry can therefore be understood as forms of collective remembering where both the universal *and* individual child is commemorated.

I argue that the institutional forms of commemoration of children who have died from abuse and neglect represent an integral part of the emotional regime that operates in relation to social work and child protection. The story of the past that they tell – especially the story of repeated failings on the part of services – provides the main moral impetus for political reform, as analysed in the next section.

The emotional politics of child rescue through reform

On 12 November 2013, Michael Gove, then Secretary of State for Education, delivered a speech at the headquarters of the National Society for the Prevention of Cruelty to Children on the subject of child protection (DfE, 2013a). The speech was widely reported in national media that evening and in newspapers the following day. The main aim of the speech was to set out a reform agenda for children's social care comprising three 'pillars of reform'. The three pillars were:

- improving social work practice;
- encouraging innovation and reducing bureaucracy;

- creating clearer lines of accountability.

These reforms were to provide a platform for later proposals to outsource child protection from the control of local authorities. The speech drew on the main themes that were discernible in political and media responses to the death of Peter Connelly in 2008 and which I have explored in-depth in the book so far. However, the emotional politics at work in Gove's speech was not the mobilisation of anger or grief, but a moral device in which the mobilisation of political action over child abuse deaths is achieved through the creation of binary discourse.

Binary discourse essentially involves the construction of reality into simple 'either/or' categories in which there is a struggle between two positions, one of which is presented as being morally superior to the other. For instance, Coe et al (2004) analysed national addresses by US President George W. Bush and the development of the 'war on terror' narrative after 9/11. They identified an archetypal example of binary discourse in the President's assertion: 'Either you're with us or with the enemy' (2004, p 234). In order that the construction of a binary discourse can be effective in political terms, it requires a 'centrally organising object' that resonates with the public and which is, preferably, easily conceived in moral terms (2004, p 235). As Coe et al (2004) argue, a centrally organising object can be an idea, an event or behaviour, but it is ideally one that people have a 'gut-level' reaction to and which is therefore likely to assist in the mobilisation of action. Child abuse can be considered a centrally organising object in these terms.

Gove's speech is a good example of how binary discourse can be used to evoke through language a particular moral stance, opposition to which is then positioned as morally wrong. The starting point of Gove's speech was the construction of an either/or category of politician in which politicians are either interventionist *or* non-interventionist:

> There are really – at heart – just two schools of politicians.
>   Not left and right.
>   But those who believe in intervention. And those who don't. (DfE, 2013a)

These two categories were presented as being mutually exclusive: it is not possible for a politician to be non-interventionist on some issues and interventionist on others. Most importantly, for the purposes of this chapter, as the narrative of the speech developed, the categories were clearly morally coded as interventionist equals morally good, non-interventionist equals morally bad. In the first instance, these categories are related to foreign policy interventions. As in David Cameron's (2008a) article analysed in Chapter Two, the use of the unifying 'we' as an appeal to affinity was important in Gove's speech too: 'Faced with crises and disasters abroad some of us believe that we should – whenever we can – act decisively…. Others prefer not to act' (DfE, 2013a).

Following a section of the speech in which there was a focus on the reforms his department had pursued in education policy, the attention shifted to children's social care and specifically child protection. Here, the interventionist category was associated with the (morally right) impulse to rescue in contrast with the non-interventionist failure to protect. However, the continued use of the term 'we' also conveyed a sense of a shared moral responsibility for failings:

> But there is one other area which is my responsibility in government where we have not yet intervened vigorously enough.
> The protection of our most vulnerable children.
> We have not intervened to rescue those children who have been suffering the most in our society. (Gove, 2013)

There was then a roll-call of the names of children who had died in recent years as a litany of pain and failure, into which Gove injected a powerful sense of his personal mission to see change. Whereas David Cameron's message of accumulated grief and anger spanned the years between the deaths of Maria Colwell, Victoria Climbié and Peter Connelly, Gove's focus was his own, more recent, experience of such deaths in the political sphere:

> My time in politics so far has been punctuated by moments when all of us have been left speechless – because a child's cries were never heard.
>
> Peter Connelly
>
> Khyra Ishaq
>
> Hamzah Khan

Keanu Williams

Daniel Pelka

All children who cried out in pain – and we never listened.
And never acted. (DfE, 2013a)

While the memories of individual children are invoked through naming them, they are yoked together as the universal child whose cries of pain went unheeded. There is no explicit mention of social work because it is not necessary to name it. The element of the story concerning the social worker who did not act has already been vividly told and retold through media and political accounts of the deaths of these children. Social work failings are brought to mind as a function of the recollection of children who have died. It is here that the importance of the roll-call of names as a form of commemoration is exemplified. Through its use, both the past and future are organised rhetorically. While the continued use of the universal 'we' in the speech again implies wide responsibility for failings, the earlier construction in the speech of a binary discourse around intervention suggests that neither Gove nor the rest of 'us' who would intervene are really morally implicated. Gove's sense of mission to see change is then personalised by his reference to his own experiences as a child in care and, crucially, his own positive experience of social workers:

> As someone who started their life in care, whose life was transformed because of the skill of social workers and the love of parents who were not my biological mother and father but who are – in every sense – my real mum and dad, this is personal. A child's opportunity to flourish should not be a matter of chance – it should be the mission which guides all our actions.

For Gove, then, the task of reform was not a rational-managerial one but an emotional one. The way this brief personal insight was offered in a speech announcing policy reforms is a good example of how the political has become more entwined with the personal to the extent that it represents a form of 'emotional labour' (Richards, 2007). One message of this speech was that Gove had a deeply personal and emotional investment in the reforms he sought to pursue and as such could be considered more trustworthy than if his ambitions were purely ideological. As Richards (2007, p 99) argues: 'There is both a stronger imperative to take on emotional labour in a personally-oriented and explicit way.... And there is greater opportunity for influence through the undertaking of this labour.'

In the analysis of the political rhetoric deployed by David Cameron in Chapter Two, being appalled by the death of Peter Connelly was logically equated with anger and a desire to see 'the buck stop somewhere'. To not be angry was to not be appalled. The binary discourse at the beginning of Gove's speech established the morally right position as being the one that supported the 'interventionist' reform agenda set out in the rest of the speech. Those who might disagree with the reforms were logically cast as non-interventionists; not 'with us', so 'against us'. They were thereby positioned morally as people who would continue to ignore children's cries of pain.

The rhetorical positioning of 'interventionist' versus 'non-interventionist' in the speech reflects a willingness to present a political discourse of hope and certainty about the possibilities for the prevention of fatal child abuse. This discourse in turn reflects the political necessity of always being, or appearing to be, in control in the face of 'a consistent stream of failures, scandals and disasters which challenge and threaten organisations, suggesting a world which is out of control' (Power, 2004, p 10). The need to appear in control can also be linked to the rise of risk management systems and the 'reputation risk' associated with them, which can be identified across private and public organisations, both inside and outside the health and social care sectors (Power, 2004). Gove's speech characterised failure as belonging in the past, and as being rooted in a moral choice 'not to listen; not to act'. Strong political leadership on the issue was characterised as heroic, compassionate and derived from personal experience; a rhetorical device that defined others, by exclusion, as occupying inferior moral terrain. But how can the more interventionist stance advocated in the speech be reconciled with the pact that the liberal state makes with its citizens 'to defend the autonomy of families' (Dingwall et al, 1983, p 244)? The answer is twofold: first by targeting the 'right' families for intervention and second by recruiting the 'right' people into social work.

Reconstituting social work as heroic

In a major section of the speech, Gove addressed the reforms he proposed to make to social work training and education. He initially constituted social work as heroic, but the heroic social worker was cast in terms of what the *role* involves and the demands made upon them. While the speech ensured that it gave credit to the current workforce and the 'many, many superb social workers' that already exist, Gove went on to emphasise that 'we are still not recruiting enough great people into social work and we are not training existing social workers well enough' (DfE, 2013a). The antidote to this problem was presented in the speech in the form of an 'explicitly elitist' new programme of social work training that would attract 'very impressive people'. The prestige that should attach to social work is therefore not seen as fundamentally derived from the nature of the work that it involves. It would be derived from the calibre of person who will newly populate the ranks of social work. Social work will be transformed because the people who will be social workers in future will be good people who have the courage to intervene.

Most important of all, the new social workers of the 'Frontline' scheme will have, according to the speech, 'intellectual abilities, and a level of emotional intelligence, or common sense, which are out of the ordinary'. Imprinted on this representation of the new social worker is the message that they will not be subject to 'the rule of optimism'. They will not be fooled by deceitful parents, or those disguising the torture they are inflicting on their child behind closed doors. These social workers will know which homes to visit; which doors to insist are opened and which may remain firmly shut; and which parents to pursue through the courts and which to leave alone. They will know when to exercise the rule of optimism, and when the rule of pessimism should apply. The speech identified the target for pessimistic intervention as the lying, drinking, drug-taking, workshy, promiscuous underclass mother, in the following, thinly veiled terms: 'Neither is it easy to see through the sometimes manipulative – and sometimes evasive, dishonest or disingenuous – behaviour of some adults as they lie about their drinking, their drug use, their efforts to find work or – most critically – which men have access to their house – and their children' (DfE, 2013a).

The idealised social worker of Gove's speech that will tackle these parents is further illustrated in the following leading article about the new initiative that appeared in *The Independent on Sunday*. The article followed the Conservative Party Conference in 2013 at which David Cameron had led a round of applause for social work:

> It has been suggested that David Cameron was badly advised to have spoken about social workers in his speech to the Conservative Party conference last week. His staff must have known, it has been said, that two terrible court cases were listed for the week – cases that would once again

cause the country to shake its head at the failure of social workers and other agencies to share information and to act on basic warnings, such as a newborn child not seen by a GP [general practitioner].

We disagree. It is precisely because the harrowing cases of children killed by parents are so hard in practice to prevent that the Prime Minister should lend his precious authority to finding ways to raising the capability of child protection services, and should use his public platforms to promote the cause.

The Independent on Sunday first supported a scheme, modelled on Teach First for teachers, to recruit the best graduates into child social work, when it was proposed by Josh MacAlister in October 2010. To their credit, Mr Cameron and Gove took up the idea as quickly as they could, given that it is more important to get it right than to do something for show.

A year ago, we reported that the Government had approved the scheme, now called Frontline, and today we report that 1,000 people have registered in the first week that applications have been open. The recruitment website is explicit that child social work is not a 'nice, comfortable office job' and that '99 per cent of us would run in the opposite direction', but these 1,000 applicants are the first wave of the 1 per cent who have the courage to try to turn around children's lives. That first wave will go through several stages to select just 100 people to start on the scheme next summer. The qualities required have been demonstrated by their absence in the cases of Keanu Williams and Hamzah Khan: teamwork, leadership, optimism and, above all, confidence. What is needed in child protection is people who can stand up to manipulative parents and who have the self-belief to work with the police and the courts. (*The Independent on Sunday*, 6 October 2013, p 40)

In painting this picture of the 'first wave' of the new heroic social worker of the future, the social workers of the past and present were specifically constructed as people whose courage in the face of trying to turn around children's lives may be doubted.

In the next, final section of this chapter, I turn attention back to processes of commemoration to show how politicians seek to memorialise individual children through reform and the inquiry process. MPs do this as a function of what I call 'emotional interest representation', by acting as emotional envoys on behalf of their constituents. Their activities also reflect the total political and cultural repudiation of the idea that child deaths cannot always be prevented.

The emotional politics of interest representation

The names of some children who have died from abuse or neglect become more memorable than others in the sense that their names become attached to major policy and legislative reform. The dynamics of the processes that differentiate them from other children who die under equally appalling circumstances are, in part, linked to the relationship between communities, politics and the press at the local level and policy making and the press at the national level. Butler and Drakeford (2003, p 93) argue that scandals involve the 'active transformation of local events into national issues'. In their detailed account of the inquiry into the death of Maria Colwell, for example, they emphasise the significance of the emotional response of the immediate neighbours of Maria's family and other local residents. The neighbours' response was driven, the authors speculate, by grief or perhaps collective guilt. Few of the anxieties voiced by neighbours at the inquiry appeared to have been expressed to services involved with the family at the time (Field-Fisher, 1974, p 8). In any event, the 'heightened emotional temperature' in the community was widely reported in the local press. Crucially, Butler and Drakeford (2003, p 93) conclude that '[i]t was the anger, the indignation and the persistence of the "mothers of Maresfield Road" that ensured that the moral landscape of the Colwell case was opened up to others'.

In this section I explore a further dimension of this opening up of the local landscape to others, and that is the role of local constituency MPs.

The role of MPs in the UK has long been linked to representation in the form of seeking redress for grievances on behalf of their constituents, with origins of this role dating back to the 13th century (Searing, 1985). Parliament thereby had its roots in emotional experiences of anger and distress at injustice, oppression, wrongful acts and injury that were felt locally but projected into a national forum. In the 19th century, the emphasis shifted to a politics defined by parliamentary debate and grandstanding on big issues of the day. However, the ancient role of the 'good constituency member' was reinvigorated by the development of the welfare state and the expanding functions of central government (Searing, 1985). The post-war period saw a rapid increase in the amount of individual constituency casework undertaken by MPs, with less emphasis on representing constituency issues in Parliament. Of the new MPs elected in 1997, only 13% identified their most important activity as 'checking the executive' compared with 86% for whom 'being a good constituency member' was more important (Gray, 2005, p 58). The number of letters received by MPs has increased year on year, with the advent of email adding to the volume significantly. The increase has also been reflected in government activity in the form of high volumes of ministerial letters to MPs in reply to their queries on behalf of constituents (Gray, 2005).

The shift to casework has been associated with the benefits that incumbent MPs believe it brings in terms of securing re-election, which in turn is part of the generally increased focus on constituency work by political parties and the development of the 'permanent election campaign' (Gray, 2005, p 63). But the shift has also been associated with the satisfaction that MPs get from achieving results from their casework, in contrast to activities in Parliament and the daily round of 'ineffective debate' (Gray, 2005, p 60). A key area of the individual casework undertaken by MPs involves dealing with complaints about local council services, where the role of local councillors has been subverted. This is due partly to the superior resources available to MPs, but it also stems from the perception of MPs by constituents as individuals who wield greater political power and the growing appreciation of the way national policy making is translated at a local level (Gray, 2005). The relationship between MPs and the local media, particularly newspapers, is a critical one and produces a scaled-down version of the politics–media–politics cycle that was analysed at the national level earlier in this book.

In his classic analysis of the role of the 'good constituency member', Searing (1985) identified two types. The *welfare officer* type is concerned to represent their constituents at an individual level and operates as an 'amateur social worker', sometimes to the extent of being available at all hours for constituents with personal problems. For welfare officers, the role provides them with a sense of competence and fulfils a sense of duty that is derived from protecting and looking after people, with emotions comparable to 'those of a family doctor of the old-fashioned kind' (1985, p 377). The *promoter* type is concerned with the constituency's collective needs such as in local industry and schools. In both cases, their dominant concern is to bring local troubles into the national arena:

Welfare officers and promoters are tribunes who shout for their people. But they shout for constituents' needs rather than for their political opinions. And they shout where they are most likely to be heard – at Westminster. This pleases their constituents, since this is what their constituents believe they should be doing. (Searing, 1985, p 371)

Awareness on the part of politicians that the deaths of certain children will attain a higher profile than others is evident in political discourse such as the exchanges that can be observed in Parliament. These exchanges demonstrate that a significant feature of emotional politics is not only the power dynamics in national policy making. Also central is the relationship between these and the political dynamics between and within local councils and committees, parliamentary constituencies, their MPs, the local press, and how all these social actors 'speak for' the populations they serve.

Lauren Wright and the fight for recognition

During the year that followed the conviction of her stepmother and father for her manslaughter on 1 October 2001, Lauren Wright's name appeared in the UK national press 112 times. On 36 of these occasions, her name was mentioned in association with Victoria Climbié, whose guardians had been convicted of her murder and child cruelty in January of the same year, attracting a great deal of political and media attention. The circumstances of Victoria Climbie's death were the subject of the Laming Inquiry (2003). While not attracting significant national media attention, the death of Lauren Wright was deeply significant at a local level and this was reflected in the local and regional press coverage it received. This included a campaign by the *Evening News* (Norfolk) for a full public inquiry into the case and for the resignation of the Director of Social Services in Norfolk.

The campaign for a public inquiry was supported by the local MP, Gillian Shephard, and the political struggle became focused on how far the ongoing inquiry into the death of Victoria Climbié should also encompass the death of Lauren Wright or whether there should be an entirely separate process. In stating the case for an inquiry in a House of Commons debate in October 2001, the MP was particularly scathing of the response she had so far received from the Department of Health, communicated to her via the national press. In the following extract, the rational-bureaucratic argument that it would be impractical to hold a public inquiry into each child's death was set against the demands of

Gillian Shephard's constituents. The inquiry represents political and public recognition of the unique value of Lauren Wright's life and so the rejection of the demand was met with rage:

> The Minister, whom I am glad to see here, will want to explain how Department of Health officials could have rejected my call for an inquiry before it reached her desk. She may even care to dissociate herself from their chilling words. I quote from *The Times* of 2 October: 'It would not be appropriate to hold a public inquiry into all the child killings that happen each year.'
>
> My plea is supported by nigh on 1,000 readers of the *Fenland Citizen*, a local newspaper, who have taken the trouble to petition the paper to indicate their support, and by the 98 per cent of the Norwich-based *Evening News* readers who, in a telephone poll, demanded a public inquiry. That has been the unanimous message from the countless letters, telephone calls and e-mails that I have received from members of the public. I am delighted to see that my hon. Friend the Member for North-West Norfolk, who supports me, is here, and there is strong cross-party support for a public inquiry. (House of Commons Debates, 2001a, col 223WH)

Gillian Shephard argued that Lauren Wright's death had resonated nationally and conveyed her concern that it may just be 'bolted on' to the inquiry into the death of Victoria Climbié:

> People from all over the United Kingdom have contacted me to express their disgust at the circumstances of Lauren's death, with its revelations of failure of professional judgment and liaison.... Nor will we be fobbed off with attempts to bolt this case on to another appalling case, that of Victoria Climbié. We are sick and tired of hearing about procedures, strategies, reports and restructuring. In the name of the thousands of vulnerable children at risk across Britain, the Minister should today demonstrate her concern by announcing an immediate public inquiry into the case of tragic Lauren Wright. (House of Commons Debates, 2001b, cols 224WH–225WH)

The outcome of the debate was reported in the local newspaper in the following terms:

> It seems a messy compromise to roll further thoughts about Lauren Wright's death into a public inquiry into the death of another child abuse victim, Victoria Climbié. But that was the decision of health minister Hazel Blears as our Norfolk MPs turned up the heat yesterday. (*Evening News*, 17 October 2001, p 8)

This assertion serves to emphasise the symbolic and cultural importance of inquiries and reviews into child deaths. The pressure that they should be national and public testifies to a function that goes beyond 'finding out what happened' and 'learning lessons'. It points to their much deeper function in serving to memorialise the dead child, producing a unique and permanent record of their lives and the circumstances of their death, which can then be witnessed by the whole nation. Child abuse deaths are, as Provan (2012) has argued, a 'nationed crime'. The story of the inquiry may also be the only time when experiences are reported in any coherent sense, since 'outside of the reports such lives and identities remain partial and fragmented' (Prior, 2003, p 63). Crucially, an inquiry in which the focus is the necessity for the reform of formal services at that national level may also serve to assuage the guilt and fear of retribution that is felt within local communities. The intensity of such emotions is illustrated in the following extract from a regional newspaper:

> Villagers in Welney remain tight-lipped about their knowledge of events leading to Lauren's death.
>
> It is a silence that reflects the decision of many to keep quiet about the schoolgirl's suspected abuse when she was alive....
>
> Three villagers did summon up the courage to stand by their convictions and alert social services to Lauren's plight.
>
> Perhaps a louder collective voice may have prompted a different outcome. (*Eastern Daily Press*, 2 October 2001, p 7)

Despite the failure to secure a public inquiry, Gillian Shephard was successful in promoting legislative change in the form of an amendment to the Education Act that was progressing through the House of Lords at the time. The amendment was to ensure that schools had a legal duty to have in place formal child protection procedures.

Shephard's colleague in the House Lords, Catherine Ashton, pursued the amendment vigorously on her behalf and was eventually able to conclude as follows: 'As I said ... we cannot bring Lauren back ... I think that the amendment will help to ensure such a tragedy could not happen again....' (House of Lords Debates, 2002, col 1460). The amendment was heralded as a political victory for Gillian Shephard in the press, and while she undoubtedly gained from the case in political terms, it is equally true that this opportunity probably only arose because of the groundswell of local feeling that she was then able to represent on the national political stage.

In the next section of the chapter the focus is on reaction to the death of Daniel Pelka in 2012, which, at the time of writing, involved a local campaign to establish 'Daniel's Law' to make it mandatory for professionals to report suspected child abuse (Bates, in *Coventry Observer*, 10 April 2014).

How many children must perish? 'The Lessons of Daniel Pelka in Coventry'

Following the convictions of Daniel Pelka's mother and her partner for his murder at the end of July 2013, the local MP, Geoffrey Robinson, not only drew sharp comparisons with the death of Peter Connelly but also invoked the same feeling and framing rules. The idea of common sense was contrasted with bureaucracy; compassion was equated with anger. These were used to attribute shame directly to the head of the children's services, Colin Green, and to demand his resignation. The MPs comments were widely reported in the national press, including in the following article, which appeared in the *Daily Mirror* under the headline 'Heads must roll':

> Mr Robinson, who represents Coventry North West, described Daniel's death in March 2012 as 'horrifyingly reminiscent' of the infamous Baby P case in 2007. He said: 'Mr Green takes with him the indelible stain of Daniel's cruel death, which his department failed to prevent.'
>
> The MP also accused teachers and health workers of 'badly letting down' Daniel. He asked: 'Where were these individuals when Daniel needed them most? Bureaucracy triumphed over common sense, care, and compassion.'
>
> 'Those who failed Daniel must examine their own consciences, and conclude whether it is appropriate for them to remain in their posts.' (Fricker, 2 August 2013, p 19)

After the summer recess of Parliament, in his initial statements in the House of Commons, Geoffrey Robinson emphasised the public response to the case he had received and its national profile, but also commented on the resistance he felt existed *locally* to raising the profile of the case any further:

> This is a public issue, and I have been astonished by the wide geographical spread of the letters of support I have received since Daniel's case became public. I have been sent letters from right across the kingdom on a scale that compares with almost any other topic during my long period in this House. This was a public case; I made the case, and then one saw the resistance building up among officials and politicians about having the issue opened in that way.
>
> I was reassured because the new leader of council, a long-standing friend of mine, issued a very good statement following this case, making her position clear. (House of Commons Debates, 2013a, col 1223)

Later, Geoffrey Robinson was able to secure a debate in the House of Commons in which he expressed the profound emotional effects of the case on him as an MP and how this personal experience had spurred him on to political action:

> This is a very important debate.... I labelled it 'The Lessons of Daniel Pelka in Coventry', which happens to be my own constituency. It is a horrid shock to MPs who have never had anything like this happen in their constituency before but have to get to grips with it as part of the job.... One thing is for sure: there has been report after report, study after study, and still we get these dreadful incidents from time to time, all too frequently.
>
> Some people say to me, 'It will always happen—don't worry about it. It's bound to happen and you can't stop it.' I find that repugnant. I cannot believe that Daniel Pelka, ... needed to die. I cannot accept it; it seems ludicrous to me. We have to find a much better way of dealing with the situation in an improved way, step by step; I am not saying that it can all be put right at once. I want to put forward four points for consideration, if not action. (House of Commons Debates, 2013b, col 992)

What is striking about this statement is the impact that such a death occurring in the MP's own constituency appears to have had. Robinson was an MP throughout the periods in which other prominent cases had come to the attention of MPs in the House of Commons, including the deaths of Victoria Climbié and Peter Connelly. To some extent, Robinson's remarks reflect a more widely occurring phenomenon, which is the tendency for the prevalence of abuse in general to be underestimated, but more specifically for the likelihood of abuse occurring 'in my neighbourhood' to be underestimated. In a Dutch survey of public attitudes towards child abuse, following the 'Savanna'[2] case that was in many respects the Dutch Baby P, it was observed that 'the dominant attitude seems to be: "I cannot exclude that child abuse and neglect occurs in my surrounding, but I do not expect it to occur" (de Baat et al, 2011, p 7).

For Geoffrey Robinson, the death of Daniel Pelka was personal, encompassing places and people that were well known to him in his constituency and for whom *he had personal political responsibility in interest representation*. This fact clearly provides an impetus for political action. However, the second most striking thing about his statement is that the urge towards political action is posited on a very specific framing and feeling rule. To accept that political action cannot produce the change necessary to prevent the deaths of *all* children is equated with adopting a moral and emotional stance which accepts that *some* deaths, such as Daniel Pelka's, are inevitable. Robinson responds to this with a visceral expression of disgust: 'I find that repugnant.' The answer to Dingwall et al's (1983) question: 'how many children must perish?' is none. However, in the continuing aftermath of Daniel Pelka's death at the *local* political level, there was evidence of a very different stance. While Coventry City Council unanimously agreed to call for action at the national level, this was underpinned by pragmatism:

> Conservative councillor David Skinner wanted more answers on the Daniel Pelka case, He said: 'It's clear there were a lot of agencies involved, but the buck has to stop somewhere – does it stops with the leader? Can the leader give an assurance that such a tragedy will not happen again?'
>
> Councillor Lucas [Leader of the Council] replied: 'There are 54 councillors – the buck stops with all of us. Can anybody give an assurance that this will not happen again? Nobody can give an assurance that some wicked parent is not going to be that clever, that evil, that calculating. I only wish I could.' (Arlott, 2014)

The contrast between this assertion and Geoffrey Robinson's visceral expression of repugnancy for the idea that deaths such as Daniel Pelka's cannot always be prevented is marked. It goes to the heart of the emotional politics of child abuse and social work and is reflected in the forms of collective remembering that were explored at the beginning of this chapter.

Conclusion

In this chapter I have extended the concept of emotional politics and illustrated three other processes that characterise it: collective remembering, the myth of political control through reform, and emotional interest representation. The roll-call device as a form of collective remembering has become an expression of the apparently infinite repetition of terrible suffering and the failure of services to prevent it. By its infinite nature, the particular story of the past that the roll-call signifies also implicitly projects forward into time, to the inevitability of future deaths and future failures. Through inquiries and serious case reviews, the unique story of what has happened to each child is told, but they are ultimately remembered 'as one' for the nature of the suffering they shared and for services that failed.

Paradoxically, in the cycle of continuous reform, the roll-call of names is used to reinforce the message that such events must never happen again and to mobilise political action to prevent them. This political action involves rhetoric in which ideas for reform are coded in moral terms, linking them to past deaths and the myth of political control in preventing future deaths. Reform is presented as the only politically legitimate and morally right response. Constructing a newly idealised workforce that can be seen as detached from the old, dysfunctional one, is often central to ideas for reform. Through the concept of 'emotional interest representation', I have shown that as well as generating emotions, politicians act as envoys for feelings that are already circulating within their local constituencies. The intense emotions about the death of an individual child can percolate from the local community through the political system, with unpredictable consequences in terms of the reforms that may or may not ensue.

The feeling rule that anger and blame are an appropriate response to the death of a child is deeply rooted and relates to the political impossibility of tolerating risk in child protection, even where these risks are impossible to eradicate. An important element in this intolerance of risk is the idea that thresholds of harm in child protection are routinely set too high by social workers. Lacking the 'common sense' to know when children are in harm's way, social workers leave them in homes which any responsible person would recognise as toxic. I explored this in Chapter Three in terms of the emotional politics of disgust and social work's longstanding identification with poverty and the so-called underclass. In the next chapter I analyse the other side of this disgust in the shape of middle-class respectability and the emotional politics of social class.

Notes

[1] Lauren Wright died aged 6 years in the village of Welney, Norfolk in May 2000. She had been beaten, starved and abused over a period of 18 months by her step-mother, who was convicted of causing her death. Her father was also convicted of her manslaughter. Lauren had been seen by social workers, police and doctors in the weeks before her death.

[2] The child known as Savanna died in the Netherlands aged 3 years. Despite being under the supervision of child protection services, she had been subject to serious abuse over a long period, mainly by her mother.

FIVE

Risk, respectability and the emotional politics of class

This chapter develops the discussion about expressions of contempt and disgust begun in Chapter Three by analysing the subject position of the respectable and responsible parent that these expressions invoke. The 'respectable' constituencies that political and media accounts assume as their audience – symbolically or otherwise – are those under scrutiny in this chapter.

In Chapter Three I argued that the moral disturbance over Peter Connelly's death and the demonisation of social workers as cold-hearted, bureaucrat folk devils was also characterised by a dramatic form of Othering of 'underclass' parenting identities, especially mothers. Underclass parents were represented as threats to the moral order and as requiring moral regulation through their identification with evil, which the story of Peter Connelly's death facilitated. I argue that the other side of the media and political discourse of disgust and revulsion at the deaths of children is the reassertion of the idea of the middle-class, respectable, responsible parent.

Within this binary discourse of 'good' and 'evil' parenting is the construction of a social work that provokes fear and anxiety on two fronts. First, it is unable to properly morally regulate the poor, marginalised mothers who are a risk to their children through either abusing them directly or through allowing risky men into their homes. But this failure raises a second, equally powerful, fear in cultural terms. The social work that has been unable to see the horror that was in plain sight – the evil and incompetent mother and the child who was being starved or tortured to death in public view – produces in the public imagination the social work that also sees abuse where none exists. Social work is thereby a putative threat to *any* parent in the country, including potentially those classed as respectable. As Cooper et al (2003, p 16) put it: 'The public is frightened of the system that has been set up to protect their children.'

This chapter explores the powerful appeal of fantasies about the threat posed to respectable parents by social work. It is argued that there are two main sources of intensified anxiety about social work in the current wave of crisis and reform in child protection. First are the shifting and unstable conceptions of parenting, respectability and what it means to be a 'good' parent, particularly among middle-class parents. Second is the mythological status of narratives epitomised by the Cleveland Inquiry,[1] which are reactivated in the media and in political discourse as warnings about the power of social work to intervene inappropriately in 'respectable family life'. The role of the politician as envoy of particular feeling rules about social work is again highlighted, but this time it is a social work to be feared for its omnipotence rather than ridiculed for its impotence.

Finally, it is suggested that paranoia about social work interventions is bound up with a deep suspicion of the local authority as a state mechanism, which is viewed as corrupt and instinctively inclined towards 'empire building'. According to this framing rule, thresholds of risk are not applied in the interests of children but instead reflect the pursuit of financial incentives and self-interest.

The next section briefly considers theoretical work on social class and mechanisms of disgust and contempt. These mechanisms are shown to produce, not only the disgusting or contemptible 'Other' but also the respectable, morally self-regulating parent.

Constituting respectable identities: the emotional politics of disgust revisited

Emotion has been highlighted as being of central importance in the way distinctions based on social class are made. Class contempt 'is complemented by approval of self and those of the same class and projection of all that is bad and immoral onto the other, which reciprocally confirms the goodness of one's own class' (Sayer, 2005, p 164, after Skeggs, 2004). A number of studies have analysed media accounts to illustrate the importance of the distinctions that are drawn between middle-class respectability and other classed identities – particularly those that provoke contempt or disgust. For example, Lawler (2004) analysed the portrayals of women in broadsheet newspaper coverage of a story about child sex abusers. She identified the class politics that was at work in the way reports drew a distinction between the 'feckless underclass' and the 'normal and desirable' middle-class women in the stories (2004, p 119). Crucially, Lawler argued that, whatever they are called, groups that represent disreputable, underclass identities are essential to the formation of middle-class, respectable ones:

> [W]hatever the nomenclature, this group is essential to the middle class because, without it, the middle class would

> be unable to define itself. Without an other against whom to mark a normalized identity, against whom to draw distinctions, the middle classes would be unable to draw the kinds of distinctions that establish them *as* middle class (and therefore as occupying a normal and desirable position). (Lawler, 2004, p 119, emphasis in original)

Similarly, in her analysis of the 'chav' figure in media accounts, Tyler (2008, p 18) observed that 'these figures are mobilised in ways that attribute superior forms of social capital to the subject positions and social groups they are implicitly or explicitly differentiated from'. Tyler further argued that the emergence of such figures of ridicule and disgust is always indicative of underlying social anxieties. In particular, she highlighted the way in which the disgusting figure of the 'chav mum' and her 'easy fertility' is caught up with specific social anxieties. These concern falling fertility rates and white, middle-class women who are criticised for 'leaving it too late' to have children (2008, p 30). In his critical commentary, drawing on newspaper reports about Peter Connelly's death, Garrett (2009, p 537) noted the class contempt in the frequent use of the underclass construct, particularly in the 'quality press', and linked this to the 'regulatory social agenda of neo-liberalism'.

In such studies, it is the emotional response of disgust that allows distinctions in class terms to be clearly made. Disgust has been theorised in a range of ways but in most accounts there is a shared idea in which it is regarded, 'not as intrinsic to the "disgusting" object, but as inhering in the *relationship* between the disgusted and the object of disgust' (Lawler, 2005, p 438, emphasis in original). Disgust has a foundation in ontological terms, in that 'part of who we are relies on *not* being (or liking) the disgusted object' (Lawler, 2005, p 438, emphasis in original). In class terms, middle-class identity can be seen as being defined in-part by possession of 'taste', which, when violated, may invoke disgust. Although disgust may be felt on a personal level, it has the power to invoke emotions that are collective. Class disgust can thereby be understood as a mechanism by which the middle-class constructs itself, and it is, in this sense, 'a means of self-constitution' (Lawler, 2005, p 443). As explored in Chapter Three of this book, the 'common sense' reaction to the life that Peter Connelly was reported to have lived was characterised by a visceral disgust and an impulse to save him that everyone in the country (except his social workers) was represented as sharing.

Anxieties about how to be respectable and processes of demarcating the disreputable as outsiders are not confined to the middle class.

As argued by Sayer (2005, p 176), '[r]espectability is sought by the dominated but largely eludes their reach. It is partially attainable by the middle classes, though precariously. It is taken for granted by the dominant'. For the white working-class council tenants in Watt's (2006) study of inner-city London, maintaining respectability was experienced as being both more important but also more difficult. Watt (2006) identified two main reasons for this difficulty:

- increased insecurity in socioeconomic terms, including the growing insecurities faced by working-class tenants in relation to employment and poverty;
- sociocultural factors relating to increased social diversity in the area and the difficulty this presents in terms of the 'demarcation of the rough/respectable boundary' (2006, p 794).

For example, while racist discourses existed among the white, working-class tenants, 'black and Asian minorities could also effectively "prove" their respectability over time and thereby legitimate their presence in the neighbourhood' (2006, p 794). Students who had moved into the area were also perplexing to tenants because, while they were perceived as belonging to a higher class position, they did not maintain respectable working-class standards, for instance with regard to personal hygiene (Watt, 2006). Such anxieties are consistent with Young's (2011) observation that contemporary moral disturbance about diversity and social class are rooted in the emergence of ontological insecurities and economic collapse, as explored earlier in this book.

In the newspaper coverage of the death of Peter Connelly, it is possible to observe the discursive construction of the respectable, self-regulating parent in relation to the disgusting and contemptible one.

The responsible 'us' versus the incapable 'them': social work, moral regulation and the middle class

In the political and media responses to the death of Peter Connelly, particularly in *The Sun*'s campaign, social workers were set against a universal 'we' made up of all ordinary parents in the country. For some commentators, the inherently 'politically correct', relativist stance of social workers was an obvious impediment to the ordinary common sense that would have prevented the tragedy. In the following article by Melanie Phillips of the *Daily Mail*, the 'ordinary middle-class family' is juxtaposed with those 'demonstrably incapable of looking after a child'. This simple binary construction of good and bad parenting illustrates how common sense was essentially defined in such articles as the ability to make absolute rather than relative judgements about (classed) parenting capacity. Phillips went on to blame social workers as a liberal professional group, who had undermined the family and deprived working-class children of the opportunity of being placed with middle-class parents:

> And while bending over backwards not to pass judgements on those who were demonstrably incapable of looking after a child, that same social work establishment refused to place children for adoption with ordinary middle-class families. Since the death of Maria Colwell in 1973, inquiry has followed inquiry into social work failings – only to be followed by one shocking case of abuse after another. Social work is plagued by low-calibre recruits, whose training is more akin to indoctrination in political correctness, working in a culture which intimidates any dissent and turns morality and common sense inside out. (Phillips, 2008)

Aside from its other themes, Phillips' account discursively constructed good parenting in terms of the capacity for *self*-regulation that goes with respectability (since 'ordinary' may be read as 'respectable'). As Lawler (2004) has noted, the differentiation of the competent 'us' from the incapable 'them' is class politics at work as it contrasts 'Other' (bad) parenting identities with middle-class (good) parenting.

Hitchens (2008) in the *Mail on Sunday* further illustrated the complexity of discursive constructions around parenting, social work and class, arguing that '[i]f Baby P had been middle-class, he'd have been taken away'. In his article it was the imagined threat to 'respectable' parents from social work that was the dominant theme. With strong echoes from the Cleveland[1] and Orkney[2] inquiries into child sexual abuse, Hitchens invoked the social work folk devils that act as 'storm troopers of the nanny state' (Cohen, 2002, p xv). Hitchens' argument was that social workers routinely falsely accuse respectable parents of harming their children *because* they are responsive to mechanisms of social control in a way that the underclass is not. Furthermore, he argued that their abuses are imagined, not real:

> Let us be plain. If one tenth part of the events that took place in Baby P's mother's house had happened in a middle-class home, the child would have been snatched away in minutes by haughty social workers.

In fact, if a middle-class Baby P had fallen off a swing and banged his head in a genuine accident, the selectively vigilant social-work squads would have been demanding his removal from the home. They are always prone to imagine abuse among the respectable, even when it's not taking place.

This is partly because of the prejudice such people usually harbour against the middle class.

It is also because they know that the middle class will co-operate with them, will obey the law, turn up at meetings and hearings, take their authority seriously. (Hitchens, 2008).

Paradoxically, according to Hitchens, it is the middle-class capacity for self-regulation that makes it vulnerable to the social worker's proneness to imagine abuse. The willingness of middle-class parents to take authority seriously and conform to the requirements of the regulatory state and its surveillance operation lays them open to the prejudices of social workers. In contrast with this view, as Dingwall et al (1983) observed in their detailed ethnographic work of child protection processes, parental cooperation with services appears to confer significant protection from further scrutiny. It is also worth noting that the prevalence of abuse experienced by upper- and middle-class children is thought to be significantly under-reported (Parton, 2014).

After the conviction of Daniel Pelka's mother and stepfather for his murder in 2013, Christopher Booker expanded on the theme of 'responsible parents' in his piece for *The Sunday Telegraph*, under the headline 'The social worker's sledgehammer misses the nut yet again':

The real scandal, of course, is not just that social workers too often fail to act where a child is being genuinely ill-treated, but that they are far too quick to seize children from responsible parents for wholly inadequate reasons.... Social workers love to defend themselves by saying, 'we're damned if we do and damned if we don't'. What they cannot understand is that in reality, both these things can be true. (Booker, *The Sunday Telegraph*, 4 August 2013)

This statement is of particular interest because, while it is mistaken in its targeting of social workers, it expresses in succinct terms the broader tensions that lie at the heart of the child protection system itself. These tensions are (if only ever provisionally) resolved in the form of the compromise that is reached between the *state* and the family:

> Uninvited surveillance is possible only as the result of a compromise which minimises the likelihood of identifying malpractice. The result is a system which is fully effective neither in preventing mistreatment nor in respecting family privacy but which lurches unevenly between these two poles. A degree of 'agency failure' is inherent in this compromise. (Dingwall et al, 1983, p 219)

Part of the 'unevenness' with which the state's compromise with families is played out is that some families will come under much closer scrutiny than others. The rule of optimism operated by the state through its child protection system serves to 'filter moral character ... leaving women and the "rough" indigenous working class as the group proportionately most vulnerable to compulsory measures' (Dingwall et al, 1983, p 102).

It is not only the classed identity of parents that was invoked in press accounts of Peter Connelly's death. Some accounts also explicitly positioned the class identity of social workers as being critical in the viability of their attempts to intervene effectively. These narratives reveal something of what Walkowitz (1999, p 6) has described in the US context as '[t]he ambiguity, fragility, and marginality of social workers' class position' and how these are 'seen in the constant struggles over who is and who is not a social worker'.

Social workers' class position

Since its earliest origins, the class position of social workers has been of fundamental importance in understanding social work's purpose and the tensions between control and care in its operation. As observed by Burnham (2012, pp 13-14), the arrangement of Poor Law, charitable and local authority organisations working together 'masked a politically fraught debate nationally about emerging state intervention into the lives of poor people'. In terms of the first social workers, their role was readily open to interpretation in simple terms: 'the charitable activities of the middle classes were a means of policing and controlling the poor' (Burnham, 2012, p 15). But the operation of early social work in the control of family life of people living in poverty was carried out not only in the homes of poor people but also in the homes of middle-class women. The moral duty vested in middle-class women to give advice to their domestic servants laid the foundations in the late 19th century for the development of social work practice in the next (Skeggs, 2004). *Advice* was the vehicle for the transmission of middle-class domestic standards to the working class, not as 'a repressive intervention but an invitation to authority'; as a power that 'is exercised through norms, disciplining, reward and manipulation of the conscience' through which control of the population could be achieved (Skeggs, 2004, p 47).

That the regulation of others has an intimate relationship with the moral regulation of the self is further supported by Hunt (1999). The binary division between respectable and non-respectable parenting involves processes of moral regulation with their origins in movements that are often initiated from 'below' rather than from above by the state (Hunt, 1999). According to Hunt (1999, p 2), the social origins of such movements are that they often come from the middle classes with women playing an important role. Moral regulation movements are also important because they 'provide classic instances of the intimate link between the "governance of others" and the "governance of the self"', such that 'projects stimulating self-governance manifest themselves in attempts to regulate others' (Hunt, 1999, p 2).

In an article in *The Independent on Sunday*, Heawood (2008) addressed the perceived cultural relativism of contemporary social workers; a theme that was also found in the articles by Hitchens and Phillips cited earlier. Heawood argued that middle-class social workers did not seem able to pass judgement on, and were overly tolerant of, the squalor in some households compared with their working-class colleagues, who were willing to take a more robust approach:

> My child protection officer friend reckons it is only really the working class social workers who are able to walk into a squalid, chaotic home and say to the family: 'This won't do, sort it out' … where the more middle-class social workers, who were more numerous in the profession, would avoid being 'judgemental' at all costs. (Heawood, 2008)

Heawood's article points to the 'cultural relativism' identified by Dingwall et al (1983, p 83) as an agency justification for permitting, under the rule of optimism, certain parenting behaviours that might otherwise be considered unacceptable. As noted in earlier chapters of this book, the theme of dirt and smell, specifically in relation to the possibilities for social work intervention within the *home*, was evident in a number of accounts.

A small proportion of commentators recognised that poor living conditions must make up a large proportion of the everyday encounters in social work. With this acknowledgement comes the idea – for good or ill – that thresholds for concern are necessarily fluid and not fixed, and risk is relative rather than absolute. For example, in *The Independent*, Orr (2008, p 18) wrote that 'social workers see dirty homes, depressed and disengaged parents, insalubrious visitors and sickly little children all the time, and naturally adjust their expectations of what an acceptable family environment is accordingly'.

For Riddell (2008b), writing in *The Daily Telegraph*, fault lay in the way 'risk' has been subverted in the reforms that followed the Laming Inquiry into the death of Victoria Climbié, so that it applied to too many children rather than just those 'at risk' of serious abuse. Invoking Cohen's (2002) 'gullible wimp' folk devil, Riddell argued that the post-Laming shift had produced social workers who are 'going into the worst homes as supportive friends rather than as hard-nosed detectives intent on sleuthing out evidence for child abuse' (Riddell, 2008, p 23).

Hunt (1999, p 2) has argued that the politics of moral regulation has become more rather than less visible with a wider range of social issues that are 'contested in strongly moralised terms'. There are few spheres where this is more true than in parenting, where it is claimed that there is a 'crisis' of identity in middle-class parenting; a crisis that is being played out largely in relation to risk. It is to an examination of the nature and extent of this crisis that the chapter now turns.

Moral regulation and the 'crisis' of middle-class parenting

It is important to acknowledge at this point in the discussion that middle-class identity is a broad landscape, in which there are significant differences. For example, there are differences:

- geographically, (the suburban and urban middle class);
- horizontally (through public and private sector employment status);
- vertically (in the growing detachment of a rich, upper-middle class) (Reay et al, 2013).

However, what is shared across this diversity is 'the privilege and relative power that comes with middle-class identity' and a shared commitment to cultural reproduction through education (Reay et al, 2013, p 18).

While it is evident that parenting practices vary according to class background, the picture is complex (Sherman and Harris, 2012). What is clear is that important shifts are perceived to have taken place in relation to parenting identities in Western industrialised countries and that these shifts are understood to be the source of considerable anxiety for some parents. The advent of 'intensive parenting', for example, has involved a shift from the noun of 'parent' to the verb of 'parenting' as an idealised occupation and a process of 'self-making' (Faircloth, 2010). A climate of 'inflated risk' has produced forms of middle-class parenting in which parents attempt to micromanage risk – often only to perpetuate a sense of insecurity (Hoffman, 2010). In a risk-centred society, 'parents feel an inexorable demand to "parent" as a risk manager' (Lee et al, 2010, p 299) and, according to Furedi (2002), parenting has become 'paranoid'. In short, the middle-class 'us' location in the 'us'/'them' dichotomy appears to be far from stable or secure.

In the burgeoning literature on parenting culture studies (Lee et al, 2014), it is argued that there is a new pervasive form of politicised parental determinism, which, as a form of thinking, is as powerful as economic and genetic determinism (2014, p 217). Parental determinism is defined as 'a form of deterministic thinking that construes the everyday activities of parents as directly and causally associated with "failing" or harming children and so the wider society' (2014, p 3). Parental determinism, it is argued, is historically specific, has emerged in a wider cultural context of risk consciousness and involves understanding the socially constructed nature of parenting. Lee et al demonstrate a growing interest in 'parenting' as the primary means through which children are brought up, as opposed to responsibility being located in the wider community and society. They do this, for example, by noting the rapid increase in sales of books about parenting (2014, p 5). However, for the purposes of this chapter, this literature needs to be considered critically. While 'parental determinism' may be new in the domain of (self)-regulation by middle-class parents, it has long been the fate of poor families, particularly poor mothers, to be subject to deterministic thinking about the threat posed to wider society through the way they bring up their children. The widening of the purview of the state in relation to parenting can be understood as reflecting the shift towards the 'social investment state' where even middle-class families are no longer seen as adequate for maximising the potential of their children as 'future workers' and law-abiding, productive adults (Gilbert et al, 2011, p 2011). As Featherstone et al (2014) have argued, when parenting is reconstituted as a job involving expert knowledge and skills rather than as an affective bond, there are particular dangers for people living in poverty. However, more importantly for the purposes of my argument in this chapter, it also means that 'all parents are vulnerable to the state gaze' (2014, p 152).

Reay et al (2013, p 3) draw attention to the fact that the traditional focus of moral panics on the working classes has now shifted so that the focus of such intense moral anxiety is on parenting in general. The crisis of middle-class parenting has been understood in relation to a moral panic about childhood in media and policy discourse, where there is a perceived over-exposure of children to consumer culture, decline in their play and self-esteem, and increased stress brought about by over-testing in education (Kehily, 2010, p 172). However, by drawing on late-modern social theory, Kehily goes further and suggests that:

> ... new practices of intimacy and the increase of risk and uncertainty in Western societies play a part in the restructuring of family relationships and childrearing practices. From this perspective it is possible to suggest that *the crisis in childhood exists as a reflection of adult anxiety and insecurity in 'new times'*. Late modern themes have implications for childhood most noticeable in the way the child is positioned as a treasured emotional investment providing security for couples in an insecure world. This conceptualisation of the child draws upon Romantic ideals of children as innocent and in need of protection. (Kehily, 2010, p 183, emphasis added)

Hacking (2003) identifies 'fear-for-our-children' as a radical change in the everyday experience of both adults and children: 'I used to park my children in their baby carriage outside the supermarket, and never thought twice about it. No matter what I believe I could not do that with my baby grandchildren' (2003, p 44). This fear arises, not from new knowledge about risk but from the increased anonymity in social relations whereby 'children are the final fundamental of our identity' (2003, p 44). More importantly, these new fears are not 'cultivated on the border' of society – they lie at the centre of it:

> That centre consists of responsible parents of all socio-economic strata. Aside from the all-too-common dysfunctional families, only someone wilfully occupying a position on the border will say to little Mary and Johnny, or even quite big Hilary and Madge, 'Stop pestering me, go over to the vacant lot five blocks away and play.' (Hacking, 2003, p 45)

In an era of socioeconomic crisis and volatility, particularly since the global economic crash of 2007, there is in class terms an intensified 'fear of falling' among the middle classes (Young, 2011, p 256). The gap between what Hacking (2003) has called the centre and the border grows bigger in cultural terms as well as socioeconomic terms. The mother who purchases Babybond foetal scanning products in pregnancy, for the purpose of 'bonding, reassurance, and foetal well-being' (Kehily, 2010, p 15), is about as far removed as it is possible to get from the mother to-be who does not attend antenatal appointments at all. Emotional responses play out in old but also new ways in terms of adult anxieties about children and their fundamental relation to individualised *and* classed identities.

In this chapter I argue that the apparent crisis of adult anxiety and insecurity about childhood and parenting has specific implications for how social work is perceived and its place in the collective imagination. This is because the moral project involving (middle-class) self-governance in relation to parenting manifests itself in an intensified anxiety about how parenting will be judged *by others*. The particular power of social work in this regard is as the ultimate arbiter of what constitutes mistreatment, with the grave consequence that 'a charge of mistreatment is equivalent to an allegation that the parents involved do not share in our common humanity' (Dingwall et al, 1983, p 219). Added to this is the power of social work – both imagined and real – to intervene directly in family life and penetrate the 'most private cells' of the home (Margolin, 1997, p 85). The potency that the idea of social work has in potentially 'moving from the office, to the doorstep, across the threshold and into the home, and moving within people's private spaces, including even their bedrooms, the most intimate corners of their lives and selves' (Ferguson, 2010, p 1103), looms large in the middle-class imagination. Furthermore, where social work is engaged in a state project that is explicitly more interventionist and authoritarian (Featherstone et al, 2014; Parton, 2014), then the *imagined* threat for middle-class parents is intensified, just as the objective, 'real' threat to poor families is increased.

The anxiety of middle-class parents is concerned at a basic level with what Sayer (2005, p 178) calls '[t]he fear of refusal of respectability and recognition'. Sayer specifically locates this fear in terms of encounters by working-class and middle-class people with class 'superiors'. Such fears are likely to be intensified still further in encounters – imagined or otherwise – between middle-class parents and social workers, whose class position is ambiguous and may be considered by parents to be inferior to their own. Anxieties may of course play out both ways, such that social workers mistakenly afford respectability where it is not due. While explicit attention to class politics is practically invisible in accounts of practice between social workers and the working class or 'underclass', it becomes one of the determinants of risk where the power dynamics are more complex. In the case of the Newcombe family in Cheshire, for example, three children were abused and neglected over a 10-year period by their adoptive parents, both of whom were doctors. The serious case review concluded as follows:

> In this case, many professionals struggled to maintain a child focus when faced with M and F's aggressive behaviour and their 'disguised compliance', and that their approach was affected by perceptions and assumptions made regarding the parents' social class, professional status, and high academic qualifications, and the attitude of M and F towards them. (Cheshire East Safeguarding Children's Board, 2011, p 21)

In the next section, the chapter explores the importance of the Cleveland affair in the cycle of crisis and reform of social work and child protection. The story of Cleveland has assumed a mythological status in the public and political imagination. I argue that the story and its retelling is an important element in the emotional regime that underpins social work and child protection. It reflects particular anxieties about the power of social workers and our capacity to 'get it wrong'. It also expresses wider fears about the putative power of state institutions at the local level to undermine family life and engage in 'empire building' in order to expand their capacity to intervene.

The myth of the Cleveland affair and the politician as envoy of fear

In 1987, two paediatricians who had recently been appointed in Cleveland began to diagnose high rates of child sexual abuse through the use of a test known as the 'anal dilatation' test. Over a five-month period, mainly May and June, they had diagnosed sexual abuse in 57 families, and a total of 121 children (Butler-Sloss, 1988, p 243). Significant numbers of the children were removed from their homes using 'place of safety orders' obtained from magistrates by the social services department. Protests by the parents and others eventually led to a public inquiry chaired by Elizabeth Butler-Sloss, which reported in 1988. The conclusions drawn by the inquiry were measured and complex. In summary, they were as follows:

- child sexual abuse was a real and serious problem;
- medical confidence in the anal dilatation test in the absence of other evidence had been excessive;
- decisions by social services to remove children had been unnecessarily hurried and had also produced a crisis in terms of the lack of resources to cope with the upsurge in cases.

Crucially, questions over the balance between false-positive and true-positive cases have never been answered with confidence although it seems that many were eventually substantiated (Munro, 2004). The fact that this uncertainty and ambiguity was never fully answered is one reason that the story of Cleveland affair retains the mythological power that it does.

Regardless of the facts of the Cleveland affair itself, my interest in this chapter is in terms of its mythological elements and particularly the story of Cleveland as it was told and is perpetually retold in the media and political sphere. Specifically, the interest here is in the story of Cleveland as narrated at the time by the local constituency MP for Middlesbrough, Stuart Bell, and how his version of what happened has resonated through time. As Parton (1991, p 114) observed, while the Cleveland Inquiry found Stuart Bell's allegations to be unsubstantiated, 'they continued to frame and dominate the agenda'. This section draws substantially on the account of events given in the Cleveland Inquiry report as well as newspaper articles and political speech. In taking this approach, the chapter again demonstrates the importance of the intertextuality between media accounts, political speech and official documents, which is a theme that is expanded upon further in the next chapter.

The first significant involvement of the media in the Cleveland child sexual abuse case was the publication of a story by the local Middlesbrough *Evening Gazette* in the middle of June 1987. The story was in response to contact from the parents of children who had been removed from their homes, and who had begun to form a parents' support group with the help of another key figure, the Rev Michael Wright. According to the sequence of events recorded in the inquiry report (Butler-Sloss, 1988), the role of Stuart Bell became prominent after 19 June 1987, when he became aware of what was happening. This was a key moment, as the inquiry report emphasised, because '[b]y Monday 22nd June, media interest was intense and national' (1988, p 161) and from that point forward the issues were played out on the national stage.

As the inquiry report went on to describe, Stuart Bell's role was pivotal as he 'became caught up in the media attention being devoted to Cleveland' (1988, p 163). The political struggle that was subsequently played out in the House of Commons over Cleveland became a significant part of the story in the 'quality press', just as it did over the death of Peter Connelly and other cases. The press coverage reflected the efforts to work through what was clearly great uncertainty and confusion about the moral rights and wrongs of the case. According to the press coverage, there was also a strong suggestion from parliamentary colleagues and others that Stuart Bell was 'playing politics' with the case for publicity. While the emergence of shared mutual interest between the press and politics was again in evidence, so too was emotional interest representation by the MP in acting as tribune on behalf of constituents. As Bell 'became deeply involved in the crisis and the perspectives of the parents' (1988, p 164), national media and political interests and the emotions that had their origins in the deeply personal experience of parents in Cleveland were mutually reinforced. This conjunction is evident from the following extract of the inquiry report: '9.4.6 The effect of the press generally was to underline and increase the importance of the story. The media assisted Mr Bell in his efforts to place the crisis in the public domain' (1988, p 169).

The main allegations made by Stuart Bell were, first, that there had been a 'fundamental attack on family life' (Butler-Sloss, 1988, p 164). Second, that Cleveland social services department had been 'empire building'; primarily in terms of the extra resources that it requested in order to cope with the upsurge of cases (Butler-Sloss, 1988, p 164). Third, Bell argued that there had been collusion and conspiracy to obstruct police involvement in the course of investigations. The main focus in the discussion that follows is on the first two of these allegations.

A fundamental attack on family life

Through his speeches in the House of Commons, press conferences and other communications with the press, and in his evidence to the inquiry, Stuart Bell explicitly argued that what was happening in Cleveland represented an attack on family life. He emphasised the extent to which the normal and everyday became nightmarish and completely outside the power of parents, such as in the following statement in the House of Commons:

Will he give the House an assurance that the specific things that happened at Middlesbrough general hospital, where children were taken in for specific ailments but were analysed and investigated for sexual abuse, will be part of the inquiry? Will the fact that parents and children were held for hours on end, and that children were woken in the middle of the night and taken to a room to be photographed, and that the police were obstructed in their duty of investigating what is a serious crime be part of the inquiry? (House of Commons Debates, 1987, col 531)

Stuart Bell's evidence to the inquiry was quoted in *The Guardian* as follows:

'What we saw in May and June was a fundamental attack on family life in Cleveland.... Many of these children are destabilised, are insecure, are unsettled; the parents are equally destabilised and unsettled and they are having serious difficulties in getting together as a family,' he said. (Sharratt, 1987)

The same evidence was quoted in *The Times* in a rather different way. In the report in *The Times*, the detail from the evidence that referred to the *particular* experience of the families in Cleveland was replaced by reference to 'the country' as a whole, as follows: 'Mr Bell ... said there had been a "fundamental attack on family life" in the country and added: "I do not withdraw a single word of my statement to the House of Commons"' (Davenport, 1987). From this account, it is possible to see the evolution from a local story about individual families to a myth about the symbolic threat to the family as a cherished institution. What happened in Cleveland was fundamental in its nature because, virtually overnight, it widened the scope of who might be considered a threat to their children. The social work gaze was no longer narrowly focused on the dirty homes of poor people and dispossessed people, but could now potentially focus on anyone, in any family, and in any home, as explicitly identified in the report. Crucially, *this* finding was not subject to any ambiguity or doubt: 'We have learned during the Inquiry that sexual abuse occurs in children of all ages, including the very young, to boys as well as girls, in all classes of society and frequently within the privacy of the family' (Butler-Sloss, 1988, p 243).

Ferguson (2004, p 159) articulated very well the dramatic impact that Cleveland had: 'In transgressing conventional boundaries, Cleveland professionals turned the world upside down.' More specifically, in the shift away from forms of assessment for abuse that had traditionally focused on the social circumstances of families and referrals by others, 'it cut through the established fields of interaction focused around marginal families to include a relatively large proportion of middle-class households' (Ferguson, 2004, p 159). Cleveland therefore represented an attack not on family life per se but most importantly on middle-class, respectable family life. As Franklin and Parton (1991) argued, Stuart Bell's advocacy went beyond those of the constituents that he directly represented and assumed the characteristics of a much wider, moral and symbolic cultural function:

> His advocacy of the parents' position struck a note with large numbers of people who seemed unable or unwilling to accept that sexual abuse of children might be as widespread as the Cleveland cases suggested. By articulating their denials, Bell calmed their fears, dispelled their anxieties and restored moral equilibrium to family life. (1991, p 24)

But Bell was not just articulating denial about child sexual abuse. He was also able to articulate a rationale for *why* the social services department and its social workers might 'see abuse where none exists'. According to this rationale, Cleveland's social services department was engaged in a deliberate project of 'empire building' in order to extend its regulatory powers. The link between the resources made available for investigating child abuse and the degree to which the state is perceived to have capacity to extend its regulatory reach into the homes of the respectable is a recurring theme in media and political narratives.

Empire building and the Cleveland myth retold

In his deeply held belief that the authority was 'empire building' and that there had been a conspiracy to exclude the police from investigating the cases, Stuart Bell reflected and reinforced a general suspicion. This was that local agencies and agents, in enacting state powers, did not always act according to their intended function; namely, in the interests of the children or families who they were charged with a duty to protect. Instead, their objectives were primarily to serve their own interests. These interests, as interpreted through the discourses around Cleveland, were evident in the social services department's attempt to secure increased resources for abuse that it had largely manufactured and thus, it was suspected, to extend its powers of surveillance.

The extent to which the myth of Cleveland can be invoked and the same story told in new ways is exemplified by the case of the Liberal Democrat MP, John Hemming. In January 2014, Hemming became the focus of a debate about social work interventions in which he publicly advised parents to 'flee the UK' rather than risk losing their children through the family courts (Doyle and Doughty, 2014). His comments accompanied a BBC *Panorama* programme entitled 'I want my baby back', broadcast on 12 January 2014. The concerns reflected the real increase in the numbers of children being subject to care proceedings, which can at least in part be attributed to the lowering of thresholds that followed the reaction to the death of Peter Connelly in 2007.

However, Hemming's reaction was based, not on concerns about this lowering of thresholds, but on an entirely different set of beliefs about why numbers may have increased. His comments reflected a set of views that he has long held and articulated publicly. His basic argument was succinctly summarised in his own words in an article for the *Mail on Sunday*, which he wrote in 2007 under the headline 'Stolen children' (Hemming, 2007). In this piece he argued that 'social workers are literally snatching newborn babies and children from good, stable, loving homes' (Hemming, 2007). He went on to describe the perverse financial incentives that he believed underpinned the practice:

> Many millions of pounds in grants are available to local councils if they hit badly thought-out Government adoption 'targets'. These grants are meant to act as an incentive to councils to find adoptive parents for older children languishing for years in care homes.
>
> The brutal truth, however, is that healthy white babies and children under the age of five are far easier to place for adoption than older children who are actually physically, emotionally or psychologically damaged by parental maltreatment.
>
> Last year, the number of children under five taken into care and swiftly adopted was more than double the number in 1995 – which strongly suggests to me that babies and young children are being deliberately taken into care in order for councils to hit their adoption targets and get their extra money. (Hemming, 2007)

The racialised dimension of Hemming's argument is evident, not only in his assertion that it is healthy *white* babies who are being taken. It is also evident in the direct comparison that he made with

Australia's 'Stolen Generations', in which the children of Aboriginal families were removed and placed with white families according to a policy of 'integration' (Hemming, 2007). The 'healthy white baby' in Hemming's account is coded in both 'race' and class terms as belonging to a 'respectable' family because it is juxtaposed with the black 'hard-to-place' child and also implicitly with the 'less white' child in a classed hierarchy of whiteness, in the sense understood by Webster (2008, p 308): 'Drawing distinctions between different sorts of "whiteness" deemed inferior or superior according to attributions of "degeneracy", "respectability", antisocial behaviour, criminality, the body, appearance and hereditability, class contempt is shown to be social and racial.'

The discourse of abused children as moral dirt, as articulated by Ferguson (2004), features prominently in Hemming's narrative, but so too does the idealised 'good, stable, loving' family that becomes the target for intervention over deliberately conceived, imagined abuse.

Conclusion

In this chapter I have explored the mechanism of disgust as it relates to the self-constitution of the middle class. The focus has been on 'respectable' but unstable middle-class parenting identities and the central importance of these in political and media discourses about social work.

Ultimately, the fears and anxieties about social work add up to the potential in the mind of *all* parents to be mistakenly designated morally 'dangerous' and a threat to the welfare of *their* child. Alongside the fear of some terrible accident or illness befalling our children lives the fear – perhaps more deeply buried but nonetheless powerful – that we may not be a 'good-enough' parent. This is fertile ground for a whole range of anxieties and fantasies in terms of who may judge us, and is in fact the basis for self-regulation. The pressure towards increased social control and moral regulation of particular groups poses a threat to all if it cannot be trusted to target the 'right' families. Children who have died under appalling circumstances – particularly where they have been 'hidden in plain sight' – serve as testimony, not to the inherent difficulty of the task, but to the apparent unpredictability or even randomness with which social workers might choose to wield their powers to intervene. Social workers who cannot spot the parent who is obviously abusing their child are also likely to be prone to see abuse where none exists. Furthermore, the power of politicians to act as envoys for feelings of fear and paranoia is clearly very great. The myth of Cleveland continues to have purchase in part because it is a myth narrated and retold, not only by the media but also by representatives who are elected to act as 'feeling legislators' on behalf of their citizens. The paradox of Cleveland is that just as it increased public distrust of social work, it damaged social work's confidence in its legitimacy (Hetherington et al, 1997).

In his detailed analysis of the Cleveland affair, Parton (1991) provided an interesting insight into why the version of events as promoted by Stuart Bell may have continued to dominate, despite his allegations being dismissed as unfounded in the full inquiry report (Butler-Sloss, 1988). The summary of the report contained no criticisms of the MP's actions or of others who had been criticised in the full report. The bulk of the summary was concerned with critical comments about the professionals involved. Most newspapers had relied on this 'reader's digest' version of the inquiry report for their reporting, leaving Stuart Bell's version of events and the emotions that went with it 'freedom to travel' in discourse terms. In this sense, the intertextuality of the inquiry report with political and media accounts of what happened in Cleveland was fundamentally important. In the next chapter the theme of the role of documents and their intertextuality is explored in depth in terms of the way documents and texts in child protection can be understood as active, and in terms of their emotionality.

Notes

[1] In 1987, two paediatricians who had recently been appointed in Cleveland began to diagnose high rates of child sexual abuse through the use of a test known as the 'anal dilatation' test. Over a five-month period, mainly in May and June, they had diagnosed sexual abuse in 57 families, and a total of 121 children (Butler-Sloss, 1988, p 243). Significant numbers of the children were removed from their homes using 'place of safety orders' obtained from magistrates by the social services department. Protests by the parents and others eventually led to a public inquiry chaired by Elizabeth Butler-Sloss, which reported in 1988.

[2] The Orkney Inquiry (Clyde, 1992) focused on events on the Scottish island of South Ronaldsay in 1991, in which children were removed from their homes following allegations of ritual child sexual abuse. The inquiry report was critical of social workers, the police and Orkney Council.

SIX

The emotionality of official documents: the serious case review as an active text

Introduction

In this chapter I argue that official documents can be understood as emotionally active in terms of the way they reflect and generate emotional responses. Specifically, the chapter will show how documents that review and analyse the events that led to the death of a child form an essential part of the emotional regime that underpins the cycle of crisis and reform. Such documents reflect and generate feeling rules that include profound regret at past actions or inactions and intense anger at the ease with which, in hindsight, the child's suffering and death might have been prevented. Documents also implant feeling and framing rules into the rationalities of practice, particularly in processes of risk and blame. Through texts such as media accounts, political statements and official documents, discourse 'travels' and its journey across the social environment can be tracked (Altheide, 1996, pp 69-70). As Skeggs (2004, p 81) has said: 'Texts are processes in which political work is done.'

The main focus of the chapter is one particular type of official document – the serious case review (SCR) report. An SCR is undertaken when a child has died from serious abuse or neglect, or when a child has been seriously harmed and there are concerns about interagency or interprofessional working. They were originally intended to act as internal reviews that could inform learning at a local level, according to 'local rationalities'. However, they have increasingly taken on a very different function, which, I argue, reflects their capacity to mobilise and generate collective emotions. These reports have had an increasingly important function in the politics–media–politics cycle in child protection in the UK. I argue that they have been particularly central in terms of the shift that has taken place from local, internal reviews of what happened in a case to public scrutiny at the national level. They now provide summary judgements on professional practice in concert with the judgement on the culpability of parents because they can be published at the conclusion of a trial. This is in contrast with an inquiry, which would not normally even commence until that point.

The chapter reports on my analysis of three SCRs carried out into the deaths of two children. First is a comparison between the two SCR reports into the death of Peter Connelly. It is noteworthy that the question of whether the first report should be made public was a major focus of the anger expressed at the time by David Cameron and others, who alleged a 'cover-up'. Comparison of the two reports shows how the disgust, anger and shame that were so evident in political and media accounts of the case, as discussed in Chapter Three of this book, were crystallised into a 'new' form of authoritative social work practice in the second review. This was partly facilitated, I argue, by the articulation of risk thresholds in absolute rather than relative and contingent terms. The rationalities reflected in the second report are no longer the local rationalities of practice in Haringey but the national rationalities of the death of Peter Connelly as a 'nationed crime'.

Second, I analyse the SCR into the death of Hamzah Khan published in November 2013. The review report and the events surrounding it illustrate the SCR as a text that embodies counterfactual emotions. These are feelings concerning 'what might have been'. They are attached to the actions or inactions in *everyday social work practice*, which, with hindsight, can be seen as fateful opportunities to save the child's life that were missed. I argue that these feelings were activated by the SCR report, particularly through the written exchanges about it between a government minister and the Independent Chair of the Bradford Safeguarding Children Board.

The chapter sets out the background concerning SCRs, their intended purpose and debates about how the reviewing process might be reformed. This is followed by a discussion about the increasing importance of the SCR in the politics–media–politics cycle in social work and child protection. First, I want to highlight the central importance of the active text for social work practice.

Social work as documented practice and the active text

It is axiomatic to state that social work is documented practice. Documents such as legislation, policies and guidance are produced in order that they should directly shape practice and how social workers undertake their tasks. The recording (electronic or otherwise) of observations, assessments, interactions and the decisions that social workers make is regarded as a cornerstone of good practice. So too are the records of professional supervision, team meetings, case conferences and the many other documented accounts of interactions between professionals and others. Added to these 'everyday' documents are the ones that are ostensibly intended to help professionals 'learn the lessons' from serious incidents, including inquiries and SCRs into the deaths of children from abuse and neglect. Other documents and texts, such as media and political accounts, although often treated as more discrete entities that lie outside the 'practice' domain, are nonetheless central to it, as already explored in earlier chapters. As such, all that constitutes 'social work' can be seen as being mediated through texts.

Documents refer not only to their intended audience but also to other documents. As Atkinson and Coffey (1997, p 61) argue, 'texts do not refer transparently to the social world. Their referential value is often to other texts.' A simple example of this 'intertextuality' is the way policy documents draw on findings from inquiry reports. Recognising their intertextuality is fundamental to understanding the sense in which documents can be considered as active. In short, '[t]exts do something rather special as coordinators of people's activities' (Smith, 2006, p 65). For Smith, texts are of interest for the role they play in structuring social relations and, as such, she rejects the idea of the text as inert and passive. Seeing documents as active involves placing greater emphasis on the role of the reader and how the act of reading constructs the meaning of a document. Smith explains as follows:

> The active text ... might be thought of as more like a crystal which bends the light as it passes through. The text itself is to be seen as organizing a course of concerted social action. As an operative part of a social relation it is activated, of course, by the reader *but its structuring effect is its own.* (Smith, 1990, p 121, emphasis added)

In this way, documents do not simply reflect 'reality' but are another means through which the social world is constructed: 'Those who use and consume documents are not merely passive actors in the communication process, but also active in the production process itself' (Prior, 2003, p 16).

Documents can be understood as active in the way that they express power relations and define social networks and how they have a structuring effect on everyday activities. This includes their 'action-at-a-distance' (Prior, 2003, p 67). The action-at-a-distance by documents may be through the way they circulate within organisations but also the 'trickle-down' effects that documents such as inquiry reports have and their intertextuality with media accounts (Warner, 2006). In my study of social workers in the mental health field, practitioners did not all have to read the report of a major inquiry into homicide in order for it to directly organise and coordinate their practice, particularly in terms of managing their fear of being personally involved in an inquiry themselves (Warner, 2006). In children's services it was not intentional that a standardised form of assessment such as the Common Assessment Framework would constrain professional practice in quite the 'tyrannical' way it appears to have done (White et al, 2009). Crucially, then, documents are active even in the absence of direct readings by social actors and their effects are easily divorced from the intentions of their authors.

Prior (2003) is keen to emphasise that documents are created in social contexts and that the production of them is collective rather than individual. This is especially true of SCRs and inquiry reports, since they are normally produced by panels or committees that comprise a number of members. The panels or committees are political entities where there is scope for considerable disagreement and struggles for power and influence. The most important illustration of this is the report into the death of Maria Colwell (Field-Fisher, 1974). The social worker member of the inquiry committee, Olive Stevenson, was unable to reach agreement on all matters with other members. She produced a 'Minority Report', which was published as part of the full report (Field-Fisher, 1974, pp 88-115). Years later, in her reflections on the inquiry into the death of Jasmine Beckford, she noted:

> Whether our differences could have been contained within one report I am not too sure. Part of the problem may lie in the relationship of the Inquiry to the chair, a relationship which Louis Blom Cooper [chair of the Jasmine Beckford Inquiry] himself characterised as 'primus inter pares' ['first among equals']. (Stevenson, 1986, p 502)

Serious case reviews and reports of inquiries are therefore best understood as *social* documents (Stanley, 2004), but also deeply political documents that produce effects that their authors can neither predict nor control. Documents from the past continue to have effects that last long after they are supposed to have been superseded by new layers of policy and guidance. In turn, newly produced documents 'speak to' those from the past and will inevitably act with them to produce effects and interpretations that are very different from those their authors may have intended.

Serious case reviews: their intended function and proposals for reform

The rationale for SCRs is set out in statutory government guidance *Working together to safeguard children* (DfES, 2006; revised 2010: DCSF, 2010, and 2013: DfE, 2013b). A review must be carried out by the local interagency group – normally the local safeguarding children board (LSCB) – where abuse or neglect of a child is known or suspected, and either the child has died or has been seriously harmed, and there is concern about how agencies and professionals have worked together to safeguard the child (DfE, 2013b, p 68). The stated purpose of an SCR is to establish whether lessons are to be learned from the case for child welfare agencies and, if so, to identify what these lessons are. To this end, SCRs are analysed on a biennial basis and their complex findings are subject to detailed and rigorous review (see for example Brandon et al, 2012).

It is instructive to compare the sections of the *Working together* documents that address the process of reviewing serious cases across time through its three most recent iterations, in 2006, 2010 and 2013. Of most relevance for this chapter are two observations. First is the shift from a focus primarily on learning in relation to the 'local rationalities' of child protection practice towards viewing the event in a national context. This is most evident in the guidance on how the SCR should be made publicly available, disseminated and scrutinised, with an increased focus on 'transparency'. Second is the related shift in the use of language, which indicates the enhanced status of SCRs as *inquiries* and their function in apportioning *blame*.

The 2006 guidance stated that an executive summary of the SCR must be made public. Beyond this, a nuanced account was given of the need to balance the right of various parties to information with complex issues such as protecting the confidentiality of those involved in the case, particularly family members of the child who had died (DfES, 2006, p 179). A considerable amount of detail was given to agencies about how to maximise learning at a local level (2006, pp 179-80). Learning at a national level was emphasised in terms of aggregated information from SCRs across the country (2006, p 180).

In the 2010 version, suspicion over the integrity of the process was evident and new layers of scrutiny were introduced. The instruction that the SCR executive summary should be published was retained and, as in the 2006 document, detailed consideration was given to the balance to be struck regarding disclosure of the report and associated documents (DCSF, 2010, p 253). The emphasis of learning lessons locally was retained. However, the full report had now also to be evaluated by the government department's quality assurance agency – Ofsted – which had powers to institute proceedings to ensure that any perceived inadequacies of the report could be addressed (2010, p 252).

By 2013, 'final reports of SCRs **must be published**, including the LSCB's response to the review findings, in order to achieve **transparency**' (DfE, 2013b, p 67, emphasis in original). The process shifted further again from its localised context in that SCRs had to be carried out by someone independent of the organisation (2013, p 66). A national panel of independent experts was formed to support the LSCBs in their tasks of applying the SCR criteria, appointing reviewers, and publishing the SCR reports, which was given heavy emphasis:

> All reviews of cases meeting the SCR criteria should result in a report which is published and readily accessible on the LSCB's website for a minimum of 12 months. Thereafter the report should be made available on request. This is important to support national sharing of lessons learnt and good practice in writing and publishing SCRs. From the very start of the SCR the fact that the report will be published should be taken into consideration. SCR reports should be written in such a way that publication will not be likely to harm the welfare of any children or vulnerable adults involved in the case. (DfE, 2013b, p 71)

The second relevant observation of the three versions of *Working together* that can be made is the use of language regarding the status of SCRs as *inquiries* and their function in apportioning blame. In 2006 it was explicitly asserted that 'serious case reviews are not inquiries into how a child died or who is culpable' (DfES, 2006, p 170). Similarly, in 2010, 'serious case reviews are not inquiries into how a child died or was seriously harmed, or who is culpable' (DCSF, 2010, p 234). This was reiterated in the second review into the death of Peter Connelly when the report emphasised that '[j]udgement about the performance of any individuals is not the remit of an SCR' (Haringey, 2009, p 4). By 2013, there was a subtle but important shift in that reviews were no longer explicitly differentiated from inquiries. There was only qualified protection for professionals, if they had acted 'in good faith': 'professionals should be involved fully in reviews and invited to contribute their perspectives without fear of being blamed for actions they took in good faith' (DfE, 2013b, p 66).

Systems thinking and the serious case review

In the 2013 version of *Working together*, an option is given to LSCBs to draw on a new, 'systems' model for undertaking a SCR, as recommended by Munro (2011) and others. A systems approach includes:

> *all* possible variables that make up the workplace and influence the efforts of front-line workers in their engagement with families. Importantly, as well as the more tangible factors like procedures, tools and aids, working conditions, resources etc, a systems approach also includes more nebulous issues such as team and organisational 'cultures' and the covert messages that are communicated and acted on. It treats these apparently softer factors as systems issues as well. (Fish et al, 2008, p 8, emphasis in original)

Fish et al (2008) identify the importance of not only learning horizontally between agencies, professionals and teams, but also 'learning vertically' between frontline staff and their managers, those at senior levels making strategic decisions, and policy makers (Fish et al, 2008, p 5). The architects of this model are realistic in their appraisal of the potential difficulties in applying it due to 'the challenge of escaping our deeply entrenched traditional frameworks for thinking about and understanding front-line practice' (Fish et al, 2008, p 6). The authors are at pains to point out that a detached view of the workplace is inadequate compared with 'reconstructing how the situation looked from the practitioner's point of view' (Fish et al, 2008, p 23). This may also underestimate the degree to which 'local rationalities' about risk have been entirely reconstituted according to the emotional politics of risk and child protection. It is hard to see at present how a systems model might operate effectively in the context of political and media discourses on risk and blame that emphasise the public shaming of practitioners. It has also been argued that the approach risks losing the lessons that might be learned from the story of the individual child and their family (Brandon, 2012, p 136).

Serious case reviews in the politics–media–politics cycle

The increasing importance of SCRs as documents that receive media attention is illustrated by noting changes in the frequency of the appearance of the term 'serious case review' in national UK newspapers. It is important to realise that these changes initially reflect the growing political pressure after the death of Peter Connelly to make SCRs publicly available. This explains why, in the year immediately before the story of Peter Connelly came to prominence in the media (November 2007 to November 2008), there were only 26 mentions of the term (LexisNexis search, 19 February 2014). In the following two years this had increased to 341 and 356 appearances respectively. However, there was then a dip in the frequency of the term's appearance in the two years between November 2010 and November 2012, with 118 and 198 occurrences respectively. Furthermore, a significant proportion of the appearances in the second year related to the SCR concerning the scandal at Winterbourne View Private Hospital for adults with learning disabilities in Bristol during this period. In the year between November 2012 and November 2013, the frequency of mentions of the term had increased significantly to 716. Over a quarter of these articles (182) referred to Daniel Pelka, who died in 2012. The criminal convictions of his mother and his stepfather concluded in 2013 and were widely reported.

The increased prominence of SCRs in newspaper accounts of the deaths of children from severe abuse or neglect is a clue to their increased importance as *news events* in their own right. In addition to the often long-awaited conclusion to the criminal trial of the parent or carer of the child who has died, the publication of the SCR report provides another rich source of detail for the media. SCRs represent every detail pertaining to the decisions that were made about a child through a chronologically ordered timeframe, sometimes starting from the birth of the child up to their death. They specifically lack reference to structural issues, so that the links between factors such as deprivation, poverty and abuse are largely lost (Brandon et al, 2012, p 135). As this chapter will later demonstrate, social actors operating within the politics–media–politics cycle have become well versed in the format of the reports and in the language of the statutory guidance; that their function is to 'learn the lessons' from the child's death.

SCRs are especially notable for the political response they produce and how this response quickly becomes 'news'. SCRs are thereby central to the politics–media–politics cycle about child abuse and social work. The author of the first SCR report into the death of Peter Connelly, Edi Carmi, argued that there has been a 'political abuse of serious case reviews since the death of Baby P' (*Community Care*, 13 December 2013). More specifically, the reviews have departed from their original function of providing 'local lessons for a local professional audience' (quoted in *Community Care*, 13 December 2013). SCRs have therefore been extracted from their 'local rationalities' so that decisions and events are instead viewed at the level of national anxieties.

Serious case reviews as textual news events

The role of the media in relation to inquiries in general has been explored in considerable depth in the literature, for example by Butler and Drakeford (2003, pp 161-7). The coverage conforms to particular patterns, as underlined in earlier chapters of this book. A pattern in media accounts is characterised by:

- a focus on the common properties of events;
- an inattention to any dissimilarity between them;
- a causal explanation that can encapsulate them all (Stallings, 1990).

In cases where a child has died as a result of extreme neglect or abuse, the pattern of reporting is quite distinctive as it follows a temporal sequence of events, in which the starting point is often the conviction of the child's killers. At this point the case represents a big news story for which the media turn to politicians for comment, especially regarding any policy implications. The initial wave of media accounts are often based on the judge's summing up at the conclusion of the trial, as explored later in this chapter in relation to coverage of the Hamzah Khan story. This is often quickly followed by the publication of an SCR. During this process, strong narratives involving great details of what happened to the child and which have been documented in painful detail during the trial are quick to circulate, together with the moral judgement contained in the judge's summing up. The details directly implicating the role of professionals in the tragic outcome are therefore produced in tandem with the judgment on those who actually killed the child. This has now become an equally important part of the exposure of details in the public domain. Opportunities for counterfactual emotions – the feelings that surround 'what might have been' – appear at virtually every turning point in the case as the details unfold.

The sensationalist media reporting that often precedes the SCR into the death of a child is matched by the intensive coverage after the report is published. This process magnifies the impact of these events in the public imagination and means that part of the organising power of SCR reports is derived from their 'intertextuality' with media accounts and court judgments as well as with other documents such as government guidance and legislation. In the next section the focus is on the two SCR reports that were carried out following the death of Peter Connelly in 2007. In this analysis I identify the discourses on disgust and moral regulation that were discussed in Chapter Three, which I argue were activated in the second SCR.

Activating 'new' authoritative practice and moral regulation

Comparative analysis of the two SCRs that were conducted into the death of Peter Connelly provides a valuable insight into how elements of the moral disturbance about his death were crystallised in texts where they could prescribe forms of practice – particularly moral judgement – in child protection. This section of the chapter shows how attributions of shame – or more specifically *shamelessness* – are central to the emotional politics that is exposed in the shift from the first SCR to the second. The comparison illustrates how 'texts are processes in which political work is done, as well as the rhetorical work of mobilizing people behind political discourses' (Skeggs, 2004, p 81).

The first draft of the first SCR into the death of Peter Connelly was completed in mid-July 2008 and the final version of it produced in November 2008 (Haringey, 2008) immediately following the conviction of his killers. The initial political response to the first SCR was positive. However, following the media and political reaction to the case, an Ofsted inspection was ordered by the-then Secretary of State, Ed Balls, which found the first SCR to be 'inadequate' (Ofsted, 2009). A second SCR panel was convened and its report completed in March 2009 (Haringey, 2009). Full (redacted) versions of both SCRs were made publicly available in October 2010, with the first report being 135 pages in length and the second 74 pages. As acknowledged in the introduction to the second SCR, it was 'conducted in the wake of a criminal trial and unprecedented media coverage and popular reaction' (2009, p 4). Given the temporal sequence of events, the critical analysis of the content of these two documents has the potential to provide invaluable insights into the intertextuality between media accounts, political discourse and the process of inquiry that an SCR entails.

It is important to note from the outset that the first SCR is not uncritical in its assessment of the professional practice in the case. In some respects its conclusions might be regarded as more critical than the second. An example of this can be seen in its forensic examination of the 'pervasive beliefs' that were held by social workers and their failure to revise their assessments in light of subsequent events (Haringey,

2008, paras 6.12.28–6.12.29). The second SCR provides a much more detailed description of the context for the case than the first report, including explicit reference to the significance of the socioeconomic context for child protection practice and the meaning this has for thresholds of risk:

> However many resources there are, the social worker is always faced with discerning the priority case from among the many which are in need but will have to manage with a lesser service or none at all ... [non-accidental deaths of children] occur more frequently in larger authorities and in those with the poorest socio-economic conditions. This is not necessarily because the families are poor but because they are harder to identify amongst the families experiencing equally difficult conditions but who do not deliberately harm their children. (Haringey, 2009, paras 2.5.4–2.5.5)

The second SCR therefore acknowledges the inherently problematic nature of decision making in child protection, particularly in a deprived authority such as Haringey. It alludes to the way children who are being abused may be 'hidden in plain sight' because of the overwhelming levels of need in their communities. However, the most important issue of difference between the two reports relates to the tone and moral language used in the second SCR and how this might relate to the nature of the moral disturbance over the case that has been discussed in earlier chapters of this book.

In comparing the evaluation of professional practice in the content of these two documents, there are important observations to be made about the moral disturbance they might be understood to reflect. First of these is the key question of where the threshold for concern about parenting should be set and second is the question of what should characterise the appropriate professional response to those concerns. These are therefore questions that essentially revolve around risk assessment and risk management. As evident in the analysis that follows, the threshold issue hinges on the *moral and philosophical* question of whether expectations of parenting capacity in some families should be lower than, or different from, the expectations that might hold for other families. This question goes to the heart of one of the two institutional devices of the 'rule of optimism' articulated by Dingwall et al (1983), which is cultural relativism. In this they included local culture such as geographical area or even individual housing estates (1983, p 58).

The two SCRs make very different evaluations of the threshold of concern set by social workers about Tracey Connelly's parenting. In crude terms, the evaluation by the first SCR can be defined as reflecting a relative idea of parenting capacity in which it should be evaluated in context, whereas the second SCR adopts a stance that is more 'absolute' in its evaluation. The second SCR explicitly states that 'the threshold of concern in the child protection system at the time was too high' (Haringey, 2009, para 3.14.4). It is highly critical of the fact that the Connelly family 'was regarded as a routine case, with injuries occurring as a matter of course, which would attract their [child protection staff's] standard and well-tried approach to the family' (2009, para 3.10.1). The response of agencies to Peter Connelly's injuries and experience of neglect 'appeared to be that this kind of occurrence was not surprising in a family *like this*' (2009, para 3.10.2, emphasis added).

This difference in relation to thresholds is highlighted in each report's treatment of an incident in which Tracey Connelly had been observed slapping one of her older children. For the first SCR, there is acknowledgement that the incident should have been reported to the police, but the language used is purely factual. In contrast, the second SCR describes the incident as 'a shocking loss of control ... a very depersonalising thing to do ... a criminal assault' and defines the authorities' response as reflecting 'the low expectations which many of the agencies in Haringey appeared to have about families *like this*' (2009, para 3.12.2, emphasis added).

A similar example can be seen in the reports' differing treatment of another issue of concern, which was the presence of dogs in the household. In the first report, the difficulty encountered in persuading Tracey Connelly to keep the dogs out of the family home is reported factually as evidence of her 'non-compliance' with social workers (Haringey, 2008, para 6.20.6). For the second SCR, Connelly's initial refusal to remove the dogs raises 'questions about her motivation for change' and her complaints about them being kept away once removed 'suggests someone who is quite shameless, and without much conscience' (2008, para 3.12.1). The evaluation is therefore no longer about the relationship she is willing to allow with services, but *who or what she is as a moral subject*. It is a conclusion surely only reached in hindsight, in the context of what she was known to have done to her son and the public, political and media reaction to it. In the designation of her as 'shameless', the report activates an emotional response towards Connelly's behaviour in which she is objectified and denied subjective status as someone who has capacity for shame. In feeling shame, a person retains the possibility of redemption. As Ahmed (2004, p 107) has argued, '[i]n showing my shame in my failure to live up to a social ideal, I come closer to that which I have been exposed as failing.'

'Authority is not a dirty word' (Blom-Cooper, 1985, p 295)

In terms of differences between the two SCRs in their evaluations of professional responses to the concerns about Peter Connelly, the most important measure is perhaps the introduction in the second SCR of the language of 'authoritative practice'. Authority and its use or abuse is a recurrent theme in inquiries and SCRs. It was a particular focus of the Jasmine Beckford inquiry in 1985, as were apparent shortcomings in social work training in terms of equipping social workers to use their authority (Blom-Cooper, 1985). The word 'authoritative' appears once in the first SCR into Peter Connelly's death and 20 times in the second, where 'principles of authoritative practice' are repeatedly invoked. An authoritative intervention is defined in the report as 'urgent, thorough, challenging, with a low threshold of concern, keeping the focus on the child, and with high expectations of parenting and what services should expect of themselves' (Haringey, 2009, para 4.2). The *moral* implications of these principles of authoritative practice are apparent. Tracey Connelly warranted this mode of relationship with professionals, not *only* because of the injuries and neglect in evidence in the care of her children, but *also* due to the 'shameless' nature of her lifestyle:

> The mode of relationship that was needed was an authoritative one, reflecting the fact that her [Connelly's] child had probably been injured with force by an adult and for which she showed little remorse or concern. All her children received neglectful care … Ms A [Connelly] intimidated the staff with her volatile emotional states so much so that they were reluctant to approach her with concerns about the children or her own anti-social behaviour. She was in rent arrears and she drank and smoked heavily with little regard for the impact of it on her children's welfare. The questions to be asked at this stage are: 'What have we got here?' And 'Who have we got here?' (Haringey, 2009, para 3.8.4)

Just as in media and political accounts, attached to the most salient point about abuse is the idea of parenting associated with specific class formations and identities. More specifically, the second SCR lends attention to the 'pathological dispositions' (Hayward and Yar, 2006) associated with constructions of the so-called 'underclass'. Tracey Connelly's smoking, drinking, antisocial behaviour and rent arrears are all given status here as a tell-tale sign of what was to come. They mirror the media and political discourse on the obviousness of the risks she posed to her son as a mother and the fact that the threshold for removing him should have been reached on these grounds alone. A powerful area of intertextuality between the media accounts (as analysed in Chapter Three) and the production of the second SCR report is in the reinforcement of a 'common-sense' link between these behaviours and parenting, which *self-evidently* falls well below the threshold of 'good-enough' parenting. The 'low threshold of concern' that characterises authoritative practices draws into its purview this wider range of behaviours. In turn, these are implicitly connected to the binary constructions of us ('good') and them ('bad') parenting in media and policy, which are invariably classed and gendered categories of risk. Under these conditions, while a rule of optimism may continue to apply to the 'us' side of this binary, a rule of pessimism should apply to 'them'.

In tracing contradictory policy discourses on the family under New Labour, Morris and Featherstone (2010) highlight the significance of reaction to the death of Peter Connelly. They argue that the case focused concern on how far social workers should be intent on 'fixing' families rather than removing children (2010, p 563). As already discussed, the 'Baby P effect' signalled a significant lowering of thresholds for care proceedings. It is clear that social work practitioners can reflect rather than resist dominant discourses about personal responsibility for poverty and deprivation. In their study of social workers and service users, for example, Grover and Mason (2013) found that some social workers utilised gender and class stereotypes about working-class mothers being promiscuous and neglectful, and had fixed ideas about the intergenerational transmission of neglect. In the context of policy responses that have emerged since the economic crisis of 2007, it is argued that social work has been mobilised as part of 'a divisive and authoritarian project against those most vulnerable' (Featherstone et al, 2014, p 19).

In the next section I analyse the SCR into the death of Hamzah Khan. The focus is on the emotionality of hindsight bias and more specifically the way that reports and reviews generate powerful counterfactual emotions. By this I mean the emotional sense of 'what might have been' as alternatives to the events that led to the death of a child.

What might have been: the hindsight fallacy and counterfactual emotions

Hindsight bias has been identified by Munro (2011, p 18) as a key element in the effort to manage uncertainty in child protection, which is one of the main drivers of change in the system. Hindsight bias is generally viewed as a cognitive bias, which is linked to heuristics, or mental 'short-cuts' in judgement and decision making (Kahneman et al, 1982). It is also linked to counterfactual emotions, such as regret and disappointment. Counterfactual emotions are the emotions that result 'when reality is compared to an imagined view of what might have been' (Kahneman and Miller, 1986, p 136). In this section of the chapter, the focus is on the emotionality of SCRs as documents that are active in the way they both embody and generate particular emotional effects. A great deal of discussion has been devoted to the problems with hindsight bias in SCRs and inquiries. The fallacy of hindsight bias has been succinctly defined as follows:

> If a decision involves risk, then even when one can demonstrate that one has chosen the unarguably optimal course of action, some proportion of the time the outcome will be suboptimal. It follows that a bad outcome in and of itself does not constitute evidence that the decision was mistaken. The hindsight fallacy is to assume that it does. (Macdonald and Macdonald, 1999, p 22)

The whole premise upon which the first SCR into Peter Connelly's death was regarded as flawed was that it had failed to identify 'mistaken decisions' in the way that had become politically necessary during the course of media and political outrage. As explored above, the first report did not capture the emotional intensity of the reaction to events and the second report constructed the past in a way that was more consistent with the public, media and political outrage that had ensued. The pitfalls involved in hindsight bias in the context of child protection are particularly well illustrated in the following lengthy extract about hindsight bias, based on a reading of the report of the inquiry into the death of Kimberley Carlile[1]:

> Here Blom-Cooper (with colleagues) is considering the events which led to the death of Kimberley Carlile. They cite, and then comment on, the social worker's perception of the end of one interview:

> "*I walked with the family to the door of the building, and watched as they walked across the road to where their old car was parked. I still have a clear mental picture of the way in which they all walked across the road and got into the car, parents holding children by the hand, children leaping around in the car as they got in, laughing shouting and playing happily with each other. It was almost an archetype for a happy family scene.*
>
> Far from being reassured, [the social worker] should have been alive to the risk of being manipulated. Plainly he had been deceived..." (London Borough of Greenwich 1987 pp.111–112)
>
> Plainly? Certainly, with hindsight, we know that family was not a 'happy family', but even with hindsight we do not know that 'manipulation' and 'deception' were present in that scene since even dysfunctional families can have happy moments. The implicit criticism is sustainable *only* with the benefit of hindsight; the invited contemporaneous counterfactual is not plausible: 'It was almost an archetype for a happy family scene. So I realised I was being manipulated, and forthwith arranged for the child to be taken into care.' (Macdonald and Macdonald, 1999, pp 23–24, emphasis in original)

In distorting judgement about the predictability of events, hindsight bias performs an important emotional function because it provides a reassurance that what happened could have been prevented were it not for human error. As Munro (2011) has emphasised, hindsight bias serves to make the sequence of events that led to the adverse outcome seem clear and it is hard not to feel they were entirely predictable: "'How could they not have realised that x would lead to y?'" (2011, p 18). Hindsight bias has led to a focus on human error as an adequate explanation for bad outcomes, which has driven system change in child protection towards controlling the behaviour of practitioners (Munro, 2011). But more importantly, the reassurance that events were predictable if only practitioners had got it right extends to the possibilities for the prevention of future tragic outcomes. The hindsight bias of the SCR and inquiry report, and the counterfactual emotions involved, are of fundamental importance in the emotional politics of social work and child protection because they help to activate the 'false hope of eliminating risk' (Munro, 2011, p 134). Among the emotions that are activated by SCRs are regret, anger and shame. Feelings of regret revolve around 'the imagined view of what might have been' when we reflect on opportunities that were missed that would have changed the course of events.

Tragic beyond words

The SCR into the death of Hamzah Khan was published on 13 November 2013 and was immediately met with very negative reaction from government ministers, with strong echoes of the reaction to the first SCR into Peter Connelly's death in 2008. The negative reaction took the official form of a letter sent from Edward Timpson MP, Under-Secretary of State for Children and Families, to the Independent Chair of the Bradford Safeguarding Children Board, Professor Nick Fros. The letter requested further clarification with regard to 10 questions concerning the findings of the SCR.

The starting point of Timpson's letter was to assert that scrutiny of decisions in *public* is a prerequisite for lessons being learned and for preventing future 'mistakes'. This assertion illustrates the way in which SCRs have been extracted from their function in addressing local rationalities of risk and decision making and are now documents that are much broader in their scope:

> It is important that we ensure rigorous public scrutiny in instances where children are seriously harmed or died under neglectful conditions. As the Secretary of State emphasised yesterday, this is not to seek out scapegoats, but to be clear about what happened in the past and try to ensure that similar mistakes are not made in future.
>
> With this in mind, I have deep concerns over the Hamzah Khan serious case review. (Timpson, 2013)

Timpson's letter then went on to ask a serious of 10 questions, chiefly revolving around why the children in the household were not assessed at various points and why other particular actions were not taken. The following two examples from the 10 illustrate the tone of the queries, in which the minister's concerns are literally underlined:

> December 2006: one of Hamzah Khan's siblings spoke to police about domestic violence at home and the police referred him to children's social care. The child was returned home. <u>Was the child assessed? If not, why not?</u>
>
> March 2007 – one of Hamzah Khan's siblings – it is not clear in the SCR whether it was the same one – was

remanded by magistrates and placed with foster carers for two nights then returned home. <u>Was the child assessed by children's social care? If not why not?</u> (Timpson, 2013, emphasis in original)

At the end of the letter after listing the 10 specific questions about the case, it stated the following:

> All of these were missed opportunities to protect the children in the house.
>
> It is tragic beyond words that by the time a health visitor did trigger concerns about the whereabouts of the younger children in the household, who were missing from health and education services altogether, Hamzah Khan was already dead.
>
> It is essential that answers to the questions above are put into the public domain so that the people of Bradford and the public are reassured that you have been clear enough about the past to ensure that such mistakes will not be repeated in future. (Timpson, 2013)

This section of the letter is a good illustration of the emotionality of the counterfactual of regret and the sense of tragedy that attaches to 'what might have been'. The tragic nature of the missed opportunities partly lies in their simplicity. None of them, as actions in their own right, would apparently have been difficult to undertake. The anger and disbelief, and ultimately the construction of these missed opportunities as *mistakes*, are mobilised by disbelief and anger that such simple steps were not taken. In turn, the shame that is activated in relation to professionals' practice in the exchange is a *collective* shame. This is because this SCR does not stand alone; it is one of a series in which the same mistakes are apparently repeated. Collective shame '"involves being publicly exposed as incompetent, not being in control, weak and potentially even disgusting *in the eyes of others*"' (cited in Allpress et al, 2010, p 82).

A demand in the House of Commons for an independent inquiry into Hamzah Khan's death from the local Bradford MP, George Galloway, was met with reassurances from Edward Timpson that he had made the request for further information. However, the extent of ministerial anger and disapproval of the SCR was conveyed through the media where, once again, the interests of politicians and the press were conjoined:

A Department for Education source yesterday dismissed the report as 'useless' and 'a rubbish document', adding that it was 'worrying that local agencies don't realise how poor an investigation this is'. (Brooke and Levy, 2013, in *Daily Mail*, 14 November)

Review of 'mummified boy' failures has glaring absences, says minister. (Malnick, 2013, in *The Daily Telegraph*, 14 November)

Little Hamzah is failed again; Report into how starved lad, 4, was let down by the system is slammed by Government. (Thornton, 2013, p 33, in *Daily Mirror*, 14 November)

The response to Edward Timpson's letter was a very detailed 11-page report compiled by officers at the Bradford Safeguarding Children Board, together with a letter from Frost in which he explicitly referred to the issue of thresholds, as follows:

A constant theme throughout the SCR is that the threshold of concern was not reached within agencies to trigger a child protection investigation, under Section 47 of the Children Act, 1989. If expectations are changing and agencies are expected to significantly lower this threshold, this will have a great impact on resources nationally. (Frost, 2013)

These exchanges, together with the details provided in the original SCR report and the detailed report that followed it, encapsulate the differences between thresholds in how they are conceptualised in practice, in policy and in the public 'everyday', common-sense sphere. But most fundamentally, the difference between these conceptualisations is in how they might relate to the operation of hindsight bias. For anyone operating in practice, there is a daily round of information gathering and very high levels of uncertainty about which pieces of information might be important and which might prove insignificant. There are also large numbers of children to whom such information applies, each of whom are essentially competing for priority. For the minister or journalist into whose hands a SCR report falls, there is an 'only child' about whom there is absolute certainty about an outcome that is 'tragic beyond words'.

Personal politics and emotional labour

As noted in previous chapters, politics in recent years has been characterised by the presence of more politicians with young families. I argue that this is significant for the emotional politics of child protection because of the confluence of feelings about what being a parent means and what it should entail, and processes of identification. Edward Timpson is another leading politician whose credibility as a politician and as a minister has been linked directly to his personal experience. In an interview for *The Guardian* (Rustin, 2014), Timpson talked about his own experience as a father of three young children, but also his childhood experience in a family that fostered children: "'I've obviously thought about this a lot and I've come to the conclusion that I wouldn't be children's minister and I wouldn't have gone into family law if my parents hadn't fostered," he says' (Rustin, 2014). While the journalist commented that Timpson's approach to policy was refreshing, the article also observed 'a degree of political calculation, since he knows constituents are interested' (Rustin, 2014). The blend of policy making as emotional labour with its origins in personal experience, and the crafting of an image for public consumption, are all in evidence in the article.

Conclusion

The main focus of this chapter has been the SCR as a specific type of document that is ritually produced and which has become central to the emotional politics of social work and child protection. I have argued that SCRs are emotionally active in the way they increasingly serve to generate and coordinate effects between the political sphere, the media and practice. The feeling rules that politicians generate, or act as envoys for, can be read into SCRs as documents that come to embody emotions such as shame, disgust and regret for what might have been. Far from being a static, rational account of the events that led to the death of a child, the SCR moves through time to animate the past and shape expectations of the future. As Ahmed (2004, p 13) puts it: 'The emotionality of texts is one way of describing how texts are "moving", or how they generate effects.'

Through hindsight bias, SCR reports produce a sense in which different decisions *could easily have been made*. In this way, the reports activate anger and reinforce the belief that preventing child abuse is common sense that could be enacted 'by anyone other than a social worker'. They reinforce the message that only common sense stands between social work practice and good decision making. By extracting them from the local rationalities of practice, SCRs have been implanted into a national system of scrutiny and ritual punishment through shame. The phrase 'learning the lessons' generally places a positive connotation on the idea of learning from past mistakes. This was the original purpose of the case reviewing system. I argue that the link between regret and shame produced by hindsight bias places a very different connotation on the phrase, which is more akin to 'being taught a lesson' in a way that entails ritual punishment through public shaming.

The chapter has also highlighted the intertextuality between documents, in terms of both their action across time but also between different domains of production and consumption. This is particularly true when understanding the effects of each new layer of policy reform and documented practice. The Laming Inquiry into the death of Victoria Climbié (2003) and New Labour's policies on *Every Child Matters* (DfES, 2004a; 2004b) that followed were invested with hope for the future that was to prove deeply problematic in the perfect storm of emotion and politics that erupted in late 2008 with the death of Peter Connelly. The hopes that are activated by successive reforms, and the infinite possibilities for prevention to which they aspire, are the light that casts a shadow in the form of the next inquiry or SCR.

Note
[1]   Kimberley Carlile died aged 4 years in 1986 in Greenwich, London. She had been abused over a period of at least nine months, starved and beaten to death. Her stepfather was convicted of her murder and her mother of assault and cruelty. Kimberley's death was the subject of an inquiry, in which social workers were heavily criticised (London Borough of Greenwich, 1987).

SEVEN

Comparative perspectives: cultures of difference and convergence

Introduction

So far in this book I have analysed the concept of emotional politics in the context of Britain. Britain, particularly England, can be regarded as an 'extreme case' in terms of the public hostility directed at social workers, and therefore worthy of detailed attention. However, it is by no means unique. Intense media, political and public scrutiny of social work following the death of a child from abuse and neglect is also found elsewhere. In this chapter my attention turns to case studies from other countries to consider how collective emotions in these contexts might do political work through texts, political rhetoric and media discourse in the way I have outlined in the book so far. The case studies are drawn from Australasia, the Netherlands, Sweden and New York in the United States (US). These were selected because they each highlight in different ways various dimensions of emotional politics discussed so far. Of necessity, consideration of each is brief and the focus is narrow in so far as these are all 'developed' countries or states. But by also drawing on the findings from the much more detailed comparative studies carried out by others, there is evidence on which to base a preliminary argument about the wider nature and significance of emotional politics.

I argue that, while there are important and significant differences between the countries in terms of the structure of child welfare services and professional ideologies of professionals, there is evidence of certain common features in terms of the nature of emotional politics that is at work. This commonality can be identified in relation to three of the main organising features of emotional politics that I have highlighted so far in my discussion:

- the meaning of the child in political, cultural and socioeconomic terms;

- the significance of difference, diversity and rising levels of social inequality, especially in a global context of neoliberal governance and economic insecurity;
- the so-called emotionalisation of politics, which can, in part, be observed through politicians acting as feeling legislators and envoys of emotion in representing the interests of citizens.

The value of undertaking comparative work on child welfare and protection systems has been summarised by Hetherington as follows:

> By looking at differences, and using the power of making comparisons, we can begin to identify the 'taken-for-granted'. This may lead us to question some of the assumptions on which our system rests and to become more aware of the aspects of the system that we value most highly. As we become more aware of the reasons why our system has developed as it has, positive changes may become more attainable. (Hetherington, 2002, p 1)

I argue that there is another dimension of the 'taken-for-granted' that comparative work potentially makes visible. This concerns the way different systems are increasingly shaped by the same pressures, particularly those that emanate from the movement of tectonic plates in global economic terms. These reverberate well beyond the boundaries of nation states. As Featherstone et al (2014) have emphasised, increased and growing inequality is a common feature across diverse systems, with profound emotional as well as other costs. Concern about the organisation of services using complex systems that are primarily geared towards managing risk to organisations is also widespread across 'Anglophone' countries of Australasia, North America and the UK (Featherstone et al, 2014).

Of particular interest in terms of the argument I develop in this chapter is that cross-national studies of child welfare and child protection have entailed thinking more deeply about *culture*. Culture has been identified as the most important source of the differences in functioning between child protection systems cross-nationally; more so than their structure and professional ideology. As Hetherington has argued:

> Culture influences and expresses expectations of the various roles that should be played by the state, the family, and by the community in relation to the child. These expectations

find expression in the functioning of child welfare systems. It is in this context that the social worker represents the state. (Hetherington, 2002, p 14)

While definitions of culture are many, it 'seems to refer to values, practices, emotions and artefacts, as well as institutions and "ways of doing things"' (Freeman and Rustin, 1999, p 13), all of which are invested with meaning. Culture therefore encompasses emotion, or what Garland (1990, p 195) terms 'structures of affect and what might be called emotional configurations or "sensibilities"'. In terms of gaining greater insight into aspects of emotional politics, such as the collective remembering of children who have died from abuse and neglect, comparative studies do appear to offer useful insights. Two of the selected case studies in particular – New York City and Sweden – also offer insights into how positive change might be attainable in a British context.

Before considering the four case studies, the chapter highlights relevant findings from comparative studies of child welfare and child protection systems. These have suggested that there may be a process of convergence under way in some respects in terms of the emotional components of the relationship between parents, the state and children.

Complexity and convergence across child welfare systems

A comparative study of responses to child abuse in nine different countries in the 1990s identified two broad orientations: family service and child protection (Gilbert, 1997). In the family service approach, child abuse was conceptualised as 'the manifestation of family dysfunction stemming from psychological difficulties, marital troubles and socioeconomic stress', all of which may be considered responsive to professional interventions (Gilbert, 2012, p 532). Belgium, Denmark, Finland, Germany, the Netherlands and Sweden were countries in which this broad orientation was most prominent. In contrast, the child protection approach 'framed abuse as the harmful behaviour of malevolent parents, which called for legal investigation and public measures to control deviant, if not outright criminal, behaviour' (Gilbert, 2012, p 532). This approach characterised systems in England, Canada and the US. Two decades later, in a follow-up study of the same nine countries plus Norway, Gilbert (2012) observed that there had been convergence and blending of these two approaches but also the development of a third approach. In this 'child-development' or child-focused orientation, the state's role in taking responsibility for child development was the focus.

The child-focused orientation borrows features of both the child protection and family service orientations but it is qualitatively different (Gilbert et al, 2011). It is variously shaped by ideas relating to 'the social investment state' in which children are seen as future workers in terms of their potential to become law–abiding and productive adults, with the family alone being viewed as no longer adequate for the task of maximising this potential (Gilbert et al, 2011, p 253). The child-focused orientation is also shaped by contemporary processes of individualisation, where children are regarded as current citizens in their own right, equal to adults, and their right to a happy childhood is seen as a social justice issue (Gilbert et al, 2011, p 254). These two influences of social investment and individualisation are in tension and emphasised in different ways in different countries:

> The three orientations provide a broad representation of alternative definitions of the problem, modes of intervention and relationships between parents and the state, which are currently emphasized in varying degrees. They afford an abstract picture of how the functioning of child welfare systems, once divided between protection and service orientations, has become more varied and complex since the 1990s. (Gilbert, 2012, p 533)

In successive comparative studies in Europe and North America, it has been shown that child welfare services have expanded in all of the countries studied and more children and families now come under the purview of services compared with in the past (Gilbert, 1997; Gilbert et al, 2011). The authors have emphasised the difficulty in assessing how far this expansion reflects changes in the incidence of abuse, increased awareness of child abuse and/or broader definitions of abuse and changing thresholds for intervention. There is evidence, however, of a change in how children's position in society is viewed. Whether the expansion of services is interpreted as an attempt to improve prevention and thus the lot of children in need or more as increased mechanisms of social surveillance, both interpretations 'imply a changing set of relationships among the state, parents, and children' (Gilbert et al, 2011, p 248).

In all of the countries scrutinised there has been an increase in the use of formal procedures, a 'pervasive spread of bureaucratic mandates', together with increased use of various technologies and tools to support evidence-based practice (Gilbert et al, 2011, p 249). These changes need to be understood as operating 'in a highly volatile atmosphere, where without warning, practices come under critical public scrutiny' (Gilbert et al, 2011, p 251). 'The challenge of operating in the public spotlight' is far from being unique to the British child welfare and protection system, and in terms of intense media coverage of cases of fatal child abuse there are many parallels with the experience of other countries including Belgium, Canada, Germany, the Netherlands and Sweden (Gilbert et al, 2011, p 245).

These developments need to be understood in the context of much wider social, political and economic change, not least the global financial crisis since 2007. There are general trends towards neoliberal governance, shifting awareness of risk and uncertainty in the 'risk society', and shifts from public/collectively organised welfare systems towards private, market-driven arrangements (Gilbert et al, 2011, p 244).

The emotional politics of these changes, particularly financial insecurity, are widely and deeply felt. As argued by Young (2011), and as discussed in earlier chapters of this book, the volatile socioeconomic climate has produced a 'fear of falling' and moral indignation among social groups that have previously felt secure:

> Such a moral indignation readily flows over into politics, whether enhancing the growing power of the extreme right-wing parties of Europe or the teabaggers of American Republicanism....
>
> The vortex of prejudice set in such a vertiginous current of economic distress engenders a plethora of moral panics. The financial crisis engenders the lives of the poor and of the culturally diverse as regular and convenient targets. (Young, 2011, p 257)

Disparities between groups based on social class, 'race' and ethnicity are evident across child welfare and protection systems. In some instances these reflect the changing populations of, for example, Nordic and North European countries, which have become more diverse in recent years, largely due to inward migration (Gilbert et al, 2011, p 250). In other countries there is a long history of racism rooted in colonialism and European settlement that is then expressed to a greater or less marked degree in all institutions, including the child welfare system. Aboriginal children in Canada, for example, continue to be greatly over-represented in every level of the system, as do Native American and African American children in the US. As argued in the next section of the chapter, case studies from Australia and New Zealand illustrate the continuing power of processes of colonialism.

Australasia (focusing on Australia and New Zealand): colonial discourse and mechanisms of blame

Australasia has been shaped by the forces of colonisation that began some two hundred years ago and this is central to understanding the development of social work and child welfare systems in the entire region (Beddoe and Fraser, 2012, p 431). Anger plays a central part in ongoing legal and political processes of claim, denial and response in addressing 'legacies of empire' (Lane West-Newman, 2004, p 189). In terms of the emotional politics of child abuse and social work, there are poignant examples that stand out as case studies of the deeply emotional nature of the processes at work. In Australia, the story of the Stolen Generations of Indigenous children removed from their families in order to 'integrate' them into white society continues to reverberate (Beddoe and Fraser, 2012, p 430). Fear and anger are passed down through generations of women, and are lived out in the contemporary context of discrimination. This is poignantly expressed by Briggs (2014) in her account of her own experience as an Aboriginal mother: 'The fear I carry and the aversion I feel towards governmental departments is due entirely to inter-generational trauma. My mother carries this fear, my grandmother carried this fear, my great-grandmother carried this fear. These fears are real – Australia's track record in this speaks for itself.'

These fears are not the abstract fears directed at the imagined social worker discussed in Chapter Five of this book. They are firmly located in embodied experience and the continuities of colonial practices: 'Aboriginal women have been told for the better part of two centuries that they are neglectful and not fit to raise children' (Briggs, 2014). Between 1910 and 1970, up to one in three Indigenous children were forcibly removed, and so *all* Indigenous families would have been affected in one or more generations over the past century (Allpress et al, 2010, p 79). This history involves the familiar themes of child protection, including dirt and cleanliness, particularly in the home, with systems of surveillance that were identified with men. Briggs (2014) recounts her grandmother's 'fear of the dreaded "welfare man", a government employee who could come to your house and demand to be let inside to ensure your house was clean, that there was adequate food available, that the children were going to school'. In terms of its continuities into the present day, Briggs also locates the racism of colonial discourse in an everyday, interpersonal politics of respectability and shame in which processes of 'disidentification' – 'I'm not like you' – operate:

> There are broader issues at work here. I am seeing all the telltale signs of respectability politics at play. Politics that are othering black women, shaming them for their economic status and for the colour of their skin. Politics that point a damning finger at Aboriginal women who exist outside the margins of perceived respectability. Politics that cater to white conservative thought via the black men (and some black women) who hold up their hands in vehement agreement with policies that hurt black people immeasurably ... 'look at me, I'm different, I'm not like these black people, I think like you'. (Briggs, 2014)

For Briggs, discourses of risk in child protection are racialised rather than classed in terms of who the targets for surveillance are:

> When the poor white woman across the road – in exactly the same boat I am and with the exact same monetary issues – does not have the extra burden and worry of people turning up on her doorstep to question her parenting, then that initiative walks like a racist duck, and quacks like a racist duck ... when it comes to programs that affect Aboriginal mothers, I can be 95% sure that the government will go with the most invasive, detrimental and shaming plan. (Briggs, 2014)

A formal apology for the Stolen Generations was made on behalf of the nation in February 2008 by the then Prime Minister Kevin Rudd. Ahmed asks: '*What does saying sorry do and what does it commit the nation to?*' (2004, p 116, emphasis in original). In answer, she argues that an apology for the past allows restoration of 'civil society' and defers responsibility for present injustice. The apology allows restoration of national pride because, 'in political rhetoric, "sorry" moves to "regret" by passing over "shame"' (2004, p 120).

New Zealand and the 'bad Maori mother'

In New Zealand, there are powerful arguments that child abuse has been constructed as a 'Maori problem', with a particular focus on Maori mothers, and with explicit links to the welfare benefit system (Beddoe, 2013). In turn this has been linked to a national neoliberal political agenda and specifically the perceived need for austerity measures and to justify stringent cuts to welfare spending (Beddoe, 2013). In press coverage of particular cases, Beddoe (2013) has identified a 'racialised underclass discourse linked to child maltreatment' in themes on class disgust similar to those discussed in Chapter Five of this book. Beddoe (2013) argues that the focus of disgust in constructions of the 'vilified and folkloric "bad Maori mother" reflects colonial discourse about disturbance of the ideals of a perfect nation' (after Provan, 2012).

Provan (2012) analysed the ritual use of a 'roll-call' of names of children who have died from abuse, noting that names that were recognisably Maori were more likely to be selected for inclusion. As discussed at length in Chapter Four of this book, the political work that is done through the ritual roll-call of children's names is important to understand with regard to the emotional politics that is in operation. In this context, the selection of Maori names is part of the mechanism by which the Maori mother is demonised and becomes the focus of blame, not only for child abuse, but also in a wider cultural sense:

> The image of the 'bad Maori mother', the 'mother who failed to protect', carries with it, I will argue, all that is uncanny, 'homely' within the nation, everything that should be hidden that continually comes to light. Ultimately, I will argue that 'the mother who failed to protect' stands accused of failing to protect Pākehā from knowing about all that is unwanted within the nation, about all that prevents the fantasised 'homelike' nation from being possible. (Provan, 2012, pp 188-9)

The racialised discourse of child abuse in the New Zealand press has a long history and can be seen as part of a broader discourse in which simplistic racial dichotomies of a colonial press are maintained (Keenan, 2000). In his analysis of newspaper accounts of the death of Hine Karaitiana-Matiaha[1] and a number of other children, Keenan (2000, p 6) shows how child abuse has been framed by the press as a 'singularly Maori phenomenon'. Keenan points to the fact that senior politicians have sometimes rejected this narrative outright. The Prime Minister at the time, Helen Clark, apparently 'pointed to the fact that should have been obvious to most people – that child abuse was not specific to Maori families' (Keenan, 2000, p 7).

Keenan's (2000) article provides a good example of the importance of active texts and their intertextuality in relation to the politics of emotion around child abuse. The title of the article uses a newspaper headline – 'Hine's Once Were Warriors Hell' – which references the book *Once were warriors* by Alan Duff, published in 1991 and produced as a film in 1994. Duff's portrayal of a poor Maori family, living in an urban area and experiencing unrelenting violence and abuse, was a significant 'textual moment' in New Zealand at the time. The book 'made an immediate and profound emotional impact, more for its perceived social realism than for its literary merit' (Brown, 1999, p 141). 'Once Were Warriors' has subsequently become a shorthand for a skein of concerns that can instantly be identified with Maori communities and which are portrayed as having deep – and therefore impenetrable – roots in Maori history and culture. The power of the book as a text that activates emotions, particularly shame, is evident in political discourse around child abuse, for example in responses to the deaths of Chris and Cru Kahui.[2]

In 2006 there was a great deal of press coverage in New Zealand following the deaths of Chris and Cru Kahui. There was particular outrage at the initial refusal of the family to cooperate with the police investigation and the shorthand of Once Were Warriors was invoked. Helen Clark in this case was quoted in the press as saying:

> There are a lot of things happening which are working, but from time to time you get a case like this which looks like Once Were Warriors played out again and results in the death of small children and it focuses everyone's mind again on 'is this the best we can do?'…. (*The New Zealand Herald*, 27 June 2006)

In the same article, the Maori Party co-leader, Pita Sharples, was reported as lending his support to the characterisation based on the family's behaviour: 'He said it was not until he had witnessed their behaviour that he realised what had earlier been described as *Once Were Warriors* by Prime Minister Helen Clark existed in New Zealand' (*The New Zealand Herald*, 27 June 2006). In an article reporting on an interview with Alan Duff about the case, the book's author located the quality of shamelessness in Maoridom as a whole: 'We've got to instil values. Maoridom from the top down has to be told that it's shameful to hit your kids, it's shameful not to make sacrifices to give them better future, it's shameful not to want to advance yourself' (Cheng, 2006).

In a number of the press accounts of the deaths of children from abuse and neglect the narrative that is at work is in part about *national* guilt and shame for child abuse deaths. This narrative is not just about 'the state of the nation' in relation to child welfare, but also about the issue of how to intervene 'behind closed doors' and instil collective responsibility. In this instance the concern is not with intervention by services but by neighbours: 'A Maori community leader and child advocate wants New Zealanders to stop turning a blind eye to child abuse and dob in their neighbours' (Tahana and Vass, 2008). But the way this article ends is very telling. The sense of a nation posing a risk to its children through collective inaction is gone as the focus falls – through the voice given to police officers – on a specific community and the belief in its propensity for child abuse: 'A police officer involved in the case described parts of Rotorua and outlying areas as "festering sores" for child abuse' (Tahana and Vass, 2008).

In the next section, our attention shifts to the Netherlands, where the idea of the 'universal parent' is invoked with particular force along with the political impulse to rescue children through more assertive forms of surveillance and intervention.

The Netherlands: from interventions 'as light as possible' to 'as heavy as needed'

In a speech to the United Nations in New York on 25 September 2009, the Netherlands Minister of Foreign Affairs, Maxime Verhagen, told of the impact in his country of the deaths of two children from severe abuse and neglect. The first phase of the speech is a poignant example of the *political* version of the double-bind of 'knowing yet not knowing' about child abuse. As reported in inquiries into social work practice where a child has died: 'sometimes the child exists and sometimes the child doesn't exist – it is not one or the other but both' (Cooper, 2005, p 8). Verhagen echoes this; abused children may be hidden from sight, both nationally and globally, but we all know they are there:

> Seven years ago, the Netherlands was shaken by the story of four-year-old Rowena Rikkers.... Two years later, our country was shocked again by the death of three-year-old Savanna. She, too, died at the hands of her caregivers after extended physical abuse. Their tragic fate seems too cruel to be true, and yet it happened.
> Unfortunately, all of us know of such tragedies. All our societies witness violence against children.... And

sometimes their suffering is invisible to us. But we know they are there. Millions of them. Scarred for life. (Government of the Netherlands, 2009)

The expression of virtual disbelief in the existence of the world in which the two girls died is particularly evident in the speech, as is the still powerful emotional response that their deaths invoked. It expresses what Cooper (2005, p 9) describes as the central difficulty that child abuse presents us with collectively: 'we know that terrible things are happening, but the pain of knowing is too great for us to be able to sustain our attention'.

The speech conforms to the ritual pattern of providing a roll-call of names of children who have died, citing deaths in countries including Austria, the Democratic Republic of the Congo, India, the US and Yemen. While the causes of death of these children were very different, their brief appearance in the speech provides an emotional backdrop for an appeal to political action. This call to action, like the other examples of political rhetoric analysed in this book, particularly in Chapters Two and Four, is based on an appeal to what 'we' all feel as parents. As Ahmed (2004, p 192) puts it, the pain of the children in such accounts 'is universalised through the imagined loss of *any* child as a loss that could be my loss'. The following section of Verhagen's speech ends with an assertion about the necessity and possibilities of using political power to exert change in a global context:

Violence against children breaks our hearts as mothers and fathers. We want to protect our children. And what we wish for our own children, we wish for every child in the world. Everyone who has ever held a baby in the arms will understand what I am saying. New life is a miracle that should be treated with care and respect. As politicians, we have the ability to do something about this horrendous problem. We have the power to act. And we must. (Government of the Netherlands, 2009)

But for the politician, just as for the social worker, the pain of knowing presents very real practical difficulties when converted into intervention 'on the ground'. In the closing section of his speech, quoted below, Verhagen returned to the national context of the Netherlands and revealed the national reflection that took place after the deaths of the two girls. In emotional terms, the questions the nation asked might be rewritten as: where should shame for these acts be felt? But he also highlighted the dilemma that defines the central tension in policy and social work practice; that of determining where the threshold lies for exerting powers to intervene in 'the most private cells' of the home. In this instance, not only is the child who died brought to mind; so too is the child who survives lesser forms of maltreatment, at great cost to both the individual *and* society:

> In the aftermath of the tragic deaths of Rowena and Savanna, emotions ran high in the Netherlands. We asked ourselves: could these tragedies have been prevented? Could child welfare institutions have done better? Would that have made a difference? Where did responsibility begin and where did it end?
>
> It is estimated that every year, 100,000 Dutch children suffer from abuse or neglect. Not every case is as severe as the two I just mentioned. But the physical and psychological consequences of violence against children are extremely serious, both in the short and in the long term, both for the individual victim and for society at large. This raises the question: *to what extent can the government exert control over what happens behind closed doors, in a private setting?* (Government of the Netherlands, 2009, emphasis added)

The 'Savanna effect' was reported widely in the Dutch media in the years following her death in 2004. It is apparent that, for a number of years at least, the threshold for intervening was lowered significantly. Like the reaction to the death of Peter Connelly in England in late 2008, there was a significant increase in the numbers of children removed from home and also an increase in the numbers of suspected cases of abuse reported to authorities (Kamerman, 2005; van Dongen, 2007). According to figures from the Netherlands Youth Institute (2013), there were increases in child protection activity including family supervision orders and custodial placement authorisation during the period immediately following the Savanna case in 2005–08. However, this effect was not attributed to an increase in problems experienced in Dutch families, or simply to an increased awareness of child abuse arising from the intensive media coverage of the case. It was more specifically related to the fact that the family supervisor (social worker) was prosecuted for culpable homicide and grievous bodily harm by culpable negligence. As Kuijvenhoven and Kortleven (2010, p 1165) observed: 'the prosecution assumed a relationship between failing practice and the fatal event, taking the step that the inquiry reports hesitated to take'.

Noteworthy in terms of comparison with Britain was the role of the press. Just as in the UK, disproportionate attention is given in the Netherlands to extreme cases of individual abuse rather than the more mundane, everyday risks faced by vulnerable children (Knijn and van Nijnatten, 2011, p 224). However, in the reporting of fatal child abuse such as Savanna, Kuijvenhoven and Kortleven (2010) observed that there were striking differences. While criticism was directed at agencies and the system as a whole, there was barely any focus on individual professionals and demand for the prosecution of the social worker involved did not come from the public or the media. Support for the prosecution was very low and where newspapers supported the prosecution, they did so 'in a rather nuanced manner' (2010, p 1166). This nuanced manner is in stark contrast to the reaction of the media following the death of Peter Connelly in the UK, where coverage included *The Sun's* front-page publication of photographs of social workers and headlines such as 'Blood on their hands' (12 November 2008) and 'Have they no shame? Go now' (1 December 2008). Although the social worker in the Netherlands was eventually acquitted a year later, there is little doubt that the prosecution had a major impact on how thresholds of risk were applied by professionals during this period (Kuijvenhoven and Kortleven, 2010).

The increase in child protection figures seen between 2005 and 2008 in the Netherlands began to decrease from the end of 2009 in what has continued (up to 2013) as a downward trend (Netherlands Youth Institute, 2013). However, the 'risk-averse' characteristics of professional practice appear to have remained and, as in the UK and elsewhere in Europe, there has been a shift to more formalised procedures and computerised systems in the effort to combat 'human error' (Edemariam and Rooseboom, 2008).

A further interesting comparison with developments in the UK is in terms of computerised systems for monitoring children. While plans for such a system in England and Wales were abandoned, Child Indexes were introduced in the Netherlands as an early warning signal about children 'at risk'. In their critique of the system, Penders and Lecluijze (2014) highlight the emotional politics at work. While not doubting the authenticity of the emotional reaction of politicians, since 'sincere worry for the fate of children in the Netherlands' was the catalyst for change, they stress the zero tolerance for risk that this imported into the system and the implications it had for more assertive interventions:

While the death of these children has offered a powerful momentum for Dutch politicians to implement this system, we cannot help but ask whether it was sufficiently justified to infringe on children's parents' and child welfare professionals' lives this way. From the beginning the system was associated with unrealistic expectations, including total prevention of any future infanticides and 'no child falling between two stools.'

Child welfare is an institution under pressure. Public trust in child welfare is heavily influenced by child deaths and the growing pressure upon the institution to provide risk-free lives for all of our children. The real tragedy is that in the pursuit of total risk-prevention, and in the pursuit of better and safer lives for Dutch children, child welfare professionals were stripped of their autonomy, every child is now a potential 'child at risk', and collaboration between caregivers is obstructed by bureaucracy, all without a decent public justification.

Dutch child welfare is being corrupted not because of financial dependencies or external interests. In fact, (almost) everybody works hard and means well. It is a continuous and misplaced trust in ICT [information and communication technology], technology and accountancy that gave birth to this tragedy. (Penders and Lecluijze, 2014)

Clearly with strong parallels with developments in the UK, reaction to the death of Savanna in 2004 signalled an increased emphasis on bureaucratic measures, and compliance with procedures, technical aids and risk assessment procedures (Kuijvenhoven and Kortleven, 2010). The pressure to place the child at the centre of practice that has become so familiar a call in UK reviews and inquiries can also be discerned in Dutch inquiries. Also discernible is an increased emphasis on more assertive forms of intervention. In Dutch childcare policy in the past, the best interests of the child were believed to be served by maintaining the relationship between parents and children for as long as possible, with interventions as 'light as possible'. This principle is now reformulated as providing care 'as heavy as needed' (Kuijvenhoven and Kortleven, 2010, p 1163). The 'new agenda' in child protection in the Netherlands has seen an extension of the criteria for intervention, which 'creates a playing field for intervening "behind the front door" of any family' (Knijn and Nijnatten, 2011, p 237).

Turning now to the Swedish system, I argue that it is possible to observe in sharp relief the emotional dynamics of national shame about the past and how these relate to a shift in the balance between child protection and family welfare-oriented services. The Swedish system is also of particular interest because of the role that local politicians have in making decisions about individual child protection cases; a model that I return to in more detail in the concluding chapter.

Sweden's two ghosts that haunt the system

Sweden is an interesting case study because of the important symbolic status the country is often felt to occupy in the 'collective political imagination' of other nations, particularly within Europe (Colla, 2013, p 12). It is frequently cited as a model for other countries for policy development. Britain's 'free school' policy, for example, was modelled on a similar system in Sweden (Gove, 2008). Perhaps the key to understanding the particular dynamics of the relationship between the state, professionals and the family in Sweden's child welfare system lies in understanding 'the interaction between the myth and the image Swedes have of themselves' (Colla, 2013, p 17). There is also a perceived gap between the image and reality. Sweden is often cited as the exemplar state that made a transition from the harshness of an industrial class society to an egalitarian society based on welfare principles (Cocozza and Hort, 2011). However, it is argued that this is an idealised image and that 'for those on the margins of society ... it is closer to hell' (Cocozza and Hort, 2011, p 89).

The dichotomy between perceived over-zealous intervention, on the one hand, and reluctance to intervene, on the other – so familiar in the history of child protection in Britain – is also a feature of depictions of Swedish services. In Sweden, this dichotomy has been described in terms of 'two ghosts' that haunt child welfare and protection service (Cocozza and Hort, 2011, p 90). The first ghost is a legacy from the 1980s. This period was characterised by high rates of children being removed from home (Cocozza and Hort, 2011, p 90). Sensational headlines in the German newspaper *Der Spiegel* (1983) coined the term 'Kinder-Gulag' to describe the phenomenon and compared the Swedish system to the detention of political prisoners. The 'lingering response to the odious characterisation' of Sweden as a children's Gulag (Gilbert, 2012, p 535) almost certainly accounts for the second of its ghosts. This took the form of a more cautious approach to intervention and the subsequent depiction of social workers and other child welfare workers in the media as 'overly cautious, unenterprising, and even incompetent in taking care of the best interest of children' (Cocozza and Hort, 2011, p 90). As in Britain, the welfare of children in Swedish civil society is a deeply emotional affair and social work is characterised by turns as being both impotent and omnipotent.

One of the most interesting features of the Swedish child protection system in terms of emotional politics is the way it is organised at the local level. This organisation includes the direct involvement in decision making of representatives who are appointed by political parties. Sitting on local committees, appointed representatives are charged with using their own experience as lay-people to make decisions. This includes decisions that have the most serious implications in terms of the level of intervention and the costs incurred. In their study of the implementation of this system, Forkby et al (2013) argue that this process of decision making legitimises child protection services and relieves pressure on the social workers who have to implement the decisions. They argue that this system may account for the fact that there is not the intense media scrutiny around social workers in Sweden that there is in England. The involvement of appointed representatives affects the political system in mutually beneficial ways. Just as child protection is influenced by politics, so the child protection system has an impact on the political system. Forkby et al argue that the capacity for these arrangements to directly inform political and public discourse about particular groups may have been underestimated. The importance of one aspect in particular may have been overlooked, and that is:

> the insight that elected representatives can gain and use in their double roles as laypersons and politicians, as members of different political groups, to more or less directly anchor their statements about society's most vulnerable individuals in experience and to make public the conditions the vulnerable members of society face. (Forkby et al, 2013, p 10)

A significant proportion of the respondents in their study reported that their experience on social service committees enhanced their credibility and enabled them to influence general policies. The authors also discuss the political implications of the concept of 'common sense', which is associated with the lay contribution to the committees. As I have argued in Chapter Three, common sense can be invoked simply as a mechanism for blanket condemnation. In their analysis of the Swedish system, Forkby et al acknowledge the deeply problematic and contested nature of the concept of 'common sense'. They note its vagueness and how it is relative to class background, culture and professional experience: 'the "common sense" of members of the committees is obviously quite distant from that of those who traditionally have been treated with morally negative sanctions, e.g. poor single mothers' (2013, p 10). However, they advocate one possible remedy for this in the form of widening the constituencies involved in committees to include service user representatives.

The involvement of service users in a more radical sense has been a feature of developments in New York City's child welfare system, which, like Britain, has been characterised by a punishing and accelerating cycle of crisis and reform. It is to this that the chapter now turns.

The US – New York City and the rollercoaster of child welfare

In February 2014, an article in the New York *Daily News* reported on the death of Myls Dobson, aged four years.[3] The article chronicles in some detail the sequence of developments that have occurred in New York's child welfare system over the past several decades. These developments include:

- successive attempts to rebrand the child welfare department;
- the direct impact of child deaths on resource levels;
- the way in which successive mayors have stamped their personal authority on change.

In particular, the article maps the relationship between the political aspirations of successive mayors to reform the system. It hints at the hope and optimism that accompanied each of these layers of reform, with the message they were ultimately – and inevitably – destined to disappoint. The article positions the child welfare system as wholly and consistently problematic; a state of affairs that is encountered anew by each mayor, who then each embarks on his own set of remedies. The political impossibility of risk and the politics of control are inscribed in each reform. The article begins with a roll-call of the names of other children who have died and thereby instantly charts the narrative of despair in a system that has been reformed so often over several decades yet still failed to prevent Myls' death:

Lisa Steinberg, Elisa Izquierdo, Nixmary Brown, Marchella Pierce, Myls Dobson.

These innocent children died horrific deaths that sickened the public, haunted caseworkers and cops and cast a harsh light on the agency that was charged with protecting them.

Every mayor from Ed Koch to Michael Bloomberg has tried to fix the city's troubled child protection unit, the Administration for Children's Services. Its name has changed four times since the 1960's [sic] – each rebranding part of a city effort, usually spurred by tragedy, to make systematic changes that would keep at-risk children safe.

Each effort at reform ultimately failed to close all the gaps, and each new mayor has again had to grapple with the dilemma of how to fix an agency charged with protecting the city's more vulnerable population – children at risk of abuse and neglect.

One week into Mayor de Blasio's tenure, he was confronted with yet another unspeakable tragedy: the Jan. 8 death of Myls Dobson. (Otis, 2014)

This article reflects what Tobis (2013, p xxiii) terms 'the rollercoaster pattern of child welfare', in which advanced systems replace a more primitive one that came before. However, these successive reforms have either been ones that fail to address the underlying, more fundamental issues or, in the case of more positive reforms, they have been 'revised, diminished, or defunded' (Tobis, 2013, p xxiii). In Tobis' analysis, the fundamental causes of this crisis–reform–crisis pattern are located in the contradiction between the system's 'nominal goal' of supporting families and protecting children and the priority given to the social control function of the system – in particular the regulation of mothers, and especially black mothers (2013, p xxv). This regulatory function of the system is represented by a pervasive regime of investigation and the removal of children, which produced widespread fear in some communities, particularly African-American, immigrant and Latino communities. As Tobis (2013, p xxv) observed: 'That is exactly what a child welfare system focused on social control seeks to accomplish.'

Appreciating the cultural and political significance of the mayor of New York City as figurehead is fundamental to understanding the emotional politics of child protection in the city. The significance of the role of mayor in emotional terms was perhaps most poignantly demonstrated by Mayor Rudy Giuliani following the attack on the World Trade Center in September 2001. Here we can see the politician as 'feeling legislator' in exactly the context described by Hochschild (2002). While the realities of his role as hero of events in New York in that period have been hotly disputed, there can be little doubting his symbolic status, as epitomised by his selection as *Time Magazine*'s person of the year in 2001 under the headline 'Mayor of the world' (Pooley, 2001): 'Giuliani took to the airwaves to calm and reassure his people, made a few hundred rapid-fire decisions about the security and rescue operations, toured hospitals to comfort the families of the missing and made four more visits to the apocalyptic attack scene.'

The death of six-year-old Elisa Izquierdo in 1995,[4] not long after the beginning of Giuliani's term of office as mayor, had exposed significant failings by the city's child welfare system. The political fallout from Elisa Izquierdo's death – or rather the perceived need to *avoid* such fallout – prompted the mayor to set up the Administration for Children's Services (ACS). He appointed Nicholas Scoppetta to lead the 'new' agency and a zero-risk policy was implemented in the following uncompromising terms: 'Any ambiguity regarding the safety of a child will be resolved in favour of removing the child from harm's way' (Tobis, 2013, p 19). Scoppetta is described by Tobis (2013, p 69) as belonging to 'the old school of child welfare reform' and this is linked explicitly to his personal experience of foster care from the age of four. The numbers of children removed from their homes and placed in foster care rose from 7,949 in 1995 to 11,453 in 1997 (Tobis, 2013).

In his account of change in New York's child welfare system, Tobis' central argument is that part of the solution lies in the involvement of parents, young people and their allies in shaping policies. Over time, a growing movement for parent participation in child welfare decisions was eventually embraced by the ACS. The impact of the movement was striking. One effect was that, by 2003, the number of children removed to foster care had reduced to 6,901. Tobis notes that there were also fewer child deaths in the same year compared with 1997.

Fundamentally, however, the problems in New York City's child welfare services stem from a much deeper and chronic malaise, which relates to the expression of compassion in America's system of modern governance:

> Americans declare their concern for poor children by supporting a massive system to report abuses and remove children from their families, rather than a program that would help struggling families by improving the difficult environments in which they live and reducing the stresses

in the home that contribute to abuse and neglect. (Tobis, 2013, p xxvi)

This underlying problem is not of course unique to the US. I would argue, along with others (Featherstone et al, 2014), that there are many parallels with current trends in Britain. We may therefore also have something to learn from strategies that were deployed in New York City to improve the lot of families caught up in the system. I consider some of these strategies in greater detail in the final chapter of this book.

Conclusion

Based on their comparative research, Hetherington et al argued that 'child protection systems seem both to express and to demonstrate fundamental aspects of a country's culture and political philosophy.' (Hetherington et al, 1997, p 177). Historical, cultural and political factors are intertwined with and reflected in social attitudes towards childhood, children and the family, as well as the legal system and professional cultures. This means that 'Each system and its associated practices emerged as unique, as having its own holistic character which is an outcome of the complex *interaction* of many forces and factors.' (Cooper, 2002, p 130, emphasis in original). I argue that fantasies about the nation state (Rose, 1998) and about who 'we' – as a 'universal parent' – imagine ourselves to be in relation to children form part of this complex interaction of forces. So too does the emotional regime with its 'feeling rules' (Hochschild, 2002) and emotional stratification system through which blame, anger, shame and other emotions are identified with some groups rather than others. In this respect, the ascendancy of neoliberalism and conditions of global economic crisis are increasingly key elements in shaping child protection and child welfare systems. It is in this sense I argue there is evidence of convergence as well as difference.

Through my brief analysis of case studies from different countries there are a number of features of emotional politics that can be highlighted. Tensions between 'child protection' and 'child welfare' orientations are expressed through the universal emotional prism of a profound unwillingness to accept risks to children in the form of parental neglect or abuse. Equally however, in all of the case studies to some degree, there was an unwillingness to face the *structural* nature of the risks faced by children – particularly those that arise directly from the poverty and disadvantage their parents endure and the everyday hardships it produces. Like Britain, mechanisms of disgust and contempt in relation to poverty, or more specifically for poor people, as well as racism were in operation in the underclass discourse in the New Zealand press. The social control function of New York's child protection system can essentially be read as a means of regulating certain groups – particularly Black mothers.

In Australia and New Zealand, colonialism continues to shape the child welfare system in terms of who is considered a risk, to whom and why. The political and economic regime of colonialism was mirrored in an emotional regime of disgust and shame that is sustained by contemporary structures including the child welfare system. This is true even in the absence of the more systematic abuses epitomised by the 'Stolen Generations'. Briggs' (2014) account of inter-generational fear, shame and anger is more significant for what it tells us about the here-and-now than for what it tells us about the past. The apology made by the Australian Government in 2008 to the 'Stolen Generations' of Aboriginal children warrants particular attention in relation to the emotional politics of collective guilt and shame.

The Swedish experience of national shame over its Kinder Gulag casts light on the way social workers have since been depicted as over-cautious in terms of their reluctance to intervene in family life. Tensions that are familiar from the British context, between over-zealous and more cautious approaches to child protection that have their origins in scandal, were explored in this case study. In the Netherlands, reaction to the death of a child known as Savanna bears many similarities to the Victoria Climbié and Peter Connelly cases in Britain, particularly in its long-term social and political impact. The history of New York's child welfare system serves to further illustrate the central importance of political leaders in sustaining the myth of political control that the mayoral figure exemplifies. Like Britain, political leaders in each case study had a key role to play as feeling legislators in generating or reflecting collective emotional responses.

Two of the case studies considered in this chapter – Sweden and New York – have offered pause for thought in terms of the way their child welfare system is organised or has been challenged. Both are examples of the different ways in which the gap between key constituencies in the child protection system has been effectively closed. In Sweden, there is a closer interplay between the political sphere and child protection where political representatives are actively involved in decision-making. In New York, following a strong parent activist movement based on anger at injustice, service users have a much stronger voice in the system and a means to challenge it. In very different ways, these two examples suggest ways in which the current form of emotional politics in Britain may be challenged and its most damaging effects ameliorated. Such ideas are considered in more detail in the next, concluding chapter of the book.

Notes

[1] Hinewaoriki 'Hine' Karaitiana-Matiaha died in July 2000 at the age of 23 months. She had been severely beaten, scalded and possibly sexually abused. Two stepsisters of her mother were convicted, one for manslaughter and a second for wilful ill-treatment.

[2] Christopher Arepa and Cru Omeka Kahui were twin boys who died aged three months in June 2006. Both died from serious brain injuries. Their father was charged but found not guilty of their murder.

[3] Myls Dobson died aged four years in January 2014. He had been beaten, tortured and starved over a number of weeks. His father's girlfriend, who had custody of Myls while his father was in prison, was charged with murder (awaiting trial at time of writing). Following the case, there was an unsuccessful attempt to change the law regarding supervision of children when their parents are arrested.

[4] Elisa Izquierdo died aged six years in November 1995 in Manhattan. She had been beaten and tortured for a prolonged period up to her death. Her mother pleaded guilty to second degree murder. Elisa's death led to 'Elisa's law' which restructured child welfare services, balancing accountability of services and individual rights to privacy.

EIGHT

Towards a new emotional politics of social work and child protection

Introduction

The main argument of this book has been that the cycle of crisis and reform in child protection is driven by collective emotions that do political work. I have shown how emotions are reflected and activated through political rhetoric, the media and official documents. Emotions in this sense are structured, embedded in institutions and stratified. These emotional structures are now so deeply rooted in our political and cultural life that it might be assumed that they are fixed and impervious to change. However, I argue that this is far from true. The aim of this final chapter is to show how the current form of emotional politics can be challenged and how a different emotional politics might take its place. The main focus of the chapter is the British context. However, many of the recommendations I make about the power of alliances and new forms of public and political engagement to create change will apply in other contexts too.

Social work has a vital role to play in producing the changes that are necessary and as a social work academic this is the main constituency I am addressing in this chapter. However, I also argue that change is only possible through alliances with others who have a stake in the child protection system. The most problematic of these constituencies, and the one I argue we should be less concerned about than we are at present, is the media. The most important constituency comprises the parents and children who come into contact with child welfare or protection services or who might do so in future. This is the broader 'we' addressed by this chapter. The most powerful of the constituencies includes the politicians whose rhetoric and actions I have shown to be of such profound importance in shaping emotional politics. I argue that closer engagement between social work and the political sphere is of vital importance. Finally, the chapter also engages with the wider political context to argue that the problem of social work and child protection is symptomatic of a bigger crisis, which lies in the relationship between the state and society.

In the next section I briefly summarise the main findings and arguments of the book. Following this I focus on how change might be achieved and, specifically, how different ways of thinking and feeling about social work and child protection might be envisaged. The basis for this is a 'new' emotional politics of social work based on a solidaristic notion of compassion and a stronger public institutional role for the profession.

The main arguments of the book

The emotional politics of social work and child protection that has been articulated in this book can be understood on a range of levels. I have shown how stories about the deaths of children are caught up in the politics–media–politics cycle in which politicians can speak for others and reflect or generate particular collective emotions. Media stories about child abuse deaths are first and foremost *news* stories and as such are intimately connected to the political environment. Politicians act as emotional envoys on behalf of others at a range of levels:

- at national and international levels;
- in terms of their ministerial portfolio as Ministers of State;
- on behalf of their constituencies as city mayors or MPs;
- as local councillors.

Through their speech acts they produce a nation or a constituency as a subject that feels emotions such as guilt and anger at the death of a child. Political leaders are instrumental in telling us how to think and feel about child deaths but more importantly, who we should feel angry at and who should feel ashamed.

Responses to the deaths of children from abuse and neglect reflect wider cultural anxieties and fears apart from the reaction to a child's suffering and the failure to prevent it. Their stories also support powerful narratives about particular groups and the emotions that attach to them. I have argued that moral disturbance about an expanding 'underclass' and those categorised as Other is a key component in the urge to retell stories about child abuse deaths in their current form. The emotions of disgust and contempt that are discernible in newspaper accounts are not only responses to the appalling acts of abuse and cruelty to which children have been subjected. They are also responses to the way communities in which children have lived are perceived: the 'welfare ghetto', the 'moral wasteland', the 'festering sore'. These constructions are in turn also constitutive of subject positions of respectability.

In producing a universal, idealised child who is mourned as the object of pity in each story of suffering and death, told and then retold, media and political constructions also produce real children who *cannot be seen and cannot be helped*. The living child who might be the subject of compassion remains 'hidden in plain sight'. They are unrecognisable as the potential victim of abuse and neglect, because the real world they occupy is a marginalised world that is largely viewed with contempt, disgust and as being beyond moral redemption. In the 'welfare ghetto' of political and media discourse, living children are caught up along with their parents in a world that, according to this discourse, is largely hated and despised. Far from being viewed as 'innocents' in a world of poverty and disadvantage, children are implicated as the future 'dangerous Other' in visions of the expanding threat posed by a culture of dependency and moral degeneration. The dead child is rescued in metaphorical terms from this discourse, as a universal child that in death could be mine – could be any of ours – their name memorialised and added to the roll-call of names that make up 'the sad army of little children'.

The book has highlighted how news stories about the deaths of children from extreme abuse or neglect constructed social workers as folk devils who are divorced from the otherwise shared common currency of grief and anger. Social workers were portrayed as the *only* citizens who would not have felt moved to rescue the child. In response, new political zeal was introduced to the process of reforming social work education to produce a new breed of social worker to replace the old, toxic version. The increased hostility and anger towards social work have not been directed at its efforts to help the all-too-real, living, suffering child and their family. They have been focused on its failure to save the idealised mythical child whose fate stands out as *obvious* to us all in death. It is here that the photographic images of children who have died are of such profound, symbolic importance. The photographs connect us to that child and to the possibilities for what might have been. I have also shown how official documents such as inquiries and serious case reviews activate these emotions of regret. They specifically activate the counterfactual emotions that are felt when we consider 'what might have been' and the apparent simplicity with which tragedy could have been prevented. When case reviews are extracted from their local rationalities, this effect is amplified.

In Chapter Seven, through the brief analysis of several international case studies, I have shown how Britain is far from unique. The chapter demonstrates how the concept of 'emotional politics' is helpful in identifying the particular structures of feeling that circulate around and within every system of child protection. The snapshots highlighted how the different groups that become the focus of collective emotions such as anger and disgust reflect the particular socioeconomic, political, historical and cultural contours of the landscape in which they are located. As other comparative studies of child protection have shown, these landscapes are rapidly changing, and to some degree converging, particularly under conditions of global financial uncertainty and neoliberalism.

In the next section I articulate how social work's own structure of feeling might change in terms of who or what its main focus of concern is. This structure of feeling revolves around social work's close proximity to suffering, the politics of compassion that flows from that and social work's as yet unfulfilled promise in undertaking a public institutional role.

Social suffering and the politics of compassion: the public institutional role of social work

As already discussed at length in the book, social work is charged with translating the power of the state to intervene in family life through close proximity to families in the home and the wider community. Expression of this power includes 'authoritative' forms of intervention where social work acts as a means of surveillance and moral regulation. However, it is through its proximity to suffering that social work also reflects 'the deeper understanding born of knowing people in distress *at first hand*' (Stevenson, 1974, p 2, emphasis in original). To a large extent, this deeper understanding, like practice, has been articulated through increasingly abstracted, codified statements about professional values and codes of practice. Through this process, I argue, when we talk about our 'values' as social workers, we have increasingly been talking to ourselves. What has been lost through this aspect of professionalisation is the sense in which social work has a *public* role. That role is to articulate the deeper understanding that it gains from working in close contact with those who are distressed and marginalised. As Holland (2014) argues, we have become physically detached from the communities we seek to serve. But just as importantly, social work has become symbolically detached from a society in which we have a public role to play in keeping it alive emotionally to the everyday experience of others. The capacity for social work to do this derives directly from the 'liminal', intermediary position it occupies. Social work has been preoccupied with the difficulties inherent to this status of 'in-between-ness', not least as it is the root cause of the acute discomfort expressed in the phrase 'damned if we do, damned if we don't'. I argue that the 'voice of social work' that matters is not the one that tells society about the difficulties that arise from this status of being 'in between'. What matters is the voice that articulates for society *what is uniquely visible from this position.* This includes a different narrative about those who have been marginalised and who invoke disgust and fear. It is a narrative that affords service users subjectivity, dignity and most importantly the right as citizens to be seen and heard.

The public institutional role of social work is to articulate different feeling rules about social work and the communities with which social work is largely engaged. To do this it is necessary to extend certain elements of our own politics to a much wider audience, and to do so with renewed energy. The most important element of our politics that I argue we need to communicate to others is the politics of social suffering. Social suffering serves to focus attention firmly on *power*, as articulated by Kleinman et al (1997, p ix): 'Social suffering results from what political, economic, and institutional power does to people and, reciprocally, from how these forms of power themselves influence responses to social problems.' By attending to suffering, I mean refocusing our energies away from talking about who we are or even what we do, and towards talking with compassion about those who receive support or other interventions from social workers. In this sense, I am reiterating what Stevenson stated 30 years ago:

> I am persuaded that social work is one of the ways open to us to combat those aspects of technology which work 'to subvert the evolution' of compassion and sensitivity and is one of the ways by which we can strive for knowledge which leads to greater understanding. Do not mistake this, which is really an affirmation of faith, for an omnipotent claim for social work or complacency about its present operation. Many others (playwrights such as Bond at least) will play a part in developing the sensitivity to distress and suffering essential to the preservation of human dignity. And the development of highly complex organisations to 'deliver' social work and social services poses problems which demand the highest level of intellectual ability and with which we are only beginning to grapple. But those who commit themselves to social work contribute, in my

view, to the *sensitization* of our society. (Stevenson, 1974, pp 1-2, emphasis added)

While social work may have a role to play in 'sensitising society' it remains somewhat unclear how we might do this. The answer to the question of what we might 'do' politically lies to some extent in how we define compassion in the face of suffering. If compassion is only to be defined in relation to individually felt, subjective experience then it takes us little further than the professional value statements that have ultimately become abstract and self-referential. But defined in the collective, emotionally political sense, compassion becomes a very different organising prospect. It is linked to what might be achieved *together* with others. Hoggett expresses this meaning of compassion in the following way:

> Central to my argument is the need to move away from a concept of compassion which is infused with the sentimentality of pity towards a concept which is more akin to solidarity. In other words, I argue for the fusion of compassion towards social suffering with anger at the injustices which underlie that suffering. Moreover, I will argue, perhaps counter-intuitively, that whereas idealisation of the suffering other appears to be crucial to liberal perspectives a solidaristic notion of compassion is one directed towards a flawed human subject, both victim of circumstance and, always to some extent, an agent of both their own misfortune and salvation. (Hoggett, 2006, p 146)

The link between the status of 'victim of circumstance' and 'agent for change' is of central importance. While the parents of children with whom social work comes into contact retain responsibility for their own actions as parents, others also bear responsibility by virtue of their role in creating 'the intolerable conditions under which some parents and children must live' (Tobis, 2013, p xxv). As Featherstone et al (2014, p 104) have argued, 'family poverty is a form of societal neglect'. This wider social responsibility was recognised by some right from the first wave of crisis and reform after the death of Maria Colwell in 1973 when Barbara Castle, then Secretary of State, argued: 'It is right that we should feel shocked and angry at the social conditions which breed the circumstances in which she [Maria Colwell] lived and died' (quoted in Greenland, 1986, p 170). The emotions of shock and anger are here directed at the structural inequalities that produced particular social conditions. The everyday frustration for social workers of working against major social and economic barriers is expressed very well by the following senior social worker quoted in Holland's (2014) research. On a day-to-day basis, it is hard to judge the effectiveness of any interventions they might make at the level of individual children:

> I don't think children's services or the voluntary agencies have the punching power to deal with the long established problems that are here ... but without an intervention that seriously looks at [unemployment, poverty and low aspirations], and this is beyond children's services and it's beyond the voluntary agencies that are here, because what we're doing is continually applying, um, plasters that come off within a couple of weeks ... I don't even know how you test it, nobody's even looking at whether our interventions do anything to make things better for children in any systematic way anyway I don't think. (Quoted in Holland, 2014, p 395)

Through the notion of compassion that is oriented towards the human subject as *both* victim of structural and institutional power *and* also agent of their own destiny, it is possible to see how a number of alliances and new networks or relations might operate. Such alliances and networks can be established or further developed by a range of individuals or bodies, including The College of Social Work, chief social workers, academics, senior managers, and trades unions. Before discussing ideas for such alliances it is important to identify the broader political and institutional context within which social work might exercise its enhanced public institutional role. This context is characterised by a distancing between the state and society.

Mind the gaps

Featherstone et al (2014) have articulated very clearly the problem of distance and its effects in the context of child protection:

> Within the past few decades, under both Conservative and Labour administrations, greater distances emerged between individuals, groups and communities; these were physical and psychological and affected everyone.... This distancing has had pernicious effects on the relationship between child and family, social work and families themselves, and

between the state and the intimate space of relationships.
(Featherstone et al, 2014, p 13)

In part, this distancing has been the outcome of the demise of intermediary institutions in British civil society, as argued by Cooper et al (2003). As the systems relating to child welfare and protection have become increasingly legalistic and proceduralised, the mechanisms by which the worst effects of such changes might have been ameliorated have instead been weakened. Community associations, tenants' associations, social clubs and trades unions; all of these various layers of institutions, 'which once organised and mediated civil society in its relationship to the individual, the family and the state' have been in decline (Cooper et al, 2003, p 22). As I discuss later in the chapter, it has also been argued that the breakdown of intermediate institutions is one cause of the increase in 'anti-politics' and general falling rates of participation in politics (Kenny and Pearce, 2014). Furthermore, collective engagement has not just been lost in real terms; it has also been lost 'as a legitimate part of the political imaginary' (Massey, 2011, p 37).

This distancing effect has not only led to a breakdown in solidarity, more specifically it is closely connected to revitalised political discourses based on binaries of 'us' and 'them', which have in turn bred deeper suspicion and distrust, as I have discussed throughout this book. It is significant that politics has very little direct engagement with the families it develops policies for *from the perspectives of those families.* As Morris and Featherstone (2010, p 563) emphasise: 'Policies have not been rooted in dialogue with vulnerable and marginalised families about their needs and the challenges they experience, nor has there been any dialogue around what risks they consider they pose.'

The growing distance between the state and society has meant that politicians who do not wish to engage with child protection dilemmas 'on the ground' have no real need to. By this I mean engagement with decisions that are directly concerned with protecting children while at the same time protecting the rights of their parents as citizens. In saying this I want to emphasise that there *are* politicians who are actively involved. But at present there is not, in the institutional sense, any buffer operating in the sphere of politics against its general detachment. One result is that politicians in their involvement with child protection have been much more concerned with the dead than they have with the *living*. The absence of political engagement with the nature of the issues and decisions involved and the context for these has produced, I argue, the almost complete refusal to publicly acknowledge that in any system of child protection or child welfare, regardless of the professionalism of the social work and social care workforce that exists, *some children will perish*. Instead, a succession of senior politicians have calibrated the value of the workforce against the zero-tolerance position that any death is one too many. When Power (2004, p 63) argues that there is a need to move towards a new 'politics of uncertainty', it is largely as an antidote to the obsession with reputation risk that has so shaped public and civic life. In the context of the emotional politics of social work and child protection, a new politics of uncertainty would entail recognising and acknowledging publicly that the hope of eliminating risk is indeed entirely false.

It is important to note, as Parton (2012) does, that despite all its detractors, social work's dominance in child protection only seems more, rather than less secure. I suggest that the distancing of all other constituencies from the domain of child protection has been accepted by social work more easily than it should. Despite the increasing isolation and discomfort that comes with its increasingly dominant position, social work seems to have accepted it. This is arguably due to the professional power that it brings and the obvious advantages of an occupational role that is securely and exclusively 'ours', by which we can engage in the increasing acquisition of expert, exclusive knowledge. The long-term problem is that this knowledge is not set to deliver the kinds of certainties that are most sought after.

The weight of evidence about the failure of 'objective' risk assessment to deliver as promised (Houston and Griffiths, 2000) serves to highlight the fact that, ultimately, evaluations of parenting remain complex and contingent. They also remain stubbornly rooted in values and moral judgements. While it may be easy to reach 'common-sense' agreement about extreme acts of abuse and neglect, reaching consensus about what it means to be a good or a bad parent on almost every other level is unlikely to get easier. The debate about smacking children serves to illustrate the point crudely but quite well. Questions of culture, class, gender, age and ethnicity all converge on this one issue in ways that are almost infinite in their complexity. What is appropriate chastisement for one parent is tantamount to abuse for another and there are all shades of opinion in between these polarised positions. Addressing the complexity of such questions about parenting in dialogue as a society seems to have been abandoned. Just as there is little meaningful political engagement in the complexity of the issues, so there is also little meaningful public engagement, particularly in relation to issues relating to diversity and difference around parenting. The question of the creation of spaces in which such dialogue might take place is addressed towards the end of this chapter.

Social work and the media

In terms of its relationship with the mainstream media, social work has become increasingly preoccupied with itself and how it is represented. This is hardly surprising given the intensified levels of hostility it has endured. However, I argue that this is not the way forward. Directly persuading the media to present 'good' stories about social work is unlikely to be successful, partly because the news *in general* is not characterised by good news, only bad. The death of a child through severe abuse or neglect is a 'good' news story because it contains all of the narrative elements that the news requires. As I have shown throughout this book, it allows journalists to explore a range of powerful narratives in the context of a tragic outcome, in which the mythological elements of good versus evil can be pored over in great detail. Social work's bad press is as a lead character in a story that the media wants to tell and which, furthermore, resonates powerfully in cultural terms. In this respect it is important to acknowledge that the moral disturbance over child deaths does not arise simply because of the media. Stories of children who have died from severe abuse and neglect would be deeply disturbing and would cause moral disturbance no matter how they were told. The realities of human suffering and the intense vulnerability of the children involved, together with the ease with which the abusing parents can be cast as evil, are more than sufficient to warrant media attention. But the specific *'story about reality'* – in the sense of *whose* story is told, *how* it is told and *which values* are reflected in that story – is much more open to challenge. It is here that the role of politicians is of fundamental importance. We need to spend less time and invest less energy trying to directly influence the media's portrayal of social work and more time forming closer and more meaningful alliances in the political sphere, both locally and nationally, along with other groups. I argue that it is through these alliances and the *alternative* discourses they have the potential to produce that mainstream media stories will ultimately be reframed.

An important potential outlet for alternative narratives is through new media and social media, where the wide dissemination of material that comes direct from those involved is becoming increasingly cheap and accessible. The use of social media in social work is growing in a range of contexts: in practice, in social work education (Westwood, 2014) and as a means of bringing the unmediated realities of social work practice into the public domain. However, such accounts normally constitute 'human interest' rather than news stories and, as I have emphasised throughout this book, it is social work as a *news* story, with all that goes with this, that is problematic. The use of social media in responding to such news stories appears to reflect and magnify mainstream media accounts more than it challenges them.

The problem of how the media (mis)represent the people with whom social work comes into contact should, I argue, be of greater concern to us than how social work is (mis)represented. The diversification of media represents a major source of potential empowerment for service users – not just independently but also in alliance with social workers. Technological change makes it possible for the perspectives of service users and the nature of the problems they face to reach a much wider audience and to challenge prejudices. One model for such a strategy is in the parent activist campaigns in New York in the 1990s (Tobis, 2013). Parents caught up in the child welfare system produced their own publications to tell their own stories and to monitor New York's child welfare system. Founded in 2005, *Rise* magazine, for example, contains 'stories written by and for parents affected by the child welfare system' (www.risemagazine.org). The main aims of the magazine are to challenge negative stereotypes of families affected by the child welfare system, support parents through advocacy, and guide policy makers and practitioners to become more responsive to their needs. The story of parent activism and advocacy in New York during this period also serves as a model for how stronger alliances between social work professionals, academics and parents and children who are service users can be formed. Such alliances take on special significance in a period when the child protection project is an increasingly authoritarian one, as discussed in the next section.

Social work, parents and children: the emotional politics of 'authority' and trust

The theme of 'authority' and the failure of social workers to exercise it appropriately has been a recurring one throughout the waves of crisis and reform in child protection. As highlighted in Chapter Six, the concept of 'authoritative practice' received a particular focus in the second serious case review into the death of Peter Connelly in 2007. The inquiry into the death of Jasmine Beckford in 1984 observed that social workers in general were failing to accept their authoritative role (Blom–Cooper, 1985). In her response to this observation, and the repeated references in the inquiry report to the social workers in the case as naive, Stevenson pinpoints the balance between trust and suspicion that constitutes encounters between social workers and families in the following terms:

> [S]hrewd observation is not at all the same as systematically approaching clients with distrust. That is a hopeless road to travel. Rehabilitation should not be attempted if there is not a measure of trust. It is a contradiction in terms. One of the hardest tasks for social work educators and students is to balance negative realism, including a recognition of deceit, with positive realism, that clients often struggle valiantly to perform parenting tasks against intolerable pressures. It is realism without rejection which is the goal. (Stevenson, 1986, p 504)

Stevenson is here (re)asserting the fact that social work most often involves working with people for whom parenting is carried out in the context of 'intolerable pressures' and where establishing trust is a prerequisite for change. Such trust, I argue, is dependent on the recognition of two things that are often presented as being mutually exclusive but are not:

- parents can be the agents of change in their own lives;
- many of the intolerable pressures they face stem from social injustice and particularly structural inequalities over which they (and indeed social workers) have little or no control.

Featherstone et al (2014, p 2) are of course right to argue as follows: 'the social justice aspect of social work is being lost in a child protection project that is characterised by a muscular authoritarianism towards multiply-deprived families'. There is an important emotional component to this shift. Just as it entails social work's potential if not actual disengagement from *anger* at the injustices faced by families, it risks producing a social work that joins in the general contempt for people living in poverty rather than for poverty and the conditions it gives rise to. Contempt is inevitable if conditions are too readily understood as being solely the result of individual inadequacies rather than having their roots in structural inequalities and social injustice. A social work that has been displaced from communities and the everyday existence of families it works with, so that it parachutes into homes from a workplace that is entirely separate, represents a particularly damaging form of detachment. As Featherstone et al (2014, p 112) have argued, 'social workers need to change where they are sitting' and they propose a range of models for how this might happen.

Holland (2014) illustrates the vital importance of social work's reinstatement into local neighbourhoods in her qualitative case study of a neighbourhood in Wales. She explores the concept of child protection and child welfare being 'everybody's business'. She concludes that social workers should adopt more of the attributes of community workers by being located – physically and socially – in local neighbourhoods. Through her analysis of the three 'spheres' of child safeguarding (local residents, statutory services and community services), Holland describes the way positive relationships between these spheres depend on availability and approachability, which have spatial, temporal and biographical features. In her study, community workers and leaders were valued by local residents for being in close proximity to the communities they served and thereby having good local knowledge. They were available and able to provide continuity in their work with parents, and were often recognised for their own stories, as being people who had encountered difficulties themselves. An informal style was seen as important, particularly in engaging people who were especially marginalised. Finally, they were valued as generalists who were able to help with virtually any problem rather than refer people on to other services. In contrast, formal social services were described in largely negative terms and were identified most strongly with *unpredictability* in terms of how they might respond to referrals. Holland (2014, p 398) argues for the involvement of local residents in the planning of safeguarding services. Local residents have valuable observations to make, Holland argues, as people who potentially might make referrals or based on their own direct or second-hand experience of child welfare and protection services. Specifically, partnership working should be facilitated between the three spheres of safeguarding, including local residents, so that there is more engagement and greater consultation with the local community.

Hetherington et al (1997) identify the importance of a flexible continuum between support and protection and the creation of intermediate spaces with increased involvement of the wider community. The flexible continuum involves creating an open door policy for families seeking support. It reflects the authors' view that the concept of 'thresholds' is 'essentially conservative' (Hetherington et al, 1997, p 183) in that it serves the system rather than the complex configurations of needs, risks, support and protection that are the focus of working with any family: 'The English preoccupation with criteria and thresholds is essentially about keeping people out of a service system with the implication that the system is malign; it is better not to be involved' (1997, p 182). The authors also identify the need for intermediate spaces, both outside the legal framework and within it. Mediation services and family group conferences are two examples given as ways to 'revitalise the centrality of trust and negotiation as the medium through which conflict is resolved, and acceptable plans are made for children at risk' (1997, p 182).

Not only is it important for there to be greater involvement from the community in child welfare, it is also legitimate to ask that those elected to represent the interests of citizens should be involved to some degree in decisions.

Social work and the political sphere: towards a politics of uncertainty and engagement

Cooper et al (1995) make the important observation that social work in the UK has not always been so weak in terms of its political influence. In the 1930s, social work was identified as the means through which the welfare state would respond to its citizens. Its relationship with the Labour administration of Harold Wilson in the 1960s was particularly strong but it was also unique to that period. Its influence declined gradually from the mid-1970s onwards (Cooper et al, 1995). Since this period there appears to have been little attempt to revitalise social work's links with the political sphere. While there may be limited opportunities, or indeed desire, for influence along the same lines as in the past, I argue that there will be new opportunities in coming years. This is due to the perceived crisis of trust in politics in Britain (Seyd, 2013), the prevailing view that democracy across Europe is in serious trouble (Armingeon and Guthmann, 2014) and the so-called 'emotionalisation' of politics (Richards, 2007), which hitherto I have only addressed as problematic. There are several ways in which the gap between social work, service users, communities and the political sphere might be brought closer together. I will discuss just two ideas very briefly here; one is in terms of the potential alliance between social work and those politicians who are more aligned with the orientation that social work has towards social problems, and the second is in direct decision making.

As discussed in Chapter Four, through their surgeries and casework, many MPs in Britain have frequent encounters with people who are experiencing severe hardships. The role of MPs as directly elected representatives of their constituents is already highly developed. The expansion of their casework role since the Second World War has been a direct consequence of the establishment of the welfare state in terms of the right of citizens to seek redress for grievances. It is important to understand that, while government ministers and their departments, Parliament and the national media are preoccupied with national and international policy issues, there is a whole tier of politics operating at the local level. For the majority of elected representatives, the politics of their constituency is the politics with which they are primarily concerned, and not purely out of self-interest. I argue that in the fraught emotional politics of the relationship between the public sphere of the state and the private sphere of the family, theirs is a role that has been allowed to drift to the margins while social work has increasingly taken centre stage on behalf of the state. Through their constituency casework, their relationships with elected local councils and the local media, MPs are in a particularly powerful position. There are undoubtedly among these politicians those who might act more vociferously as emotional envoys and tribunes *for* social work and the families and communities with whom social work is primarily engaged.

The second way in which the gaps between the political sphere, social work and society might be closed is the potential for closer and more formal engagement by politicians in the nature of decisions made by social workers. One model for this approach was discussed in the last chapter. Sweden has a system of child welfare and protection in which there is direct involvement of representatives from elected political parties. The appointed representatives sit on child protection committees and are directly engaged in decision making. This interaction between politics and social work is said to have reciprocal benefits for policy making and civil society, particularly in the way social work is perceived (Forkby et al, 2013). As Cocozza and Hort (2011) suggest, it is by no means a perfect system. However, even *discussing* the idea of direct political involvement in decision making at the local level linked to national parties would almost certainly change the nature of the current conversation about child protection in this country.

Finally, I turn to the wider context for social work's engagement in the political sphere and the altering of state–social relations. This includes the prospect of new forms of participatory democracy and challenges to the current direction of public sector reform towards marketisation and privatisation.

Social work, neoliberalism and the politics of public participation

The impossible space that social work occupies between the private sphere of the family and the public sphere of the state, and between 'us' and 'them', places it at the heart of a deeper political paradox. That is the paradoxical nature of modern democracy itself, in which there exists two competing traditions, which can *only* exist in tension:

> On one side we have the liberal tradition constituted by the rule of law, the defence of human rights and the respect of individual liberty; on the other the democratic tradition whose main ideas are those of equality, identity between governing and governed and popular sovereignty. (Mouffe, 2005, p 3)

Mouffe is at pains to argue that the irreconcilability of these competing liberal-democratic traditions is not a destructive contradiction but an ongoing tension, which has to be negotiated and stabilised. In the shift from the post-war social-democratic settlement to the present neoliberal 'settlement', 'equality has lost out, hands down, to liberalism' (Massey, 2011, p 36). Crucially, this is a liberalism that applies unevenly, in what Wacquant (2010) has characterised as the 'Centaur state'. The Centaur state presents 'a comely and caring visage toward the middle and upper classes, and a fearsome and frowning mug towards the lower class' (Wacquant, 2010, p 217). As Parton (2014) argues, this duality has taken a particularly aggressive and punitive form under the coalition government of 2010 onwards, with significant consequences for social work and child protection. The current neoliberal settlement is not, however, the final settlement in the competing traditions of liberalism and democracy.

Earlier in this chapter I emphasised, as many others have done, the importance of social work being reinstated in communities, both physically and symbolically. There is a broader political context within which the concept of child protection being 'everybody's business' can be understood. The argument in favour of local involvement in services is not just that it will improve services and people's experience of them. Such involvement can also be seen as having an important connection to the way democracy can or should function. This is particularly true in democratic societies that are increasingly complex, diverse, unequal and apparently subject to declining levels of political engagement among their electorates. The continued rapid shift towards marketisation and centralised control in public services under the global project of neoliberalism is not inevitable. Among ideas to counter the 'common-sense' politics of neoliberal agendas there are movements for public services that are based on participatory democracy and relational forms of welfare. There is little space to explore all these ideas in detail here, but Angel (2014) provides a useful account of ideas for a new agenda on public services and Cottam's work (2011) also warrants close attention. Cottam argues that the welfare state requires reinvention so that it is characterised by being shared, collective and relational. One of her five principles for relational welfare is particularly apt for my purposes here and that is the need for politics to 'facilitate the dialogue', as follows:

> Politics needs to create the conditions for new forms of creative, developmental conversation – just as between the front line and families – beyond the traditional political meeting, the focus group or the complaint form. It is through this new conversation that something shared, collective and relational will grow. (Cottam, 2011, p 144)

In their paper 'Toward a democracy of the emotions', Hoggett and Thompson (2002) address problems that have been identified with creating political processes of participation that can accommodate diversity and difference. The focus of their paper is deliberative democracy, which they define as follows: '*A series of interlinked public spaces in which all citizens can participate in an ongoing free and fair debate leading to reasonable agreement – or even rational consensus – on matters of public concern*' (2002, p 107, emphasis in original). Drawing on psychoanalytic ideas, they argue that deliberative democracy needs to give closer attention to the affective dimensions of the use of public spaces for debate. These are always present and strong emotions will often undermine principles of deliberation in such forums. Feelings such as fear will intrude on the process. In arguing for a 'democracy of the emotions', Hoggett and Thompson (2012) propose that the spaces for deliberative democracy should be structured, not around the concept of 'rational argument', but as spaces where citizens can 'reveal their needs and express their emotions in a process of coming to what might be thought of as a "good enough" understanding of their fellows' (2012, p 107). They argue that understanding group emotions is the basis for a 'passionate rationality' on which citizen participation might be based.

Conclusion

My main objective in this final chapter has been to suggest ways in which a new emotional politics of social work and child protection might emerge. Change depends not only on what we are saying, but also who we are in dialogue with and the feelings that we can activate. I have argued that there are different conversations that can begin on both sides of the state–society divide that social work must operate between. Our dialogues with the political sphere and with the public sphere can be significantly strengthened, both separately and together. As a profession, we may not have lived up to the particular ambitions that were set out for us at the beginning of the modern era of social work and the welfare state. The words of Clement Attlee (Prime Minister of the 1945 Labour government) in his 1920 book *The social worker* are as pertinent today as they were then:

> The social service movement of modern times is not confined to any one class, nor is it the preserve of a particular section of dull and respectable people. It has arisen out of a deep discontent with society as at present constituted, and among its prophets have been the greatest spirits of our time. It is not a movement concerned alone with the material, with housing and drains, clinics and feeding centres, gas and water, but is the expression of the desire for social justice, for freedom and beauty, and for the better apportionment of all the things that make up the good life. It is the constructive side of the criticism passed by the reformer and the revolutionary on the failure of our society to provide a fit environment where a good life shall be possible for all. (Attlee, 1920, pp 2–3)

With innovative approaches to both public and political engagement, social work might not only improve its image but, much more important in my view, we might make the contribution to public and political discourse in Britain that social work has always promised.

APPENDIX

Using qualitative document analysis techniques to analyse media and political accounts

The ideas in this book are based largely on qualitative documentary research. The main types of document I analysed were:

- newspaper articles;
- inquiry reports and serious case reviews into the abuse or neglect of children;
- political statements taken mainly from *Hansard* records (including parliamentary debates and ministerial statements);
- official speeches obtained from government department websites;
- a small number of blogs and published letters.

I selected newspaper reports as the main source of media account because they were, in research terms, the most relevant, meaningful and retrievable documents for analysis (Altheide, 1996). The newspaper article is the medium where hostility towards social work has been particularly vigorous *and* where the relationship between the media and politics is most readily observable, given the longstanding nature of the relationship between politics and the press in general. This relationship is discussed at length in Chapter Two. While the newspaper accounts were almost all written by journalists, there were also articles written by individual politicians that were published in local and national newspapers and some of these have been analysed in considerable detail. All of the material quoted in the book is publicly available and as such my interpretation of it is open to scrutiny.

I undertook the research over a period of six years between 2008 and 2014 with varying degrees of intensity. While the initial focus was the political and media response in 2008 to the death of Peter Connelly, my focus widened to other cases in Britain and then also encompassed a comparative approach with international case studies, as reported in Chapter Seven. The study therefore shifted from a single case study to a multiple case study. That the research has spanned this length of time has been one of its strengths. As Altheide (1996) argues, patterns and their meaning in documentary research emerge over time through a process of constant comparison. During this time I used different approaches to analysing large sections of the data, reflecting the fact that I accumulated more material over time and as ideas developed and new cases emerged. For example, the initial focus on categorising the 'moral talk' of politicians shifted as I became interested in a more thematic analysis using critical moral panic theory, which informs much of the discussion in Chapter Three. I briefly describe each of these approaches, but first a general note about analysing documents and media texts.

Analysing documents and media texts

In terms of their potential use in social research, documents are often viewed as having a clear advantage over other forms of data because they are static and 'lack reactivity' (Padgett, 1998). This suggests that the meaning of a document can be regarded as relatively fixed in a way that materials from primary methods of data collection such as face-to-face interviews cannot be. Consequently, documents have traditionally been regarded as potential sources of information for social scientists primarily in terms of what they *contain* (Prior, 2003). However, interest among social scientists has increasingly shifted away from viewing documents as inert or static records of events towards considering their production and consumption and seeing documents as situated and social products (Prior, 2003, p 26). Through detailed investigation, documents enable understanding of changing meanings and social definitions. In this sense, the study of documents can be a route towards the study of culture 'or the process and the array of objects, symbols, and meanings that make up social reality shared by members of a society' (Altheide, 1996, p 2).

In this study, I used methodological techniques that would enable me to discern and make explicit the main themes in the press coverage by locating patterns in the way different aspects of the story were represented. By analysing and comparing newspaper accounts with other documents, such as political statements and serious case reviews, it was possible to trace cross-referencing, the intertextuality of documents and the nature of their relationship to one another, and their activating effects.

Identifying relevant documents

I identified relevant newspaper articles by using simple search terms in the LexisNexis database of UK newspapers. As Greer and MacLaughlin

(2012) have observed, LexisNexis needs a 'methodological health warning', not least because it is incomplete. I believe I was able to identify and fill any gaps with hard copies of newspaper articles. For the purpose of carrying out qualitative analysis on a discrete topic, and the impressionistic quantitative measures I utilised, this was more than adequate. For example, we do not need to know by *exactly* how many articles *The Sun* newspaper's coverage of Peter Connelly's death exceeded that of other newspapers to know that its coverage was much greater. I identified key dates for the most intensive periods of media coverage, which normally began on the day that the criminal trial of parents responsible for the death of their child concluded. For example, press restrictions on media reporting of the death of Peter Connelly (then known only as 'Baby P') had been in place for the duration of the criminal court proceedings and these were finally lifted on 11 November 2008, when his mother and her boyfriend and their lodger were all convicted. The dataset of newspaper articles about the death of Peter Connelly was by far the largest, but the pattern of intense coverage following the conclusion of the criminal court case was the same for the other cases that were investigated. Cross-referencing of one case to another was also evident in newspaper accounts, for example, references to Victoria Climbié increased in late 2008 compared with the year before, as reports referred back to her death when reporting on Peter Connelly's in the same London borough.

I identified significant political statements and debates through searching *Hansard* records online, using multiple search terms, normally using either the name of a child or the name of the politician for references in debates and statements. There was significant cross-referencing from newspaper articles to parliamentary debates or significant statements, which was a key indicator for where to search in *Hansard* by date where indicated. I collected inquiry reports and serious case reviews in portable document format (pdf), which are searchable using keywords as well as being amenable to thematic analysis.

In addition to the technical approaches to analysis, as described here, I was able to draw on particularly relevant theoretical work as a guide to identify key themes. This included Ahmed's (2004) work on cultural politics and emotion and Skeggs' (2004) work on the political rhetoric of class. Also, the more recent theoretical work on the idea of moral panic (Critcher, 2009; Young, 2009, 2011) provided invaluable analytic tools in relation to themes around social class, parenting and social work that were discernible in the documents.

Technical aspects of the data analysis

Analysing moral talk

In this approach, the analysis of data was based broadly on methods for coding moral discourse developed by Lee and Ungar (1989). Rather than formally 'test' these methods, the aim was to draw on the categories that Lee and Ungar developed to take their ideas forward in an exploratory way. This approach to data analysis is particularly evident in Chapter Two. The potential value of the approach is that morality is explored as a way of talking – including 'talking' in its printed form (Lee and Ungar, 1989, p 693). Moral talk involves the creation of moral categories, such as the categories of 'pro-life' and 'pro-choice' in abortion debates. Crucially, moral talk is conceived of by Lee and Ungar (1989, p 712) as an 'action-oriented' medium: 'Our methods provide systematic categories for the various roles or stances taken by the moralizer seeking to evoke through language the feeling rules and emotion work leading to moral action.'

The methods that Lee and Ungar develop involve coding moral discourse on three levels. In the first level – the analysis of topic and voice – 'topic' refers to the 'moral notion discoursed by the sentence' while 'voice' addresses the question *'Who is really doing the moral talking?'* (1989, p 696, emphasis in original). In discourses such as media accounts, coding of 'voice' includes the speaker of the moral claim even if it is being reported second hand.

In the second level, categories of 'moral stance' relate to the way language creates an emotional distance to an event. This distance ranges from 'a dispassionate statement of "facts" to a ringing call for righteous action' (1989, p 703). In terms of the moral stance it represents, talk can be coded as 'giving information', 'beating the breastplate of righteousness' or 'urging to action'. 'Giving information' includes information that is 'asserted as data' – as if the information is purely factual. In a moral stance coded under 'beating the breastplate of righteousness', there is a category of 'legitimation', in which one's own moral position is presented as going beyond mere opinion to become the position of 'the good' (versus 'the bad' of the opposing view). There is also 'challenge and vilification', in which the moral talk involves insults and an implication of moral dangerousness. In the moral stance of 'urging to action', the moral entrepreneur can 'call', 'warn' or 'threaten'.

In the third level of coding the focus is on the direction of moral rhetoric appeals. Under this category there are codes for appeals to 'logic', 'rights', 'fairness and goodness', 'feelings' and 'affinity'. These categories are largely self-explanatory. In 'appeals to affinity', moral rhetoric is used in 'an appeal to act like a member of one's kin and kind' (1989, p 711). An 'appeal to logic' is where logical reasoning is deployed, and so forth.

Open, axial and selective coding

I analysed material using a three-stage process regarded as providing an appropriate foundation for the rigorous analysis of qualitative data (Neuman, 1997, after Strauss, 1987). I started with 'open coding' of a smaller sample of documents, in order that a mass of data could be condensed into initial categories to produce a list of themes. At this stage of coding, I used further word searches and the LexisNexis facility to review the 'expanded list' of articles, which shows article headlines and occurrences of the key search terms in context.

The next stage of analysis was 'axial coding'. I read hard copies of batches of articles around critical dates to code for the theme categories that had been identified in open coding, adding to and amending the coding list where required. I coded mainly at the level of sentence or paragraph and left large amounts of data uncoded. For example, there were extensive, graphic and repetitious descriptions of the injuries sustained by children with chronologies but very little of this material was relevant for the purpose of the study. This approach to coding is consistent with normal practice in qualitative research, where '[t] he degree of detail in coding depends on the research question, the "richness" of the data, and the researcher's purpose' (Neuman, 1997, p 423).

In the final, 'selective coding' phase, I scanned articles again, selecting cases that illustrated key themes and, where necessary, reviewed and amended coding categories. Since I was operating as a sole researcher, the coding was not systematically repeated by another researcher. However, in the qualitative-interpretivist tradition of research, the idea that the interpretation of texts must be directly shared is not assumed (Krippendorff, 2004). Instead, 'qualitative researchers ... must rely on their ability to present a clear description, offer a convincing analysis, and make a strong argument for their interpretation' (Manheim et al, 2002, p 317). For Guba and Lincoln (1994), access to data for the reader is also important in establishing 'trustworthiness' of analysis. To my knowledge, all of the materials and secondary data that I have utilised in this research remain publicly available. In the event that any reader has difficulty accessing any of it, I would be happy to assist.

References

Abbott, D. (2013) 'Daniel Pelka's horrendous death: the buck-passing must stop here', *The Guardian*, 18 September.

Ahmed, S. (2004) *The cultural politics of emotion*, New York, NY: Routledge.

Aldridge, M. (1994) *Making social work news*, London: Routledge.

Allen, G. and Smith, I.D. (2008) *Early intervention: Good parents, great kids, better citizens*, London: The Centre for Social Justice/The Smith Institute.

Allpress, J.A., Barlow, F.K., Brown, R. and Louise, W.R. (2010) 'Atoning for colonial injustices: group-based shame and guilt motivate support for reparation', *International Journal of Conflict and Violence*, 4(1), 75-88.

Altheide, D.L. (1996) *Qualitative media analysis*, Thousand Oaks, CA: Sage Publications.

Anderson, B. (2008) 'The night a grim malaise was hammered home', *The Sunday Telegraph*, 16 November.

Angel, J. (2014) *Moving beyond the market: A new agenda for public services*, London: New Economics Foundation.

Arlott, G. (2014) 'City councillors put aside party divides at children's services meeting', *Coventry Telegraph*, 10 April.

Armingeon, K. and Guthmann, K. (2014) 'Democracy in crisis? The declining support for national democracy in European countries, 2007-2011', *European Journal of Political Research*, 53, 423-42.

Atkinson, P. and Coffey, A. (1997) 'Analysing documentary realities', in D. Silverman (ed) *Qualitative research: Theory, method and practice*, Thousand Oaks, CA: Sage Publications, 45-62.

Attlee, C. (1920) *The social worker*, London: Bell & Sons.

Ayre, P. (2001) 'Child protection and the media: lessons from the last three decades', *British Journal of Social Work*, 31, 887-901.

Balls, E. (2008a) 'Wakefield Express column', *Wakefield Express*, 14 November, p 10, www.edballs.co.uk

Balls, E. (2008b) 'Power of your feeling is clear', *The Sun*, 27 November, p 10.

Barbalet, J. (2002) 'Introduction: why emotions are crucial', in J. Barbalet (ed) *Emotions and sociology*, Oxford: Blackwell, 1-9.

Barbalet, J. (2006) 'Emotions in politics: from the ballot to suicide terrorism', in S. Clarke, P. Hoggett and S. Thompson (eds) *Emotion, politics and society*, Basingstoke: Palgrave Macmillan, 31-55.

Beddoe, L. (2013) ' 'Making a moral panic - welfare reform, racism and "feral families" in New Zealand: doing the work of the state?', *Social work research in New Zealand*, blogpost: http://socialworkresearchnz.wordpress.com/2013/08/31/making-a-moral-panic-welfare-reform-racism-and-feral-families-in-new-zealand-doing-the-work-of-the-state-3/

Beddoe, L. and Fraser, H. (2012) 'Social work in Australasia', in K.H. Lyon, T. Hokenstad, M. Pawar, N. Huegler and N. Hall (eds) *Sage handbook of international social work*, London: Sage Publications, 421-35.

Berezin, M. (2002) 'Secure states: towards a political sociology of emotion', in J. Barbalet (ed) *Emotions and sociology*, Oxford: Blackwell, 33-52.

Berrick, J.D. (2011) 'Trends and issues in the U.S. child welfare system', in N. Gilbert, N. Parton and M. Skivenes (eds) *Child protection systems: International trends and orientations*, New York, NY: Oxford University Press, 17-35.

Bird, S.E. and Dardenne, R.W. (1997) 'Myth, chronical and story: exploring the narrative quality of news', in D. Berkowitz (ed) *Social meanings of news*, Thousand Oaks, CA: Sage Publications, 333-50.

Blair, L. (2008) 'Gordon Brown on the psychologist's couch', *The Daily Telegraph*, 17 May.

Blom-Cooper, L. (1985) *A child in trust: The report of the panel of inquiry into the circumstances surrounding the death of Jasmine Beckford*, London: London Borough of Brent.

Booker, C. (2013) 'The social worker's sledgehammer misses the nut yet again', *The Sunday Telegraph*, 4 August.

Bradford Safeguarding Children Board (BSCB) (2013) *A serious case review: Hamzah Khan – the overview report*, Bradford: BSCB.

Brandon, M., Sidebotham, P., Bailey, S., Belderson, P., Hawley, C., Ellis, C. and Megson, M. (2012) *New learning from serious case reviews: A two-year report for 2009-2011*, DFE-RR226, London: Department for Education.

Briggs, K. (2014) 'Aboriginal mothers like me still fear that our children could be taken away', *The Guardian*, 20 January.

Broadhurst, K., Hall, C., Wastell, D., White, S. and Pithouse, A. (2010) 'Risk, instrumentalism and the humane project in social work: identifying the *informal* logics of risk management in children's services', *British Journal of Social Work*, 40(4), 1046-64.

Brooke, C. (2013) 'Children crawled through the waste in dirty nappies', *Daily Mail*, 4 October.

Brooke, C. and Levy, A. (2013) 'Useless! Minister slams inquiry into death of boy, 4, found mummified in family home', *Daily Mail*, 14 November.

Brown, D. (2013) 'Mother jailed for starving boy had made death threats', *The Times*, 5 October.

Brown, R. (1999) 'Closing the gaps: "Once were warriors" from book to film and beyond', *Journal of New Zealand Literature*, 17, 141-55.

Burnham, D. (2012) *The social worker speaks: A history of social workers through the twentieth century*, Farnham: Ashgate.

Butler, I. and Drakeford, M. (2011) *Social work on trial: The Colwell inquiry and the state of welfare*, Bristol: Policy Press.

Butler, I. and Drakeford, M. (2003) *Scandal, social policy and social welfare*, Basingstoke: Palgrave Macmillan.

Butler, P. (2009) 'Sharon Shoesmith emails reveal extent of media and political storm', *The Guardian*, 7 October.

Butler-Sloss, E. (1988) *Report of the inquiry into child abuse in Cleveland 1987*, London: The Stationery Office.

Cameron, D. (2008a) 'We've had a raft of excuses and no apology', *The London Evening Standard*, 12 November.

Cameron, D. (2008b) 'Excuses won't do', *The Sun*, 13 November.

Carr, S. (2008) 'Tragedy casts a shadow over the political ring', *The Independent*, 13 November.

Cheng, D. (2006) 'Warriors author slams Maoridom and politicians', *The New Zealand Herald*, 28 June.

Cheshire East Safeguarding Children's Board (2011) *Serious case review CE001: Executive summary*, Cheshire: CESCB.

Clarke, S., Hoggett, P. and Thompson, S. (2006) 'The study of emotion: an introduction', in S. Clarke, P. Hoggett and S. Thompson (eds) *Emotion, politics and society*, Basingstoke: Palgrave Macmillan, 3-13.

Clyde, J.J. (1992) *The report of the inquiry into the removal of children from Orkney in February 1991*, Edinburgh: HMSO.

Cocozza, M. and Hort, S.E.O. (2011) 'The dark side of the universal welfare state? Child abuse and protection in Sweden', in N. Gilbert, N. Parton and M. Skivenes (eds) *Child protection systems: International trends and orientations*, New York, NY: Oxford University Press, 89-111.

Coe, K., Donke, D., Graham, E.S., John, S.L. and Pickard, V.W. (2004) 'No shades of gray: the binary discourse of George W. Bush and an echoing press', *Journal of Communication*, June, 234-52.

Cohen, S. (1972) *Folk devils and moral panics*, London: MacGibbon and Key.

Cohen, S. (2002) *Folk devils and moral panics: The creation of the mods and rockers* (3rd edn), Oxford: Routledge.

Colla, P. (2013) '"Just look at Sweden!" Archaeology of a conditioned response', *Trauma and Memory: Four Monthly Review of Psychoanalysis and Social Science*, 1(1), 9-15.

College of Social Work, The (2011) *A guide to the media for social workers*, London: The College of Social Work and *Community Care*.

College of Social Work, The (2012) *Media ethics: Experiences from the social work profession*, London: The College of Social Work.

Community Care (2013) 'Serious case reviews "politically abused" since death of Baby P, claims expert', 13 December.

Cooper, A. (2002) 'International perspectives on child protection', in M. Hill, A. Stafford and P. Green Lister (eds) *International perspectives on child protection: Report of a seminar held on 20 March 2002*, 130-41, www.scotland.gov.uk/resource/doc/1181/0009926.pdf

Cooper, A. (2005) 'Surface and depth in the Victoria Climbié report', *Child and Family Social Work*, 10, 1-9.

Cooper, A., Hetherington, R. and Katz, I. (2003) *The risk factor: Making the child protection system work for children*, London: Demos.

Cooper, A., Hetherington, R., Baistow, K., Pitts, J. and Spriggs, A. (1995) *Positive child protection: A view from abroad*, Lyme Regis: Russell House.

Cottam, H. (2011) 'Relational welfare', *Soundings*, 48, 134-44.

Critcher, C. (2009) 'Widening the focus: moral panics as moral regulation', *British Journal of Criminology*, 49, 17-34.

d'Ancona, M. (2011) 'There's another deficit that Cameron has to deal with', *The Daily Telegraph*, 30 July.

Daily Express (2008) 'Cameron's shock tactics', lead article, 13 November.

Daily Mail (2008) 'Comment: the tragic face of a passing system', 15 November

Davenport, P. (1987) 'MP insists doctors conspired over sexual abuse affair', *The Times*, 17 December.

Davis, P. (2002) 'On apologies', *Journal of Applied Philosophy*, 19(2), 169-73.

DCLG (Department for Communities and Local Government) (2012) *Working with troubled families: a guide to the evidence and good practice*, London: DCLG.

DCSF (Department for Children, Schools and Families) (2010) *Working together to safeguard children*, London: The Stationery Office.

de Baat, M., van der Linden, P., Koojiman, K. and Vink, C. (2011) *Combating child abuse and neglect in the Netherlands*, Utrecht, the Netherlands: Nederlands Jeugd Instituut.

Dean, M. (2013) *Democracy under attack: How the media distort policy and politics*, Bristol: Policy Press.

Der Spiegel (1983) 'Kinder-Gulag im Sozialstaat Schweden', 1 August, www.spiegel.de/spiegel/print/d-14019042.html

DfE (Department for Education) (2013a) 'Getting it right for children in need, speech to the NSPCC by Michael Gove MP, 12 November, https://www.gov.uk/government/speeches/getting-it-right-for-children-in-need-speech-to-the-nspcc

DfE (2013b) *Working together to safeguard children*, London: The Stationery Office.

DfES (2004a) *Every child matters: Next steps*, London: DfES.

DfES (2004b) *Every child matters: Change for children*, London: DfES.

DfES (Department for Education and Skills) (2006) *Working together to safeguard children*, London: The Stationery Office.

Dingwall, R. (1986) 'The Jasmine Beckford affair', *The Modern Law Review*, 49, 489-507.

Dingwall, R., Eekelaar, J. and Murray, T. (1983) *The protection of children: State intervention and family life*, Oxford: Blackwell.

Douglas, M. (1966/69) *Purity and danger: An analysis of concepts of pollution and taboo*, London: Routledge & Kegan Paul.

Doyle, J. and Doughty, S. (2014) 'Parents should flee UK to stop social workers taking children, says LibDem family campaigner', *Daily Mail*, 13 January.

Drewry, G. (1987) 'The parliamentary response to child abuse', in G. Drewry, B. Martin and B. Sheldon (eds) *After Beckford? Essays on themes related to child abuse*, Egham: Department of Social Policy, Royal Holloway and Bedford New College, 101-14.

Driscoll, M., Ungoed-Thomas, J. and Foggo, D. (2008) 'How more Baby Ps are there?', *The Sunday Times*, 16 November.

Duff, A. (1991) *Once were warriors*, Auckland, New Zealand: Tandem.

Edemariam, A. (2009) 'When a dead child is known to us, that's the biggest horror. We knew the size of that', *The Guardian*, 6 February.

Edemariam, A. and Rooseboom, S. (2008) 'After Savanna', *The Guardian*, 1 December.

Elsley, S. (2010) *Media coverage of child deaths in the UK: The impact of Baby P: A case for influence?*, Briefing No. 8, Edinburgh: University of Edinburgh.

Faircloth, C.R. (2010) '"If they want to risk the health and well-being of their child, that's up to them": long-term breastfeeding, risk and maternal identity', *Health, Risk and Society*, 12(4), 357-67.

Fairclough, N. (2000) *New Labour, new language?*, London: Routledge.

Featherstone, B., White, S. and Morris, K. (2014) *Re-imagining child protection: Towards humane social work with families*, Bristol: Policy Press.

Featherstone, L. (2008a) 'Baby P verdict', www.lynnefeatherstone.org/2008/11/baby-p-verdict.htm

Featherstone, L. (2008b) 'Why heads must roll over Baby P failures', *Norfolk Life: Eastern Daily Press*, 21 November.

Ferguson, H. (2004) *Protecting children in time: Child abuse, child protection and the consequences of modernity*, Basingstoke: Palgrave Macmillan.

Ferguson, H. (2007) 'Abused and looked after children as "moral dirt": child abuse and institutional care in historical perspective', *Journal of Social Policy*, 36(1), 123-39.

Ferguson, H. (2010) 'Walks, home visits and atmospheres: risk and the everyday practices and mobilities of social work and child protection', *British Journal of Social Work*, 40, 1100-17.

Field-Fisher, T.G. (1974) *Report of the committee of inquiry into the care and supervision provided in relation to Maria Colwell*, London: HMSO.

Fish, S., Munro, E. and Bairstow, S. (2008) *Learning together to safeguard children: Developing a multi-agency systems approach for case reviews*, London: Social Care Institute for Excellence.

Forkby, T., Hojer, S. and Lijegren, A. (2013) 'Making sense of common sense: examining the decision-making of politically appointed representatives in Swedish child protection', *Child and Family Social Work*, published online 30 September.

Franklin, B. and Parton, N. (1991) 'Media reporting of social work: a framework for analysis', in B. Franklin and N. Parton (eds) *Social work, the media and public relations*, London: Routledge, 7-52.

Freeman, R. and Rustin, M. (1999) 'Introduction: welfare, culture and Europe', in P. Chamberlayne, A. Cooper, R. Freeman and M. Rustin (eds) *Welfare and culture in Europe: Towards a new paradigm in social policy*, London: Routledge, 9-20.

Fricker, M (2013) 'Heads must roll for 26 missed chances to save poor Daniel; MP blasts council boss over murder', *Daily Mirror*, 2 August.

Frost, N (2013) *Letter to Edward Timpson in response to queries concerning the serious case review of Hamzah Khan*, Bradford: BSCB,www.bradford-scb.org.uk/scr/hamzah_khan_scr/Ministerresponse%20to%20the%20letter%20NF%2020112013.pdf

Frost, N. and Parton, N. (2009) *Understanding children's social care*, London: Sage Publications.

Furedi, F. (2002) *Paranoid parenting*, London: Allen Lane.

Gaber, I. (2008) 'How Haringey's failures turned the Baby P case into a PR disaster', *The Guardian*, 3 December, www.guardian.co.uk/media/organgrinder/2008/dec/03/baby-p-haringey-pr/print

Galilee, J. (2005) *Literature review on media representations of social work and social workers*, Edinburgh: Scottish Executive.

Garland, D. (1990) *Punishment and modern society: A study in social theory*, Oxford: Oxford University Press.

Garrett, P.M. (2009) 'The case of "Baby P": opening up spaces for debate on the "transformation" of children's services?', *Critical Social Policy*, 29(3), 533-47.

Gilbert, N. (ed) (1997) *Combatting child abuse: International perspectives and trends*, New York, NY: Oxford University Press.

Gilbert, N. (2012) 'A comparative study of child welfare systems', *Children and Youth Studies Review*, 34, 532-6.

Gilbert, N., Parton, N. and Skivenes, M. (2011) *Child protection systems: International trends and orientations*, New York, NY: Oxford University Press.

Gillies, V. (2007) *Marginalised mothers: Exploring working-class experiences of parenting*, Abingdon: Routledge.

Gimson, A. (2008) 'The question that threw Brown off his learning curve [...] questions taken over by Cameron's fury at Baby P case', *The Daily Telegraph*, 13 November.

Golding, P. and Middleton, S. (1982) *Images of welfare: Press and public attitudes to poverty*, Oxford: Martin Robertson.

Gove, M. (2008) 'We need a Swedish education system', *The Independent*, 3 December.

Gove, M. (2013) Speech to the National Society for the Protection of Children, 12 November, https://www.gov.uk/government/speeches/getting-it-right-for-children-in-need-speech-to-the-nspcc

Government of the Netherlands (2009) Speech by Maxime Verhagen: 'Combatting violence against girls', 25 September, www.government.nl/documents-and-publications/speeches/2009/09/25/speech-by-verhagen-at-the-side-event-combating-violence-against-girls.html

Gray, O. (2005) 'MPs go back to their constituencies', *The Political Quarterly*, 57-66.

Greenland, C. (1986) 'Inquiries into child abuse and neglect (C.A.N) deaths in the United Kingdom', *British Journal of Criminology*, 26(2), 164-72.

Greer, C. and McLaughlin, E. (2012) '"This is not justice": Ian Tomlinson, institutional failure and the press politics of outrage', *British Journal of Criminology*, 52, 274-93.

Grover, C. and Mason, C. (2013) 'The Allen Report: class, gender and disadvantage', *Families, Relationships and Societies*, 2(3), 355-69.

Guba, E.G. and Lincoln, Y.S (1994) 'Competing paradigms in qualitative research', in N.K. Denzin and Y.S Lincoln (eds) *Handbook of qualitative research*, Thousand Oaks, CA: Sage.

Hacking, I. (2003) 'Risk and dirt', in R.V. Ericson and A. Doyle (eds) *Risk and morality*, Toronto: University of Toronto Press, 22-47.

Haringey Local Safeguarding Children Board (2008) *First serious case review overview report relating to Peter Connelly*, London: DfE.

Haringey Local Safeguarding Children Board (2009) *Second serious case review overview report relating to Peter Connelly*, London: DfE. Hayward, K. and Yar, M. (2006) 'The "chav" phenomenon: consumption, media and the construction of the new underclass', *Crime, Media, Culture*, 2(1), 9-28.

Heawood, S. (2008) 'The world around Baby P is wrong: why are we so afraid to say so?', *The Independent on Sunday*, 16 November.

Heffer, S. (2008) 'Britain is as depraved as in Dickens's day', *The Daily Telegraph*, 15 November.

Hemming, J. (2007) 'Stolen children', *Mail on Sunday*, 15 July.

Hetherington, R (2002) *Partnerships for children and families project – learning from difference: Comparing child welfare systems*, Ontario, Canada: Wilfred Laurier University, www.wlu.ca/documents/7203/Hetherington_Keynote_Address.pdf

Hetherington, R., Cooper, A., Smith, P. and Wilford, G. (1997) *Protecting children: Messages from Europe*, Lyme Regis: Russell House.

Hey, D. (1999) 'Be(long)ing: New Labour, New Britain and the "Dianaization" of politics', in A. Kear and D.J. Steinberg (eds) *Mourning Diana: Nation, culture and the performance of grief*, London: Routledge, 60-73.

Heyes, L. (2014) 'Social work needs positive news stories – why are they so hard to tell?', *The Guardian*, 10 January.

Higgens, D. (2013) 'Hamzah's mother "made threat to kill other children"', *The Independent*, 5 October.

Hitchens, P. (2008) 'If Baby P had been middle class, he'd have been taken away', *Mail on Sunday*, 16 November.

Hochschild, A.R. (2002) 'Emotion management in an age of terrorism', *Soundings*, 20, 117-26.

Hoffman, D.M. (2010) 'Risky investments: parenting and the production of the "resilient child"', *Health, Risk and Society*, 12(4), 385-94.

Hoggart, S. (2008) 'House shamed by row over political corpse of Baby P', *The Guardian*, 13 November.

Hoggart, S. (2009) 'When coping with loss beats winning petty points', *The Guardian*, 12 March.

Hoggett, P. (2000) *Emotional life and the politics of welfare*, Basingstoke: Palgrave Macmillan.

Hoggett, P. (2006) 'Pity, compassion, solidarity', in S. Clarke, P. Hoggett and S. Thompson (eds) *Emotion, politics and society*, Basingstoke: Palgrave Macmillan, 145-61.

Hoggett, P. and Thompson, S. (2002) 'Towards a democracy of the emotions', *Constellations*, 9(1), 106-26.

Holland, S. (2014) 'Trust in the community: understanding the relationship between formal, semi-formal and informal child safeguarding in a local neighbourhood', *British Journal of Social Work*, 44(2), 384-400.

Holmes, M. (2004) 'The importance of being angry: anger in political life', *European Journal of Social Theory*, 7(2), 123-132.

Hope, C. (2012) 'Boris Johnson says he never rode ex-police horse and is not a part of David Cameron's "Chipping Norton Set"', *The Daily Telegraph*, 2 March.

House of Commons Debates (1987) *Hansard*, 9 July, vol 119, col 531.

House of Commons Debates (2001a) *Hansard*, 16 October, col 223WH, www.publications.parliament.uk/pa/cm200102/cmhansrd/vo011016/halltext/11016h04.htm

House of Commons Debates (2001b) *Hansard*, 16 October, cols 224WH to 225WH, www.publications.parliament.uk/pa/cm200102/cmhansrd/vo011016/halltext/11016h04.htm

House of Commons Debates (2008a) 'Engagements', *Hansard*, 12 November, col 761, www.publications.parliament.uk/pa/cm200708/cmhansrd/cm081112/debtext/81112-0002.htm

House of Commons Debates (2008b) 'Engagements', *Hansard*, 12 November, col 763, www.publications.parliament.uk/pa/cm200708/cmhansrd/cm081112/debtext/81112-0003.htm

House of Commons Debates (2009) 'Engagements', *Hansard*, 11 March, col 287, www.publications.parliament.uk/pa/cm200809/cmhansrd/cm090311/debtext/90311-0002.htm

House of Commons Debates (2011) 'Engagements', *Hansard*, 8 June, col 158, www.publications.parliament.uk/pa/cm201011/cmhansrd/cm110608/debtext/110608-0001.htm

House of Commons Debates (2013a) *Hansard*, 12 September, col 1223, http://www.publications.parliament.uk/pa/cm201314/cmhansrd/cm130912/debtext/130912-0003.htm#13091227000586

House of Commons Debates (2013b) *Hansard*, 17 October, col 992, www.publications.parliament.uk/pa/cm201314/cmhansrd/cm131017/debtext/131017-0004.htm#column_992

House of Commons Health Select Committee (2003) *The Victoria Climbié inquiry report: Sixth report of session 2002–3*, London: The Stationery Office.

House of Commons Written Ministerial Statements (2008) *Hansard*, 12 November, col 58WS.

House of Lords Debates (2002) *Hansard*, 26 June, vol 636, col 1460.

Houston, S. and Griffiths, H. (2000) 'Reflections on risk in child protection: is it time for a shift in paradigms?', *Child and Family Social Work*, 5, 1-10.

Hunt, A. (1999) *Governing morals: A social history of moral regulation*, Cambridge: Cambridge University Press.

Jones, N. (2011) 'Baby P tragedy: Cameron's culpability should not be overlooked', 28 May, www.nicholasjones.org.uk

Jones, R. (2014) *The story of Baby P: Setting the record straight*, Bristol: Policy Press.

Kahneman, D. and Miller, D.T. (1986) 'Norm theory: comparing reality to its alternatives', *Psychological Review*, 93(2), 136-53.

Kahneman, D., Slovic, P. and Tversky, A. (1982) *Judgement under uncertainty: Heuristics and biases*, Cambridge: Cambridge University Press.

Kamerman, S. (2005) 'Youth stricter by "Savanna effect"', *NRC Handelsblad*, 9 December.

Keenan, D. (2000) '"Hine's Once were warriors hell" – the reporting and racialising of child abuse', *Social Work Review*, summer, p 58.

Kehily, M.J. (2010) 'Childhood in crisis? Tracing the contours of "crisis" and its impact upon contemporary parenting practices', *Media, Culture and Society*, 32(2), 171-85.

Kenny, M. and Pearce, N. (2014) 'The end of the party: how we could be heading for a post-democratic era', *New Statesman*, 1 August.

Kitzinger, J. (2004) *Framing abuse: Media influence and public understanding of sexual violence against children*, London: Pluto.

Kleinman, A. and Kleinman, J. (1997) 'The appeal of experience; the dismay of images: cultural appropriations of suffering in our times', in A. Kleinman, V. Das and M. Lock (eds) *Social suffering*, Berkeley, CA: University of California Press, 1-23.

Kleinman, A., Das, V. and Lock, M. (eds) (1997) *Social suffering*, Berkeley, CA: University of California Press.

Knijn, T. and van Nijnatten, C. (2011) 'Child welfare in the Netherlands: between privacy and protection', in N. Gilbert, N. Parton and M. Skivenes (eds) *Child protection systems: International trends and orientations*, New York, NY: Oxford University Press, 223-40.

Krippendorf, K. (2004) *Content analysis: An introduction to its methodology* (2nd edn), Thousand Oaks, CA: Sage.

Kuijvenhoven, T. and Kortleven, W.J. (2010) 'Inquiries into fatal child abuse in the Netherlands: a source for improvement?', *British Journal of Social Work*, 40(4), 1152-73.

Laming, H. (2003) *The Victoria Climbié inquiry: Report of an inquiry by Lord* Laming, Cm 5730, London: HMSO.

Lane West-Newman, C. (2004) 'Anger in legacies of empire: Indigenous peoples and settler states', *European Journal of Social Theory*, 7(2), 189-208.

Largey, G.P. and Watson, D.R. (1972) 'The sociology of odors', *The American Journal of Sociology*, 77(6), 1021-34.

Lawler, S. (2002) 'Mobs and monsters: Independent man meets Paulsgrove woman', *Feminist Theory*, 3(1), 103-113.

Lawler, S. (2004) 'Rule of engagement: habitus, power and resistance', *Sociological Review*, 52(s2), 110-28.

Lawler, S. (2005) 'Disgusted subjects: the making of middle-class identities', *Sociological Review*, 53(2), 429-46.

Leapman, B. (2008) 'We need open courts and open decisions', *The Sunday Telegraph*, 16 November.

Lee, E., Bristow, J., Faircloth, C.R. and Macvarish, J. (2014) *Parenting culture studies*, Basingstoke: Palgrave Macmillan.

Lee, E., Macvarish, J. and Bristow, J. (2010) 'Risk, health and parenting culture', *Health, Risk and Society*, 12(4), 293-300.

Lee, J.A. and Ungar, S. (1989) 'A coding method for the analysis of moral discourse', *Human Relations*, 42(8), 691-715.

Lestor, J. (1989) House of Commons Debates, *Hansard*, 27 April, vol 151, col 1155.

Letts, Q. (2008) 'Mr Cameron's vehemence was spontaneous ... and magnificent', *Daily Mail*, 13 November.

Letts, Q. (2009) 'That's enough grief ... let the melee resume', *Daily Mail*, 12 March.

Leveson Inquiry (2012) *An inquiry into the culture, practices and ethics of the press*, London: The Stationery Office.

London Borough of Greenwich (1987) *A child in mind: Protection of children in a responsible society, the report of the commission of inquiry into the circumstances surrounding the death of Kimberley Carlile*, London: London Borough of Greenwich and Greenwich Health Authority.

Lowe, B.M. (2002) 'Hearts and minds and morality: analyzing moral vocabularies in qualitative studies', *Qualitative Sociology*, 25(1), 105-23.

Lupton, D. (1999) *Risk*, London: Routledge.

Lupton, D. (2013) 'Risk and emotion: towards an alternative theoretical perspective', *Health, Risk and Society*, 15(8), 634-47.

Lyman, P (1981) 'The politics of anger: on silence, ressentiment and political speech', *Socialist Review*, 11(3), 55-74.

Lyman, P. (2004) 'The domestication of anger: the use and abuse of anger in politics', *European Journal of Social Theory*, 7(2), 133-47.

Macdonald, K.I. and Macdonald, G.M. (1999) 'Perceptions of risk', in P. Parsloe (ed) *Risk assessment in social care and social work*, London: Jessica Kingsley Publishers, 17-52.

MacKenzie, K. (2008) 'Idiots who betrayed Baby P must go now', *The Sun*, 13 November.

Macnicol, J. (1987) 'In pursuit of the underclass', *Journal of Social Policy*, 16(3), 293-318.

Malnick, E. (2013) 'Review of "mummified boy" failures has glaring absences, says minister', *The Daily Telegraph*, 14 November.

Malone, C. (2008) 'Baby P: they're ALL guilty', *News of the World*, 16 November.

Manheim, J.B., Rich, R.C. and Willnat, L. (eds) (2002) *Empirical political analysis: Research methods in political science* (5th edn), Toronto: Longman.

Marcus, G.E. (2000) 'Emotions in politics', *Annual Review of Political Science*, 3, 221-50.

Margolin, L. (1997) *Under the cover of kindness: The invention of social work*, Charlottesville, VA: University Press of Virginia.

Martin, B. (1987) 'Moral messages and the press: newspaper response to a child in trust', in G. Drewry, B. Martin and B. Sheldon (eds) *After Beckford? Essays on themes related to child abuse*, Egham: Department of Social Policy, Royal Holloway and Bedford New College, 115-30.

Massey, D. (2011) 'Ideology and economics in the present moment', *Soundings*, 48, 29-39.

Mayo, M. (1999) 'New Language, New Labour: exploring the politics of emotions', *Soundings*, 11(spring), 144-51.

McIntosh, F. (2008) 'They ticked their boxes but let Baby P die in pain', *Sunday Mirror*, 16 November.

Middleton, D. and Edwards, D. (1990) 'Introduction', in D. Middleton and D. Edwards (eds) *Collective remembering*, London: Sage Publications, 1-22.

Millar, F. (2007) 'For the sake of the children', *British Journalism Review*, 18(1), 45-9.

Milne, K. (2005) *Manufacturing dissent: Single-issue protest, the public and the press*, London: Demos.

Minogue, R. (2014) 'Unempathetic Ed's problems are not in the head', *Spiked*, 31 July.

Moeller, S.D. (2002) 'A hierarchy of innocence: the media's use of children in the telling of international news', *The International Journal of Press/Politics*, 7(1), 36-56.

Morris, K. and Featherstone, B. (2010) 'Investing in children, regulating parents, thinking family: a decade of tensions and contradictions', *Social Policy and Society*, 9(4), 557-66.

Motz, A. (2001) *The psychology of female violence*, Hove: Brunner-Routledge.

Mouffe, C. (2005) *The democratic paradox*, London: Verso.

Munro, E. (2004) 'The impact of child abuse inquiries since 1990', in N. Stanley and J. Manthorpe (eds) *The age of the inquiry: learning and blaming in health and social care*, London: Routledge, 75-91.

Munro, E. (2008) 'Lessons learned, boxes ticked, families ignored', *The Independent on Sunday*, 16 November.

Munro, E. (2011) *The Munro review of child protection: Final report*, London: Department for Education.

Narey, M. (2008) 'Barnardo's lecture: children and the criminal justice system', Barnardo's, 26 November.

Nelson, F. (2008) 'Evil and the idle', *News of the World*, 16 November.

Netherlands Youth Institute (2013) 'Child protection figures', www. youthpolicy.nl

Neuman, W.L. (1997) *Social research methods: Qualitative and quantitative approaches*, Needham Heights: Allyn and Bacon.

Norgaard, K.M. (2006) '"People want to protect themselves a little bit": emotions, denial, and social movement nonparticipation', *Sociological Inquiry*, 76(3), 372-96.

Ofsted (2009) *Joint area review: Haringey children's services authority area*, London: Ofsted/Healthcare Commission/HM Inspectorate of Constabulary.

Orr, D. (2008) 'Helpless children get trampled in the rush to pass judgement', *The Independent*, 15 November.

Ost, D. (2004) 'Politics as the mobilization of anger', *European Journal of Social Theory*, 7(2), 229-44.

Otis, G.A. (2014) 'Administration for children's services failing to prevent tragedies despite city efforts to make changes', *New York Daily News*, 9 February.

Padgett, D.K. (1998) *Qualitative methods in social work research*, London: Sage.

Parton, N. (1985) *The politics of child abuse*, Basingstoke: Macmillan.

Parton, N. (1991) *Governing the family: Child care, child protection and the state*, Basingstoke: Macmillan.

Parton, N. (2008) 'Changes in the form of knowledge in social work: from the "social" to the "informational"', *British Journal of Social Work*, 38(2), 253-69.

Parton, N. (2012) 'Reflections on "governing the family": the close relationship between child protection and social work in advanced Western societies – the example of England', *Families, Relationships and Societies*, 1(1), 87-101.

Parton, N. (2014) *The politics of child protection: Contemporary developments and future directions*, Basingstoke: Palgrave Macmillan.

Parton, N. and Berridge, D. (2011) 'Child protection in England', in N. Gilbert, N. Parton and M. Skivenes (eds) *Child protection systems: International trends and orientations*, New York, NY: Oxford University Press, 60-85.

Pascoe-Watson, G. (2008) 'March on No 10', *The Sun*, 27 November.

Penders, B. and Lecluijze, I. (2014) 'Fighting tragedies in Dutch child welfare with ICT', www.ethics.harvard.edu/lab/blog/404-fighting-tragedies-in-dutch-child-welfare-with-ict

Phillips, M. (2008) 'The liberals who did so much to destroy the family must share the blame for Baby P', *Daily Mail*, 17 November.

Philp, M. (1979) 'Notes on the form of knowledge in social work', *Sociological Review*, 27(1), 83-111.

Pidd, H. (2013) 'Amanda Hutton jailed for 15 years over Hamzah Khan death and child cruelty', *The Guardian*, 4 October.

Pooley, E. (2001) 'Mayor of the world', *Time Magazine*, 31 December.

Power, M. (2004) *The risk management of everything: Rethinking the politics of uncertainty*, London: Demos.

Prior, L. (2003) *Using documents in social research*, London: Sage Publications.

Provan, S. (2012) 'The uncanny place of the bad mother and the innocent child at the heart of New Zealand's "cultural identity"', unpublished PhD thesis, University of Canterbury, New Zealand.

Rayner, E. (1995) *Unconscious logic: An introduction to Matte Blanco's bi-logic and its uses*, London: Routledge.

Rayner, G. (2013) 'Starved to death, waiting for help that never came; another tale of unimaginable horror in 21st century Britain: mother's instinct led PCSO to dead child', *The Daily Telegraph*, 4 October.

Reay, D., Crozier, G. and James, D. (2013) *White middle-class identities and urban schooling*, Basingstoke: Palgrave Macmillan.

Reid, S. (2008) 'The woman who puts performance graphs before a baby's life', *Daily Mail*, 13 November.

Richards, B. (2007) *Emotional governance: Politics, media and terror*, Basingstoke: Palgrave Macmillan.

Riddell, M. (2008a) 'Why Baby P was doomed to die', *The Daily Telegraph*, 13 November.

Riddell, M. (2008b) 'The country now has a choice, but will it help Arron get a job', *The Daily Telegraph*, 20 November.

Roberts, B. (2008) 'Grubby scenes in Parliament', *The Mirror*, 13 November.

Rose, J. (1998) *States of fantasy*, Oxford: Clarendon Press.

Rustin, S (2014) 'Edward Timpson: "I wouldn't be children's minister if my parents hadn't fostered"', *The Guardian*, 29 March.

Sayer, A. (2005) *The moral significance of class*, Cambridge: Cambridge University Press.

Scheff, T. (1994) *Microsociology: Discourse, emotion and social structure*, Chicago, IL: University of Chicago Press.

Schneider, B. (2014) 'Homelessness: emotion discourse and the reproduction of social inequality', *Canadian Journal of Communication*, 39(2), 1-13.

Scourfield, J. and Welsh, I. (2003) 'Risk, reflexivity and social control in child protection: new times or same old story?', *Critical Social Policy*, 23(3), 398-420.

Searing, D.D. (1985) 'The role of the good constituency member and the practice of representation in Great Britain', *Journal of Politics*, 47(2), 348-81.

Seyd, B. (2013) 'Is Britain still a "civic culture"?', *Political Insight*, December, 30-3.

Sharratt, T. (1987) '"Fresh problems now for child abuse families', *The Guardian*, 17 December.

Sherman, J. and Harris, E. (2012) 'Social class and parenting: classic debates and new understandings', *Sociology Compass*, 6(1), 60-71.

Shields, S.A. and MacDowell, K.A. (1987) '"Appropriate" emotion in politics: judgements of a televised debate', *Journal of Communication*, 37(2), 78-89.

Skeggs, B. (1997) *Formations of class and gender*, London: Sage Publications.

Skeggs, B. (2004) *Class, self, culture*, London: Routledge.

Smith, D. (1990) *Texts, facts and femininity: Exploring the relations of ruling*, London: Routledge.

Smith, D. (2006) 'Incorporating texts into ethnographic practice', in D. Smith (ed) *Institutional ethnography as practice*, Lanham, MD: Rowman & Littlefield, 65-88.

Smith, I.D. (2008) 'The legacy of broken lives: dysfunctional families raise children whose destructive paths are set by the age of three', *The Guardian*, 13 November.

Sreberny, A. (2002) 'Trauma talk: reconfiguring the inside outside', in B. Zelizer and S. Allan (eds) *Journalism after September 11*, Oxford: Routledge, 220-34.

Stallings, R.A. (1990) 'Media discourse and the social construction of risk', *Social Problems*, 37(1), 80-95.

Stanley, N. (2004) 'Women and mental health inquiries', in N. Stanley and J. Manthorpe (eds) *The age of the inquiry: Learning and blaming in health and social care*, London: Routledge, 151-64.

Starkey, P. (2000) 'The feckless mother: women, poverty and social workers in wartime and post-war England', *Women's History Review*, 9(3), 539-57.

Stevenson, O. (1974) 'Editorial', *British Journal of Social Work*, 4(1), 1-3.

Stevenson, O. (1986) 'Guest editorial on the Jasmine Beckford inquiry', *British Journal of Social Work*, 16(5), 501-10.

Strauss, A. (1987) *Qualitative analysis for social scientists*, New York: Cambridge University Press.

Tahana, Y. and Vass, B. (2008) 'Nia Glassie case: "we've got to learn to nark"', *The New Zealand Herald*, 19 November.

The Daily Telegraph (2008) 'Leading article: the buck never stops', *The Daily Telegraph*, 15 November.

The Guardian (2008a) 'Child protection: learning the lessons, again', lead article, 13 November.

The Guardian (2008b) 'ABCs: National daily newspaper circulation November 2008', theguardian.com, 5 December.

The Independent on Sunday (2013) 'A ray of light in child protection', 6 October, p 40.

The New Zealand Herald (2006) 'Kahui silence disgusting, says Sharples', *The New Zealand Herald*, 27 June.

The Sun (2008) 'The Sun says: leading article', *The Sun*, 13 November.

The Times (1985) 'Catalogue of failure in infant abuse deaths', *The Times*, 27 July.

The Times (2008a) 'Words fail', *The Times*, 13 November.

The Times (2008b) 'On the other side of the tracks lies a world of careless morality', *The Times*, 15 November.

Thompson, J.B. (2000) *Political scandal: Power and invisibility in the media age*, Cambridge: Polity Press.

Thompson, S. (2006) 'Anger and the struggle for justice', in S. Clarke, P. Hoggett and S. Thompson (eds) *Emotion, politics and society*, Basingstoke: Palgrave Macmillan, 123-44.

Thornton, L. (2013) 'Little Hamzah is failed again: report into how starved lad, 4, was let down by the system is slammed by government', *Daily Mirror*, 14 November.

Timpson, E (2013) *Letter to Professor Nick Frost, Independent chair of Bradford Safeguarding Children Board*, 13 November, https://www.gov.uk/government/uploads/system/uploads/attachment_data/file/261273/Bradford_Serious_Case_Review_-_Letter_from_Edward_Timpson_-_27_11.pdf

Tobis, D. (2013) *From pariahs to partners: How parents and their allies changed New York City's child welfare system*, New York, NY: Oxford University Press.

Treneman, A. (2008) 'Shame, they cried. And they were right', *The Times*, 13 November.

Turney, D. (2004) 'Who cares? The role of mothers in cases of child neglect', in J. Taylor and B. Daniel (eds) *Child neglect: Practice issues for health and social care*, London: Jessica Kingsley Publishers, 249-62.

Tweedie, N. (2008) 'Where no one will hear you cry', *The Daily Telegraph*, 15 November.

Tyler, I. (2008) '"Chav mum chav scum": class disgust in contemporary Britain', *Feminist Media Studies*, 8(1), 17-34.

Vallely, P. (2013) 'Our love of soap opera is a real killer', *Independent on Sunday*, 3 November.

Van Dongen, M (2007) 'Jeugdzorg haalt kind eerder uit huis' [Reporting on the 'Savanna effect'], *de Volkskrant*, 4 September, www.volkskrant.nl/binnenland/jeugdzorg-haalt-kind-eerder-uit-huis~a873480/

Wacquant, L. (2009) *Punishing the poor: The neoliberal government of insecurity*, Durham, NC: Duke University Press.

Wacquant, L. (2010) 'Crafting the neoliberal state: workfare, prisonfare, and social insecurity', *Sociological Forum*, 25(2), 197-220.

Waisbord, S. (2002) 'Journalism, risk and patriotism', in B. Zelizer and S. Allan (eds) *Journalism after September 11*, Oxford: Routledge, 201-19.

Walkowitz, D.J. (1999) *Working with class: Social workers and the politics of middle-class identity*, Chapel Hill, NC: University of North Carolina Press.

Warner, J. (2006) 'Inquiry reports as active texts and their function in relation to professional practice in mental health', *Health, Risk and Society*, 8(3), 223-37.

Warner, J. (2013) '"Heads must roll"? Emotional politics, the press and the death of Baby P', *British Journal of Social Work*, first published online 4 March 2013 (www.bjsw.oxfordjournals.org/content/44/6/1637).

Warner, M. (1994) *Managing monsters: Six myths of our time*, London: Vintage.

Waterson, J. (2000) *Women and alcohol in social context: Mother's ruin revisited*, Basingstoke: Palgrave Macmillan.

Watt, P. (2006) 'Respectability, roughness and "race": neighbourhood place images and the making of working-class social distinctions in London', *International Journal of Urban and Regional Research*, 30(4), 776-97.

Webster, C. (2008) 'Marginalised white ethnicity, race and crime', *Theoretical Criminology*, 12(3), 293-312.

Welshman, J. (2013) *Underclass: A history of the excluded since 1880* (2nd edn), London: Bloomsbury Academic.

Westwood, J. (ed) (2014) *Social media in social work education*, St Albans: Critical Publishing.

White, S., Hall, C. and Peckover, S. (2009) 'The descriptive tyranny of the common assessment framework', *British Journal of Social Work*, 39(7), 1197-217.

Whitney, R. (1985) House of Commons Debates, *Hansard*, 29 November, vol 87, col 1162.

Wilkinson, I. (2005) *Suffering: A sociological introduction*, Cambridge: Polity Press.

Wilkinson, R. and Pickett, K. (2009) *The spirit level: Why more equal societies always do better*, London: Penguin.

Williams, S.J. and Bendelow, G. (1998) 'Introduction: emotions in social life', in G. Bendelow and S.J. Williams (eds) *Emotions in social life: Critical themes and contemporary issues*, London: Routledge, xv-xxx.

Wolfsfeld, G. (2011) *Making sense of media and politics: Five principles in political communication*, Abingdon: Routledge.

Young, J. (2009) 'Moral panic: its origins in resistance, ressentiment and the translation of fantasy into reality', *British Journal of Criminology*, 49, 4-16.

Young, J. (2011) 'Moral panics and the transgressive other', *Crime, Media, Culture*, 7(3), 245-58.

Index

The following abbreviation has been used – *n* = note

Index

Index